INSPIRATIONS & INSIGHTS FROM THE BOOK OF MORMON

OTHER BOOKS AND AUDIOBOOKS
BY JOHN W. WELCH

The Parables of Jesus: Revealing the Plan of Salvation

INSPIRATIONS & INSIGHTS FROM THE BOOK OF MORMON

A *COME, FOLLOW ME* COMMENTARY

JOHN W. WELCH

Cover image: © 2023 Vecteezy

Cover design by Emily Remington
Cover design copyright © 2023 by Covenant Communications, Inc.

Published by Covenant Communications, Inc.
American Fork, Utah

Copyright © 2023 by John W. Welch
All rights reserved. No part of this book may be reproduced in any format or in any medium without the written permission of the publisher, Covenant Communications, Inc., PO Box 416, American Fork, UT 84003. This work is not an official publication of The Church of Jesus Christ of Latter-day Saints. The views expressed within this work are the sole responsibility of the authors and do not necessarily reflect the position of The Church of Jesus Christ of Latter-day Saints, Covenant Communications, Inc., or any other entity.

Printed in the United States of America
First Printing: October 2023

32 31 30 29 28 27 26 25 24   11 10 9 8 7 6 5 4 3 2

FOREWORD

Welcome to this year's study of the Book of Mormon. Whether this is your first or your fiftieth time through the Book of Mormon, whether you are diving into the Book of Mormon individually or re-exploring its amazing pages either as a family or as a member of a class, we hope this handy set of insights will provide a richly rewarding experience for you, helping you strengthen your enduring faith and glorious hope in Jesus Christ.

The materials found in each chapter of this book have been drawn from a much longer set of explanations and insights, which can be found and accessed for free on the web at bookofmormoncentral.org or scripturecentral.org under Come Follow Me/John W. Welch Notes. In those longer class notes, you will find charts, graphics, chiastic structures, illustrations, footnotes, and further materials that relate closely to many of the selections included in this volume.

Additional helpful resources for *Come, Follow Me* lessons can also be found on scripturecentral.org, evidencecentral.org, and on the ScripturePlus app. Look there for these and other open resources in English, Spanish, and Portuguese. Inquiries and feedback are always welcome. Without the dedicated and superb work of researchers and writers at Book of Mormon Central, and its expanded team at Scriptural Central, making these valuable resources available would have been impossible.

Heartfelt thanks go to several very dedicated editors and assistants who have volunteered to help bring this volume to fruition, including Jackson Abhau, Cheng Hao (Nelson) Leung, Kelly Shaffer-Bulloch, Lisa Bolin Hawkins, Patricia Orr, Rita Spencer, John S. Thompson, Deanne Welch, James B. Welch, Nicholas Welch, and several others, including the editorial and production team at Covenant Communications. We all hope this book will be a welcome addition to your personal library and a great blessing to your family.

1: TITLE PAGE

The Title Page of the Book of Mormon is a great place to begin, even though it was the last page added to this ancient record before Moroni buried this work. The Title Page gives an impressive overview of the contents and purposes of the Book of Mormon.

WHEN WAS THE TITLE PAGE TRANSLATED BY JOSEPH SMITH?

While it is printed today as the first page in the Book of Mormon, it was not the first page translated by Joseph Smith. In fact, Joseph Smith once said that "the Title Page of the Book of Mormon is a literal translation, taken from the very last leaf, on the left hand side" of the plates of Mormon.[1] The Title Page was found there because it was finished by Moroni immediately after he finished writing his book of Moroni. Thus, the Title Page was translated at the end of May 1829. It was soon used on June 11 by Joseph as the description of the Book of Mormon on the application he filed to secure the copyright for the publication of the Book of Mormon.[2]

WHO WROTE THE TITLE PAGE?

The Title Page was written by Moroni. The Title Page itself states that the Book of Mormon was being "sealed up and hid up unto the Lord, . . . sealed by the hand of Moroni." Three times Moroni "finished" his work on the plates that his father Mormon had entrusted to him. The first time, he wrote Mormon 8-9 and signed off around 390 AD. Second, he abridged the book of Ether, about the people of Jared, and signed off again around 400-421 AD (see Mormon 8:6 and Moroni 10:1). Third, he compiled priesthood texts, three letters from Mormon (see Moroni 7-9), and then he wrote Moroni 10 as his final farewell around 421 AD. The Title Page in the 1840 edition of the Book of Mormon, printed under Joseph Smith's direction, ends with an explicit attribution of this text to Moroni.

Mormon's purposes are clearly reflected in the Title Page. Moroni had no doubt worked closely with his father on this massive project. Perhaps they had even discussed what this final sealing inscription should include. While Moroni mentions himself by name in the Title Page as the one who would seal the record to come forth in the Lord's time and way, it is impressive how much more Moroni honors his noble father, who had died courageously in about AD 385. After all, while Moroni could have called the book "The Book of Mormon and Moroni," he simply names it "The Book of Mormon." Drawing no attention to his own significant contributions to the volume, Moroni simply says "written by the hand of Mormon."

---

[1] "History, 1838–1856, volume A-1 [23 December 1805–30 August 1834]," p. 34, The Joseph Smith Papers, online at josephsmithpapers.org.
[2] John W. Welch, "Timing the Translation of the Book of Mormon: 'Days [and Hours] Never to Be Forgotten,'" BYU Studies Quarterly 57, no. 4 (2018): 10–50, esp. 26–29, 47–48.

DOES THE TITLE PAGE REFER TO ANY WORDS PREVIOUSLY WRITTEN BY MORMON?

Yes, it actually does. Mormon had promised his readers in Mosiah 28:17–19 that a record of the Jaredites (now known as the book of Ether) would be given "hereafter." Thus, when Moroni added the book of Ether to the plates of Mormon, he was fulfilling his father's prior editorial plan and promise. Interestingly, Moroni's wording of the Title Page draws attention to this fact, as follows.

When discussing the book of Ether, the Title Page describes it as a record of the people of Jared

        1.) "who were scattered

        2.) at the time the Lord confounded the language of the people,

        3.) when they were building a tower to get to heaven" (Title Page).

Moroni appears to be quoting here, in reverse order, from statements made by Mormon in Mosiah 28:17–19, which speak of King Mosiah's translation of a record that was discovered among a people whose history stretches

        3.) "back to the **building of the great tower**,
        2.) at the time the **Lord confounded the language of the people**
        1.) and they were **scattered** abroad" (Mosiah 28:17).

Such a reversal was an ancient scribal practice used to signal that the writer was intentionally alluding back to an earlier text.

HOW ARE THE PARTS AND WORDS OF THE TITLE PAGE ORGANIZED AND STRUCTURED?

The Title Page readily divides into two intricately balanced halves. The first half of the Title Page focuses on Mormon's work in abridging the record of the people of Nephi (which was recorded on what is now known as the Large Plates of Nephi). Moroni's key work, mentioned in the second half, mainly deals with the record of the Jaredites.

Both halves of the Title Page are each carefully constructed with four parts:

- part 1 identifies the final record as "an abridgment" of the "record" of particular people,

- part 2 announces the audiences to whom the final record was addressed and the purposes for which it was written,

- part 3 affirms the divine role involved in the record's production,

- part 4 certifies that the work is of the Lord and sealed by authority.

In the first half, Moroni states that it is "an abridgment of the record of the **[particular]** people of Nephi, and also of the Lamanites—Written to **[audiences]** the Lamanites, who are a remnant of the House of Israel, and also to Jew and Gentile—Written **[divinely]** by way of commandment, and also by the spirit of prophecy and of revelation—Written **[of the Lord]** and sealed up, and hid up unto the Lord, that they might not be destroyed—To come forth by the gift and power of God unto the interpretation thereof—Sealed by the hand of Moroni, and hid up unto the Lord, to come forth in due time by way of the Gentile—The interpretation thereof by the gift of God."

In the second half, the book is further described as "an abridgment from the book of Ether also, which is a record of the **[particular]** people of Jared who were scattered at the time when the Lord confounded the language of the people, when they were building a tower to get to heaven, which is to show **[audience]** the remnant of the House of Israel what great things the Lord hath done for their fathers; and that they may know the covenants of the Lord, that they are not cast off forever, and also to the convincing of the **[audience]** Jew and Gentile that Jesus is the **[divine]** Christ, the eternal God, manifesting himself to all nations. And now if there are faults, they are the mistakes of men; wherefore **[of the Lord]** condemn not the things *of God,* that ye may be found spotless at the judgment-seat *of Christ*."

In addition, the Title Page also manifests a strong preference for verbal triplets, ten of which appear in this elegantly balanced text.

DOES THE TITLE PAGE ALSO WEAVE IN WORDS PREVIOUSLY WRITTEN BY MORONI?

Again, the answer is yes. From his first farewell (found in Mormon 8:9–20), Moroni reused here several terms, including the solely remaining Lamanites (v. 9), knowing the true God (v. 10), condemning not the record because of imperfections (v. 12), hiding up the record by commandment of the Lord (v. 14), the power of God to bring it forth (v. 15), covenant people (v. 15), faults of man (v. 16), and the judgment of the Lord (v. 20). And, in addition, four elements in the last line in the Title Page (to be found "spotless" at the "judgment" "seat" of "Christ") are words found in Moroni 10:33–34, which mention being perfected and sanctified in "Christ," "without spot," before the "bar" of the eternal "judge." These are further marks of Moroni's signature upon this masterful text.

WHY DID MORONI WRITE THE TITLE PAGE?

Obviously, the Title Page has been carefully chosen and arranged. It clearly articulates the essentials of the Book of Mormon. It states the who, the what, the when, the why, the whence, and the wherefore of the sacred volume. Producing this concluding summation took considerable time, keen deliberation, and intimate familiarity with the entire volume. Moroni likely pondered and prayed over this text, especially as he wandered widely and kept himself out of harm's way during the twenty-one years after he had finished his work on the book of Ether. With this final one-page text in place, Moroni could rest assured that he had honorably completed the sacred assignment that his father, Mormon, had entrusted to him. Moroni could also confidently place the Title Page as his protective and authoritative seal of approval upon this masterful book of scripture. Having this clearly inspired statement of purpose in front of them, readers can know, of a surety, the unambiguously good intent of the Book of Mormon, written unto the convincing of all people that Jesus is the Christ, the eternal God, manifesting Himself to all nations, so that people may know and embrace the mercies and covenants of the Lord, who desires all to come unto Him.

WHERE IS THE EARLIEST COPY OF THE TITLE PAGE FOUND?

The earliest transcript of the Title Page would have been written by Oliver Cowdery at the end of May, 1829, as Joseph finished dictating the translation of the plates of Mormon by the gift and power of God. Unfortunately, that original manuscript of the Title Page and three-quarters of the Book of Mormon's Original Manuscript were ruined by water or mold in a time capsule in the cornerstone of the Nauvoo House.

Fortunately, the wording of the Title Page is well-attested, thanks to an official legal document filed by Joseph Smith on June 11, 1829. In 2005, a great discovery was made in the Library of Congress as people there were preparing to celebrate the bicentennial of Joseph Smith's birth in 1805. What they discovered was (1) the recorded application filed by Joseph Smith in a federal court in the northern district of New York to secure his copyright of the Book of Mormon. The filed application form includes a handwritten description of the Book of Mormon, which reproduces in full the language of the Title Page. Attached to that copyright application was (2) a preliminary printed version of the Title Page. It is the earliest printed page from The Church of Jesus Christ of Latter-day Saints. It was folded long-ways (as legal papers were folded and filed in that day), and it was dated with Joseph Smith's name on the back.

TAKEAWAYS

- **What are the stated purposes of the Book of Mormon?**
- **How does the Book of Mormon accomplish all those purposes?**
- **How can it help readers to know these intended purposes?**
- **In what ways is the Book of Mormon exactly what this world needs now?**

2: 1 NEPHI 1-5

1 NEPHI 1:1-3—NEPHI'S PERSONAL COLOPHON

As you read through the Book of Mormon, notice that its books begin with "I, Nephi," or "I, Jacob." The pattern continues with "I, Enos," "I, Mormon," and others. This pattern of Book of Mormon witnessing continues all the way to the end when Moroni ends his final statement in Moroni 10 saying, "When you get these things, ask God, and He will tell you that I have not lied. You will see me at the judgment bar, and you will know that I have told you the truth" (Moroni 10:4–5, 27, 34). These are credible, personal, urgent testimonies.

1 NEPHI 1:4—MANY PROPHETS IN JERUSALEM

Nephi explained that in the first year of the reign of Zedekiah, there came many prophets prophesying to the people that they must repent. The Book of Mormon names a few of them—Zenos, Zenock, and Nahum. We do not know exactly when those prophets lived, but maybe about this time. Additionally, in 640 BC, Huldah was preaching as a prophetess. In 627, in the thirteenth year of Josiah's reign (Jeremiah 1:1), Jeremiah began prophesying.

There were indeed many prophets in Lehi's day. We also have many prophets in our day—15, to be exact. We have prophets and apostles working together to lead and guide the children of God. Is there strength in numbers? There is, especially in crucial times. Does the Lord send a lot of prophets? If we listen to all of them, we can learn. The Lord gave fair warning to Israel. "You must repent, and if you do not, you are going to be destroyed." Lehi was just one of many taking the same message to the people. We can learn a lesson—not just about listening to the prophets, but also that the Lord will not abandon us.

1 NEPHI 1:8—GOD IS WITH US

Emphatically, in this very first chapter, Nephi states the purpose of his record: to teach the doctrine of Christ. In verse 8, there is one preposition that is particularly important. Lehi "thought he saw God sitting upon his throne, surrounded with numberless concourses of angels in the attitude of singing and praising their God." What is the difference between "with" and "by"? It is significant, because it may signal that God is with them. "With" may mean a lot more than "by." This small, unusual word choice depicts something about who God is. He is not surrounded by concourses because He needs to show off. He is surrounded with them because He is an invested partner in every one of those individuals' salvation.

1 NEPHI 1:8, 14-15—GRACE IN THE DESTRUCTION: "SINGING AND PRAISING GOD" AND ACKNOWLEDGING HIS TENDER MERCIES

Lehi saw the destruction and woe that would come upon his people if they did not repent. At the end of his vision, Lehi was overwhelmed with gratitude and reverence for the goodness of God. How? Where is the goodness in destruction? God is merciful because He will not allow those who come to Him to perish. Lehi not only saw the woe and the consequences of the inhabitants of Jerusalem continuing in disobedience, but he saw the grand promise given to those who would repent and turn from wickedness. After Lehi saw destruction and terrible things, he exclaimed, "Great and marvelous are thy works," and "Thy throne is high in the heavens; thy power and goodness and mercy are over all the inhabitants of the earth." Lehi's focus was on mercy. Nephi also focuses on "show[ing] unto you that the tender mercies of the Lord are over all those whom he hath chosen, because of their faith, to make them mighty even unto the power of deliverance." Not only will the mercies of God be a major theme for Nephi, clear to the end of the final chapter in the Book of Mormon, but Moroni will identify remembering God's mercifulness as a key step in preparing one's heart and soul to receive inspiration and revelation through the power of the Holy Ghost (Moroni 10:3–4).

1 NEPHI 1:18—LEHI PROPHESIES TO JERUSALEM CONCERNING ITS DESTRUCTION

Rationalization eventually led the people in Jerusalem to a rebellious and stubborn approach toward righteousness. We have, in the Book of Mormon, plenty of places where people like King Benjamin talk about those who come out in open rebellion against God. This type of rebellion leads to what Brother Satterfield calls a "seared conscience," where you become so calloused to what is going on, that even in your rebellion, you lose the feeling that you are rebelling. You become hard and insensitive. Shame becomes something that is not tolerated in your life or in your world. But once all shame or regret is gone, how can you possibly turn yourself around? This is when the prophets enter. Their ministry is to tell the people that it is urgent and that they must reverse their course. Lehi may well have been present when Urijah was extradited from Egypt, publicly executed, and refused a burial. Likewise, Jeremiah was arrested and was brought to the gates of the temple. Only the intervention of princes prevented Jeremiah's execution. When God then called Lehi to deliver essentially the same prophetic warning that Urijah and Jeremiah had been delivering, he must have been chilled to the bone. But he courageously answered the call and went forth, and soon found himself fleeing for his life.

1 NEPHI 2:9-10—LEHI'S EXHORTATION TO LAMAN AND LEMUEL

Laman and Lemuel had lived a very nice, very comfortable life up until their father was called to be a prophet and commanded to flee Jerusalem. They were not ready—they were still mourning all they had been asked to give up. How many of us likewise hold onto past things, obsessing over what could have been or should have been? We struggle to let go and move on.

When Lehi saw a stream emptied into the Red Sea, he said to Laman, "O that thou mightest be like unto this river, continually running into the fountain of all righteousness." He also spoke unto Lemuel, "O that thou mightest be like unto this valley, firm and steadfast and immovable in keeping the commandments of the Lord." Traveling in the Middle East, you will hear it said over and over again, "Water is life." Indeed, nothing can live in the desert without water. Lehi may have been trying to teach Laman here to see himself as a river of life, always giving to others, nothing done in selfishness. We too might benefit from seeing ourselves like the river, always giving to the world around us.

Lehi told Lemuel to be firm, steadfast, and immovable. *Firm* speaks to inner strength. *Steadfast* speaks to standing steadily fastened. *Immoveable* speaks to not being swayed or moved by outside influences. Lehi gave them words and imagery that could stay with them and their posterity forever. Indeed, the words "steadfast and immovable" were reused used by Benjamin in his closing words in Mosiah 5:15 and also by Alma in Alma 1:25. Mormon used Lehi's wording in 3 Nephi 6:14, speaking of the Lamanites who remained converted unto the true faith and would not depart from it, "for they were firm, and steadfast, and immovable, willing with all diligence to keep the commandments of the Lord." Even though Laman and Lemuel did not respond to Lehi, we see that these blessings were nonetheless extended to some of their faithful descendants.

1 NEPHI 2:16-19—NEPHI'S HEART IS SOFTENED

We learn from Nephi's words that his own heart also needed "softening." Why? He looked like a true believer from the beginning. He believed what his father was telling him. He wanted to understand the mysteries too. But it would seem that there was still some further refining necessary for him—as there is for all of us, wherever we may be on the journey of faith. There are troubled times ahead. We're warned over and over that we can't coast along. Every one of us is going to be challenged in one way or another. Nephi was inspired to start us off with his experience because his pattern is essential for us to follow. He testified that he knew that he would be blessed, no matter what lay ahead, because God is faithful to those who keep their covenants with Him. It's a beautiful testimony, and it's a good starting point for faith, as we see what's going to happen because his testimony is true.

1 NEPHI 3:28-29—BELIEVING THE ANGEL

After the failed attempts to retrieve the plates and having their lives threatened, it may have been difficult to comprehend how to accomplish the commandment of God. However, Nephi feared not, but was believing. Reading about Nephi's experience with the angel invites us to think again of our own "reference experiences"—spiritual experiences that we have had that we can go back to throughout our lives. President Henry B. Eyring has spoken about the value of keeping a record of those times when we have been touched by the Spirit and have received personal revelation and help from the Lord—our "tender mercies." It is important to anchor ourselves to a time when we knew. This is a pattern that Nephi shows us—remembering those times when he knew. When the angel of the Lord delivered the message that He would deliver Laban into their hands, Nephi believed and knew that this would happen. In contrast, Laman and Lemuel questioned the words of the angel, "How is it possible for the Lord to deliver Laban? He is a mighty man."

1 NEPHI 4:5-18—THE SLAYING OF LABAN AND OBTAINING THE PLATES

As the three brothers stayed outside the walls, Nephi crept alone into the city, at night, going back toward the house of Laban (4:5). Hearing words quoted to him by the Spirit from Exodus 21:13, saying, "Slay him, for 'the Lord hath delivered him into thy hands'" (4:11), Nephi paused and reflected further. To make it unmistakably clear that only one reason ultimately justified Nephi's action, the Spirit repeated the injunction a second time, quoting again from Exodus 21, "Slay him, for the Lord hath delivered him into thy hands" (4:12). These words of the Spirit certify that the Lord had brought together the facts and circumstances, together with the means and methods necessary for Nephi to slay Laban, and thus it was not so much Nephi, but "the Lord, [who] slayeth the wicked to bring forth his righteous purposes" (4:13). The Lord wanted Lehi and his family to have the brass plates. Nephi told his brothers they were necessary, "otherwise, how can we preserve our language for our children?" Additionally, Nephi states that the people "could not keep the commandments of the Lord according to the law of Moses, save they should have the law."

1 NEPHI 5:1-2, 8—SARIAH COMPLAINS, THEN REJOICES AS HER SONS RETURN

When the text mentions that Sariah complained, it is important to acknowledge that she was experiencing a terrible trial. As the absence of her sons stretched on, and as she envisioned the task they had been given, it was only natural that her fears would begin to mount. There is no question that the most important possession for a woman in the ancient world was her sons. Her sons were her social security and status. It was understandable for Sariah to be worried about the loss of her sons.

Upon her sons' return, Sariah's words to Lehi form a beautiful little four-part poem. It begins with "knowing that the Lord has commanded my husband" and it ends with "knowing that the Lord has given them power that they might accomplish the thing that he has commanded them." We might call it The Song of Sariah.

TAKEAWAYS

- What do you find personally inspiring about Lehi's visions in 1 Nephi 1?
- What does Nephi want his readers to feel and do by reading chapters 1-5?
- Compare Laman's and Lemuel's responses with Nephi's.
- What can people do to value the scriptures as much as Lehi did?
- In what ways was Sariah a very significant person in this story?

3: 1 NEPHI 6-10

1 NEPHI 6:4—NEPHI'S PURPOSES

"But behold, I, Nephi, will show unto you that the tender mercies of the Lord are over all those whom he hath chosen, because of their faith, to make them mighty even unto the power of deliverance" (1 Nephi 1:20). Nephi clearly states that one of his main points is to show his readers that God is merciful and that if we are faithful, He will deliver us in our trials. Yet, in 1 Nephi 6:4, Nephi gives another purpose that is larger in its scope than the first. He declares that the "fulness" of his intent is to help men (and women) come unto God and be saved. For Nephi, this was surely a spiritual concept, indicating that if men (and women) keep God's commandments, they will become spiritually closer to God and eventually be unified in purpose with Him. However, there is a very physical component as well. Those who are righteous in this life will eventually be resurrected and will be granted the privilege of physically dwelling in the presence of God for eternity. They will have been saved from the perils of mortal life and literally *come* to where God is. Nephi is sharing with readers the results of both his spiritual and his temporal journeys to teach us about God.

1 NEPHI 7:22—OFFERING SACRIFICES

We see repeatedly that every time they get back to the camp, Lehi and his family make sacrifices and give thanks unto the God of Israel. It's the first thing they do: acknowledge God in keeping them safe. There are often two areas of focus when we thank God for a gift. One is to focus on how happy we are for the thing itself. "Thanks for giving *that* to me. I'm glad that you—God—were so kind as to do that for me." The other is in an attitude of praise, an acknowledgment of the kindness behind the gift. "You were wonderful to do that; thank you, I revere you for that." Instead of saying, I'm so glad I got *it*, you are saying, *you* are so wonderful to *do* it. We must pause and remember to worship, to revere God for our blessings, as we see exemplified here by Lehi and Sariah.

1 NEPHI 8:1—SEEDS

Lehi's and Ishmael's families knew they were leaving their homeland and expected to be traveling for a long time. Wisely, they started putting together something of a seed bank, knowing that wherever they eventually settled, they would need to be able to plant seeds and harvest food for their survival. This important endeavor likely occupied much of their time. You never know what will trigger a dream or a vision. At this time when the families were focused on seeds, plants, and trees, Lehi received a prophetic vision and was inspired with a deep understanding of the Tree of Life, the mission of Jesus Christ, the love of God, and eternal life.

1 NEPHI 8:6-7—LEHI FOLLOWS THE ANGEL

The greatest lesson we can learn from Lehi's interaction with the angel is to trust the Lord. We need to acknowledge the Lord and trust in what He says. That's all part of the greatest commandment—to love the Lord and trust in Him. How many times do the words "invitation" or "invite" show up in the Book of Mormon? When Lehi stated that the Spirit *bade* him to follow Him, it was an invitation. It helps to know that the Lord presents us with options and requests. Even though there would have been undesirable consequences if Lehi had not followed the bidding of the Lord, His gentle commands were all grounded in a loving relationship. After all, the tree that the Spirit is bidding Lehi to approach is a representation of the love of God.

1 NEPHI 8:10—THE TREE OF LIFE

Just about every culture and every religion recognizes, in some way, the importance of the Tree of Life. The image of the tree of life bears a lot of weight and yields fruit in many ways. "The image of the people struggling uphill toward the tree of life is a fitting symbol for life on earth. At times, life may feel like an uphill climb, a desperate attempt to overcome the effects of the Fall and return to the Eden from which we have been cast out."[1]

1 NEPHI 8:13-18—PARTAKING OF THE FRUIT OF THE TREE OF LIFE

In his dream, Lehi looked around and saw that his family was searching. It looked like they were lost. As a good father, he beckoned them by calling out with a loud voice. Lehi did not go and get them; rather, they needed to come to him and the tree. Sariah, Sam, and Nephi chose to follow the path and partake of the tree. Laman and Lemuel chose not to do so. But Lehi invited, and he did it with a loud, clear voice so they would not miss it. Remember that if you or someone you love is lost, it is *not* the end of the story. Even those who have wandered off will be brought to the tree or given additional opportunities in the next life. The Lord continues to work with people as they exercise their agency, and He continues to beckon and do all He possibly can to try to lead them back onto the righteous path of happiness. Brigham Young once said, "How long will this missionary work go on?" His answer was, "It will go on in the next life and it will continue, and it will go on and on until every soul that possibly can be saved has been saved, and we are not going to be finished until we have reached that point."

1 NEPHI 8:19—THE IRON ROD

"If there is any one thing most needed in this time of tumult and frustration, when men and women and youth and young adults are desperately seeking for answers to the problems which afflict mankind, it is an 'iron rod' as a safe guide along the straight path on the way to eternal life, amidst the strange and devious roadways that would eventually lead to destruction

---

1 Book of Mormon Central, "Why We Still Have to Cling to the Iron Rod Even Though the Path Is Strait (1 Nephi 8:13–14)," *KnoWhy* 402 (January 25, 2018).

and to the ruin of all that is 'virtuous, lovely, or of good report.'"[2] As you're holding onto the rod, with the mist of darkness and the confusion all around, you can feel the stability of the rod. That kind of reinforcement applies to all. "In Nephi's vision, the iron rod seems to function much like a shepherd's staff—leading people to the Tree of Life just as a shepherd would use a 'rod' (Psalms 23:4) to lead his sheep to 'green pastures' and 'still waters' (23:2)."[3]

1 NEPHI 8:30—STAYING AT THE TREE OF LIFE

Interestingly, there were those who partook of the fruit but did not stay at the tree. Lehi describes others who stayed at the tree and continued to partake of the fruit. What did they do that was different from the others? "They did press their way forward, continually holding fast to the rod of iron." They did not let go of the rod. Moreover, when they finally made it to the tree, these people fell down before they had even eaten the fruit. Why? There could be several reasons. First is gratitude. Another is humility. "To fall down" in the ancient world meant literally "to bow down." In bowing down, the person did not just bow his head; he bowed his whole body and fell to the ground. In the Beatitudes, when it says, "Blessed are the poor in spirit," the phrasing can be understood as saying, "Blessed are they who bow down themselves to the earth." Whatever the reason, their apparent gratitude and humility made them different from the others who simply partook and then wandered off. Those people who stayed were the people who did not let it affect them when they looked around and saw other people mocking, ridiculing, and scorning them. They did not pay any attention to the comments of other people in the great and spacious building. They had their testimonies. They were firm. And they were grateful to God.

1 NEPHI 8:37-38—LEHI PLEADS WITH LAMAN AND LEMUEL

In the vision, Lehi pleads with Laman and Lemuel to keep the commandments. What does it mean to "keep" the commandments? One obvious definition would be to "obey." But what do you *do* when you *keep* something? You hold onto it. You treasure it. You can keep something when you protect it. In all these senses, we must *keep* the commandments. Additionally, in ancient languages, the word "keep" often means to protect or to guard. You must *guard* the commandments. You must guard them for your own good, but you also must guard them so that they do not slip into some kind of misunderstanding or errors in the way they are applied. Keeping the commandments means not only obeying them, but keeping, preserving, and passing them on to the next generation. Lehi wanted all his sons to pass the commandments on to the next generation. He clearly believed with all his heart that Laman and Lemuel had the opportunity to repent. Even though, at this point, Laman and Lemuel had rejected the tree and had rejected the path, Lehi did not believe this was their unchangeable fate. He still, with the tender pleadings of a loving father, continued to entreat them to come to the tree.

---

2   Harold B. Lee, "The Iron Rod," *Ensign*, June 1971, online at churchofjesuschrist.org.
3   Book of Mormon Central, "How Are Rod and Sword Connected to the Word of God? (1 Nephi 11:25)," *KnoWhy* 427 (April 24, 2018).

1 NEPHI 9:3-6—FOR A WISE PURPOSE

To understand the full impact of these passages, one must be acquainted with how the Book of Mormon was translated by Joseph Smith. The small plates of Nephi—on which were found 1 Nephi, 2 Nephi, Jacob, Enos, Jarom, and Omni—were not translated until the very end. After Joseph Smith had completed the translation of the books of Mosiah through Moroni, he came to the small plates of Nephi and then translated them. Imagine Joseph Smith's initial reactions. The first 116 pages of the Book of Mormon had been lost, and Joseph was devastated that he allowed that to happen. For a period of time, his gift of translation was taken from him. Finally, Joseph was forgiven, but he was instructed not to go back and retranslate the plates on which had been found the text of the 116 pages that had been lost. Instead, he was instructed to resume translating where he had left off, which was early in the book of Mosiah. Thus, the whole time Joseph Smith was translating from Mosiah to Moroni, he must have been regretting that those who would read the Book of Mormon in modern times would not have the words of Lehi.

Imagine Joseph Smith's joy when he finally got to the end of the plates and read Mormon's words regarding his inclusion of the small plates, saying: "I do this [I append the small plates] for a wise purpose; for thus it whispereth me, according to the workings of the Spirit of the Lord which is in me" (Words of Mormon 1:7). God knew fourteen hundred years in advance that those 116 pages of manuscript could become lost. Joseph's experience can teach us an important lesson. "Whatever challenges or setbacks we may suffer in our personal lives, we can . . . trust that the Lord can compensate for our weaknesses and limitations. Sometimes, like Joseph Smith and Martin Harris, we may feel that 'all is lost.' Yet through the infinite power of Christ's Atonement, all that seems lost can be ultimately and miraculously restored."[4]

TAKEAWAYS

- What lessons one can learn from the marriages performed in 1 Nephi 7.
- What might each element in Lehi's dream represent in your life today?
- Give four reasons why those who came to the tree were able to stay there.

---

4   Book of Mormon Central, "What Was on the Lost 116 Pages? (1 Nephi 9:5)," *KnoWhy* 452 (July 24, 2018).

4: 1 NEPHI 11-15

1 NEPHI 11-14—OVERVIEW: THE FOUR STAGES OF NEPHI'S PROPHETIC WORLDVIEW

Nephi's vision, which stands at the center of the book of 1 Nephi, is four chapters long. It is a powerful and unforgettable prophetic statement, which clearly portrays the future of the world, commencing with Nephi's time, then unfolding in four major stages:

- Stage 1 foresees the coming to earth of Jesus Christ, the Messiah, the Son of God (found in 1 Nephi 11).

- Stage 2 laments the rejection of Christ by most of the people He lived with, visited, and taught, resulting in their being scattered (found in 1 Nephi 12).

- Stage 3 anticipates the role of the Gentiles in preserving parts of the gospel of Jesus Christ and bringing the word of God to the remnant of scattered Israel (found in 1 Nephi 13).

- Stage 4 speaks of the restoration of the house of Israel and Christ's ultimate victory over the forces of evil (found in 1 Nephi 14).

This same prophetic worldview becomes the foundational framework which Nephi (1 Nephi 19–22; 2 Nephi 25–30), Jacob (in 2 Nephi 6–10), Abinadi, and several other Nephite prophets will subsequently use as the foundation of their worldview.

1 NEPHI 11:1—NEPHI DESIRES KNOWLEDGE

Nephi puts his account of this vision at the very center of his first book written on his small plates. There are twenty-two chapters in 1 Nephi, and the entire book appears to have been arranged as a chiasm, where elements in the first part of the book are reversed and then repeated in the second part. (See John W. Welch Notes for the chiastic structure of this book. The full texts of these Notes can be found at https://archive.bookofmormoncentral.org/book/john-w-welch-notes/6420.)

The central point of a chiasm usually contains its most important or pivotal concept. It is thus significant that chapter 11—the center point of 1 Nephi's chiastic structure—contains Nephi's vision of the coming of the Lord, the tree of life, the iron rod, and the relation of various groups to the Tree of Life, which Nephi understands is a representation of the love of God as manifested by Jesus. For Nephi, this was likely the most critical vision he ever received, and it proved foundational for him. It can be seen as a kind of Sacred Grove or Sacred Mountain experience for him. That kind of magnitude, allowing Nephi to understand things of the Spirit more fully and in a way that he had never experienced before, made this vision the focus of his first book.

1 NEPHI 11:2—THE GREAT QUESTION

"What desirest thou?" In the New Testament, when the Lord is about to heal someone, He will ask them first what it is that they want from Him. The question "What desirest thou?" precedes the miracle—in Jesus's day and still today. Nephi was specific in what he asked for. Notice that not only was Nephi's specific question answered, but much more was given. Asking is important. We should all be prepared to give an answer to the question: What do you *really* desire?

1 NEPHI 11:16—THE CONDESCENSION OF GOD

In 1 Nephi 11:16, the Spirit asked, "Knowest thou the condescension of God?" Nephi answered, "I know that [God] loveth his children; nevertheless, I do not know the meaning of all things" (1 Nephi 17). Isn't that the crucial recognition—knowing that God loves His children? Everything else can wait. Even though we do not know the meaning of all things, as long as we know that the Lord loves us and is going to see that things will turn out right, we know what really matters. That is what will sustain us.

To "descend" means to "come down." "*Con*descend" means to come down "*with* or to a level *with* another." Nephi saw the condescension of the Messiah on several different levels:

- Jesus was born as a baby, just like everyone else.

- He was born as lowly as possible.

- Jesus was baptized. He condescended to say, "I will be obedient, and I will submit myself to the will of the Father." Baptism is a symbol of death followed by being raised to a new life. So, Jesus's participation in the ordinance of baptism symbolized His willingness to submit to the will of the Father, even unto the point of death.

- Nephi saw Jesus casting out evil spirits. He was doing difficult work, interacting with some nasty elements.

- Jesus would experience pain to the fullest extent.

- Christ would die, going into the world of the departed spirits.

- Even after Christ was exalted, He *came down* among the Nephites as a glorified being.

And He continues to willingly descend (condescend) again and again to care for all those who will come unto Him.

1 NEPHI 13:26-28—PLAIN AND PRECIOUS TRUTHS WOULD BE TAKEN FROM THE BIBLE

A careful reading of these verses teaches us what was lost first. The *gospel*—the basic principles of the gospel were lost first: "they have taken away from the gospel of the Lamb many parts which are plain and most precious" (13:26). And once a basic knowledge of the Atonement of Christ and repentance was lost, what else was consequently lost? The plan of salvation.

Second, once knowledge of the plan of salvation was lost, then "many covenants of the Lord" were lost (13:26). The covenantal nature of baptism, the covenantal renewal in the sacrament, the covenant of marriage and all other temple covenants were lost. With these covenants lost, so too was the oath and covenant of the priesthood. It is not as if a few, small, unimportant truths were lost. The very foundation of the gospel was taken away.

Third, with the foundation missing, the remaining text and doctrine needed to be justified and explained. Because of this, certain writings were seen as unnecessary or even as an embarrassment. For example, the gospel of Barnabas (a very early Christian text) discusses the physical Resurrection of the Lord. That was standard doctrine until about the 3rd century, and then it became a point of contention. Why? It became a snag in the gospel fabric that was already becoming tattered. If it has become standard to believe that God is without a body and now dwells only in the heavens, then it is awkward to have scriptures that conflict with that view. Thus, it was removed from the Bible.

1 NEPHI 13:35-36—NEPHI SEES LATTER-DAY SCRIPTURE COME FORTH

When Nephi began his record, he knew he was inspired to write for "a wise purpose" (1 Nephi 9:5), but he did not know the details. Now, immersed in this grand vision, Nephi learned a little more about the reasons for keeping a record of sacred things. Here was a tender mercy for Nephi, for him to see what would be lost and to understand the scope of what he and his posterity must do. In all of this, we see the love and omniscience of God. Remember that Nephi was shown this vision hundreds of years before Christ was born, before the events of the New Testament, and certainly before those plain and precious things would be lost over the centuries after Christ's death.

1 NEPHI 13:38-39—OTHER BOOKS WILL COME FORTH

At the time when Joseph Smith translated the Book of Mormon, there were few other significant discoveries of ancient manuscripts. Nephi had prophesied, however, that other books would come forth, validating the Book of Mormon. Joseph Smith was killed in June 1844. Just two months later, biblical and early Christian texts began to come forth in rapid succession. A young man, Constantin von Tischendorf, found his way to St. Catherine's Monastery in the Sinai. There he was shown a full, fourth-century Greek Bible, which included texts like the Epistle of Barnabas, the Shepherd of Hermas, as well as other long-lost texts. Other discoveries followed, notably the Narrative of Zosimus.

Hugh Nibley called this unusual outpouring of ancient records "the peculiar blessing of our generation." In a conversation involving myself and Professor James H. Charlesworth, the content of 1 Nephi 13:39 came up. Charlesworth read it, paused, and asked me, "When was *this* written?" I said, "That would have been about 550–540 BC." He said, "No, I meant, when was this published? When did this appear in English?" I answered, "It was translated into English by June 1829, and published in March 1830." "That's impossible!" he said. "No one at that time could have known that all these many books would soon be coming forth. You," he continued, "cannot *believe* this anymore. You have to *know* it is true. You have seen it come to pass in your lifetime."[1]

1 NEPHI 14:10—WHAT ARE THE TWO CHURCHES?

The word "church" in ancient languages meant "assembly," "company," or "congregation." Thus, in Greek, the word *ecclesia* (often translated as "church") simply implied a gathering. In Nephi's vision, we learn that there are *only* two gatherings. You are either in the Church of the Lamb of God or in the church of those aligned with Satan. Nephi wrote chapter 14 with an apocalyptic view, which pertains to the end times and shows how things are going to *conclude*. In the end, there will be only two choices. You are either with the Lord or you are not.

In contrast to what Lehi called the great and spacious building (which is a big building filled with a large crowd), Nephi said of the gathering of the righteous, "And I saw that they were few" (14:12). That is not to say that a little leaven cannot enlarge the entire loaf, or a little salt cannot season an entire pot of stew. But the word "few" still tells us something about the demographics of righteousness.

1 NEPHI 15:1–10—INQUIRING OF THE LORD

After Nephi returned from his vision, he found his elder brothers "disputing one with another" (15:2) about what Lehi had told them. Nephi was exhausted. He had just seen the destruction of his people and was overwhelmed at the great Plan of Redemption he had just witnessed. And now he returned to see his brothers arguing. Nephi asks, "Have ye inquired of the Lord?" And what was their response? "We have not; for the Lord maketh no such thing known unto us" (15:8–9). This answer probably left Nephi utterly flabbergasted. How could they possibly not understand that they could ask the Lord and receive the information they needed? Of course, the Lord would talk to Laman and Lemuel! But they were not obedient. They were hardhearted, quick to anger, and filled with doubt. Nephi saw that this could have been a turning point for them, so he encouraged them to pray and learn for themselves.

---

1   Book of Mormon Central, "What Were the 'Other Records' Nephi Saw in Vision? (1 Nephi 13:39)," *KnoWhy* 376 (October 26, 2017); John W. Welch, "The Narrative of Zosimus and the Book of Mormon," *BYU Studies Quarterly* 22, no. 3 (1982): 311–332; revised and updated as "The Narrative of Zosimus (History of the Rechabites) and the Book of Mormon," in *Book of Mormon Authorship Revisited: The Evidence for Ancient Origins*, ed. Noel B. Reynolds (Provo, UT: FARMS, 1997), 323–374.

Today, we spend a lot of time with the Lord saying, "please bless . . ." "thank you for . . ." "I'm worried about my children . . ." or "help me find a job." All these things are completely fine in prayers. However, Nephi provides a great example. He may have prayed for similar things, but he also said, in essence, "Heavenly Father, please teach me something. Please help me better understand something." The Lord is very generous with answers to those kinds of questions. As we follow Nephi's prayer pattern, we will be blessed with more light; the Lord wants and needs us to have more light. He needs us to shine brighter than ever before.

1 NEPHI 15:33-36—THE WICKED WILL BE CAST INTO HELL

There's a wonderful concluding section at the end of chapter 15, in which Nephi wrote about justice and how we will all stand to be judged according to our works and be rewarded with eternal blessings. That is when he said,

> And if their works have been filthiness they must needs be filthy; and if they be filthy it must needs be that they cannot dwell in the kingdom of God; if so, the kingdom of God must be filthy also. But behold, I say unto you, the kingdom of God is not filthy, and there cannot any unclean thing enter into the kingdom of God; wherefore there must needs be a place of filthiness prepared for that which is filthy (15:33–34).

This is not to say that a human being can be considered trash. Filthiness (or impurity) are consequences of choices made and were of great concern to the Israelites. Nephi, who lived under and respected the law of Moses, would have been particularly concerned about what would be done to purify the impurities that are natural consequences of sinful behavior.

TAKEAWAYS

- **Why do you think Nephi was shown a mother holding a child (and not just the child) in order to understand that the Tree of Life was the love of God?**
- **Why do you think Nephi was shown people falling down at Jesus's feet and worshiping Him in order to understand that the rod of iron was the word of God?**
- **Nephi says those in the great and spacious building are the house of Israel who "fight against the twelve apostles of the Lamb" (11:35). Does this affect how you feel about our modern Church leaders?**

5: 1 NEPHI 16-22

1 NEPHI 16:2-5—HOW TO KEEP THE COMMANDMENTS

Nephi teaches his brothers how to keep the commandments. His formula for success can be grouped into the following three components:

- Hearkening to the Truth: To hearken means more than to just listen. It also means "to obey."

- Giving Heed to the Truth: To heed something is to give diligent and meticulous attention to it.

- Walking Uprightly: When we are obedient, we are confident and walk uprightly, knowing that we are righteous and that the Lord knows we are righteous. Thus, it is not only a matter of knowing the truth, but of doing, and of adhering to a habit in which we *walk with God.*

1 NEPHI 16:7-8—LEHI'S SONS MARRY ISHMAEL'S DAUGHTERS

Verse 8 states: "and thus my father had fulfilled all the commandments of the Lord which had been given unto him." What commandment was Nephi referring to? This surely refers, at least in part, to 1 Nephi 7:1, where the Lord commanded Lehi's sons to "take daughters to wife, that they might raise up seed unto the Lord in the land of promise." In addition, it was a general responsibility of fathers in the ancient world to see that their children were married.

How might this story pertain to us today? Do we as parents or grandparents have any kind of obligation to help our children make and keep covenants? Concerning baptism, the Doctrine and Covenants says that our children should all be baptized (see Doctrine and Covenants 18:42; 68:27–28). And if parents fail to teach that doctrine? "The sin be upon the head of the parents" (see Doctrine and Covenants 68:25; compare. 93:40, 50). Obviously, helping children keep *any* of the commandments, especially those involving entering into covenants, is part of a parent's obligation. Parents should remember always, however, that with baptism or further covenants, our children still have the choice. We ought not to take away their agency.

1 NEPHI 16:23—NEPHI ASKS HIS FATHER WHERE TO HUNT

At the end of verse 20, Nephi mentioned how his father, Lehi, began to "murmur against the Lord his God," and shortly afterwards Nephi made a new bow. Rather than complaining, Nephi went to work. However, he first asked Lehi—it being the proper order of things in families for children to honor their parents—where he should go to obtain food (16: 23). Nephi could have sought such a revelation himself, but he showed respect to his father, giving him the opportunity to lead again in righteousness. What a great lesson this is for all of us—of all ages.

1 NEPHI 16:23—SONSHIP

In his writings, Nephi uses ten names for Christ that no one else uses. This list provides an interesting reflection of his religious sensitivities. For example, Nephi calls Jesus "the Son of the Most High God," "the Son of the Everlasting Father," "the Son of Righteousness," "the Beloved Son." Here is a whole cluster of *son* names that—in all the Book of Mormon—only Nephi uses. Perhaps this use of *son* names is because Nephi had a unique understanding of what it means to be an obedient son and show ultimate respect to his father. Nephi would have appreciated the sonship of Jesus Christ. Even though Jesus was a God and had descended from heaven, He was still an obedient son.

Nephi's example of sonship is seen in the story of the broken bow. Even when his father was in a physically and spiritually weakened position and his faith was stretched to the limit, Nephi was still the faithful, respectful, obedient son.

1 NEPHI 16:26-29—HOW DID THE LIAHONA WORK?

Interestingly, this first recorded use of the Liahona was not a case of its being used to help Lehi's family learn the direction in which they should travel, but rather to help them find food. The Liahona should serve us, therefore, as a life-sustaining symbol, not just as a direction-giving instrument. It symbolizes the Lord's willingness to direct us toward physical and spiritual sustenance or nourishment. Yet, when harmony and peace were absent, this instrument could not function. We must have peace and harmony for the Spirit to fully function in our lives (see Alma 37:41–47).

1 NEPHI 16:34—ISHMAEL DIES AT NAHOM

Many Latter-day Saints have pioneer ancestors who suffered similar experiences: burying loved ones in shallow graves, knowing that their bodies would probably not be left in peace. How painful it must have been for Lehi and his family to move on, enduring the hardships of the heat, uncertainty, and dangers of many kinds. Many of us experience hard times in life and in our families. Does it help to know that there was a land of "milk and honey" at the end of the journey for Lehi and his family; that the Lord knew where He was taking these people; that they followed; and that they were in the hand of the Lord, trusting that He would watch over them?

1 NEPHI 17:35—THE DIFFERENCE BETWEEN GOD'S LOVE AND GOD'S FAVOR

Nephi said to his brothers, "Behold, the Lord esteemeth all flesh in one; he that is righteous is favored of God." We know that God is no respecter of persons, and that all men are saved by obedience to the same laws and ordinances of the gospel (see Acts 10:34–35). And yet, there is a corollary that Nephi rightly points out: While we believe that God loves all His children, we also believe that "he that is righteous is *favored* of God." Although this truth is troublesome to some people, Nephi teaches straightforward doctrine that the tender mercies of the Lord are over all those whom God has chosen, showing favor to them because of their faith and faithfulness (see 1 Nephi 1:20). His *favor* might be interpreted as the blessings He is bound (and anxious) to bestow on *all* those who are obedient. "I, the Lord, am bound when ye do what I say; but when ye do not what I say, ye have no promise" (Doctrine and Covenants 82:10).

1 NEPHI 18:3—REVELATION COMES THROUGH CONSTANT PRAYER

Clearly, Nephi did not receive just one initial revelation on how to build the ship. He went many times into the mountain to pray, and the Lord showed him many things, more things than just about the ship. The mountain was a place of revelation, and Nephi was a man who believed in prayer and revelation. At the conclusion of his narrative he affirmed: "But behold, I say unto you that ye must pray always, and not faint; that ye must not perform any thing unto the Lord save in the first place ye shall pray unto the Father in the name of Christ, that he will consecrate thy performance unto thee, that thy performance may be for the welfare of thy soul" (2 Nephi 32:9). He learned this lesson early in his life, and it was continually reinforced through his experiences.

1 NEPHI 19:6—NEPHI WRITES THAT WHICH IS SACRED

We often say that the large plates of Nephi contained a secular history, and the small plates a spiritual history, but in this verse, Nephi said, "Nevertheless, I do not write anything upon plates save it be that I think it be sacred." Possibly, to Nephi all these records were sacred because the hand of the Lord was involved. We might see a record as being more politically or economically focused, but Nephi never took God out of the equation. To put it in modern terms, whether the people prosper or perish has less to do with how the stock market is doing and more to do with their collective righteousness. To Nephi, even what we would call secular was sacred.

1 NEPHI 19:23-24—ISAIAH

In reading the words of Isaiah, (1) Nephi saw particular words and phrases as being relevant to his own world—we did "liken all scriptures unto us" (1 Nephi 19:23), both temporally and spiritually (1 Nephi 22:1, 3, 27). (2) In addition, Nephi related Isaiah's prophecies to his own prophetic worldview, informed by his great vision in 1 Nephi 11–14. Perhaps this is what Nephi meant when he spoke of reading these things not only temporally but also spiritually (1 Nephi 22:1–3). And (3) Nephi expects all his readers to see these fruitful texts as being relevant to themselves and to read them "for our profit and learning" (19:23). Getting through Isaiah is difficult, but it works better when readers try to *get things out of Isaiah*, not just *to get through it*.

1 NEPHI 21:14-16—THE LORD WILL NOT FORGET HIS PEOPLE

Is it reassuring to you today to know that God will not forget you? You have made covenants with Him, and while you may on occasion forget Him, He will never forget you. How heartening it would have been for Nephi to read aloud the promise of God's enduring love and covenant. "Yea, they may forget, yet will I not forget thee" (21:15).

1 NEPHI 21:26—THE VICTORY OF THE LORD JESUS CHRIST

This verse ends with a strong declaration of the eventual victory of God: "And all flesh shall know that I, the Lord [Jehovah], am thy Savior and thy Redeemer, the Mighty One of Jacob." There will be one shepherd who will reign in dominion and might and power and great glory. This final theme is introduced at the end of 1 Nephi 21 (compare. Isaiah 49:26). Isaiah had prophesied that Israel will be restored and that they who oppress the righteous shall be "drunken with their own blood" (Isaiah 49:26). We know that God is going to win. That is where Isaiah leaves off in Isaiah 49, and Nephi thus continues that optimistic point of view as he proceeds with his own teachings and prophecy.

1 NEPHI 22:3-5—WHERE AND HOW ARE THE LOST TRIBES LOST?

The lost tribes are "scattered" among all nations. In what sense are they lost? They are lost to the lands of their inheritance. They are lost to the gospel and its saving ordinances. They are lost to the priesthood and the blessings that flow from it. They are lost in the sense that many do not even know they are of the house of Israel. One of the reasons we send our missionaries to the four corners of the earth is to find, gather, and expand the house of Israel.

1 NEPHI 22:30-31—NEPHI EXHORTS ALL TO KEEP THE COMMANDMENTS

Nephi's concluding words here in verses 30–31, encouraging all to be obedient to the commandments and to endure to the end, are clearly related to Nephi's earlier declarations of commitment that reverberate throughout the book of 1 Nephi and draw its contents together. Nephi was a great prophet. He saw the Lord Jesus Christ. He testified in 2 Nephi 11 that he had seen Him, that Isaiah had seen Him, that Jacob had seen Him, just as Lehi had also seen Him. We have here eyewitnesses of the *premortal* Christ. Throughout his life, Nephi was a great preacher of righteousness, not only in word but also in deed: "And we talk of Christ, we rejoice in Christ, we preach of Christ, we prophesy of Christ, and we write according to our prophecies that our children may know to what source they may look for a remission of their sins" (2 Nephi 25:26).

TAKEAWAYS

- How does reviewing the main sacred stories that Nephi included in 1 Nephi help you to see the spiritual dimension in the world around you?
- In what specific and exemplary ways did Nephi obey the commandment of God to honor his father and mother?
- Recall a time you knew that God had not forgotten you (see 1 Nephi 21:15–16).

6: 2 Nephi 1-2

These two chapters begin Lehi's final instructions as a patriarch over his posterity. He speaks to Laman, Lemuel, Sam, and the sons of Ishmael, counseling them that their blessing is contingent on obeying Nephi. If they do not hearken, Laman will lose his "first blessing" as eldest son, and Nephi will step into his position. To compensate for the legal requirement that the eldest son receive a double inheritance portion (Deuteronomy 22:17), Lehi specified that Sam's portion would be combined into Nephi's: "thy seed shall be numbered with [Nephi's] seed" (4:11). Jacob was given temple responsibilities, Joseph was made a teacher, and Zoram appears to become the military leader. Lehi's division of his estate was his final effort to keep his family together in righteousness. Unfortunately, his plan did not last long. Patriarchs in our midst lay their hands on our heads to give us guidance along righteous paths. Lehi set a wonderful precedent when blessing his posterity.

2 NEPHI 1:7-9—THE AMERICAS ARE A CHOICE LAND

Lehi declares that if those who come from Jerusalem to this land "keep his [the Lord's] commandments, they shall prosper upon the face of this land" (1:9, compare. v. 20). Similar words are mentioned predominantly in Deuteronomy, the book of scripture found during Lehi's young adulthood. I believe one reason so many people in the Western Hemisphere have joined the Church is because these lands were given to Joseph and his descendants. Lehi was a descendant of Manasseh. In patriarchal blessings given throughout North and South America, the descendants of Joseph, whether Ephraim or Manasseh, are consistently declared. For further reading and discussion of this topic, see Book of Mormon Central, "Where Is the Land of Promise? (2 Nephi 1:5)," *KnoWhy* 497 (January 8, 2019).

2 NEPHI 1:30-32—LEHI BLESSES ZORAM

Zoram's blessing was to dwell in safety and prosperity if he remained aligned with Nephi. When Nephi left the land of their first inheritance, Zoram went with him. Thus, Nephi's oath and promise to Zoram, that "you shall have place with us" (1 Nephi 4:34), was intentionally fulfilled. Zoram's descendants, the Zoramites, are mentioned many times in the Book of Mormon, almost always in connection with military affairs. This seems to have been the role of the Zoramites within their wider society. Centuries later, Alma the Younger worried when the Zoramites withdrew and severed relationships with the Nephites. He feared that the Zoramites would form an alliance with the Lamanites (Alma 31:4), effectively renouncing Lehi's arrangement. Remembering Lehi's blessing, take note of the Zoramites throughout Nephite history.

2 NEPHI 2:2—THE LORD WILL CONSECRATE AFFLICTIONS FOR OUR GAIN

The word *consecrate* means to imbue with sacredness, to make sacred or holy. In this passage, Jacob's privation and suffering are acknowledged. Lehi vows that everything Jacob will suffer through in his life will be consecrated by God for a blessing to him. As a young child, Jacob experienced dangerous journeys, a near shipwreck, and lack of adequate food or water. He never knew the riches that the family once enjoyed in Jerusalem. Yet, the affliction father Lehi mentions specifically is "sorrow because of the rudeness of thy brethren." Truly, the deepest pains are those inflicted by other people. Nevertheless, Lehi said that the Lord would consecrate all these afflictions for his gain. We receive this similar reassuring promise that "all things wherewith you have been afflicted shall work together for your good" (Doctrine & Covenants 98:3).

2 NEPHI 2:3—JACOB WILL SPEND HIS DAYS IN THE SERVICE OF GOD

Jacob is being dedicated here by his father to spend his days—in other words, his whole life—serving in the temple.

In Hebrew, the same word can be translated either as *servant* or as *slave*. We don't like to think of ourselves as *belonging to* anyone else, or being *slaves* of God, yet the scriptures describe the faithful as God's "peculiar people." The English word *peculiar* comes from a Latin word, *peculia,* which means *personal property.* And indeed, we are bought with a price. We are *peculiar* because we belong to God, having been purchased by Christ's blood, and therefore we belong to Him as His servants. This is a very important part of the way in which ancient Israelite religion and the relationship between God and man were understood. All this would have applied to Jacob's consecrated state as a lifetime servant of God. Jacob became the high priest of the temple. After Nephi's death, Jacob kept the sacred records, which were then passed down through his generations.

2 NEPHI 2:8—THE MERITS, MERCY, AND GRACE OF THE SAVIOR

We might ponder what those three words mean. Lehi says that the Savior will lay down His life and take it up again by the power of the Spirit that He may bring to pass the resurrection of the dead. His victory over death gives Him the merits to be able to then make intercession for all the children of men. Therein is mercy, the intercession which allows further time for repentance to take place, and thereby grace operates, allowing mankind to be saved. Hence, all men come unto God and must stand in the presence of Him to be judged according to the truth and holiness which is in *Him.* We will not only be judged according to our works, but we will also be judged in accordance with the mercy, truth, and holiness of God.

2 NEPHI 2:11-14—OPPOSITION IN ALL THINGS, ALL THINGS CREATED BY DESIGN

The plan of salvation was set forth in the Council in Heaven. The world we inhabit is not an arbitrary, random place. Instead, we have come to do certain things, to accomplish certain purposes and objectives. As we are shown in the temple endowment, our world was not created simply for amusement, but designed as an environment in which to make serious choices. In the Creation, opposites came into being: light was separated from darkness, mountains separated from valleys, land separated from water. We learn in the temple that opposition is the fundamental characteristic of this mortal realm. Many things like obedience and disobedience, choosing Christ or choosing Satan, life or death, become fundamental choices that indicate why we are here.

Everything that comes from God is good: light, life, truth, and joy. Satan takes those away; darkness is the absence of light, death is the absence of life, falsehood is the absence of truth, misery is the absence of joy, evil is the absence of good. The existence of opposites coupled with our agency gives meaning and purpose to our mortal probation. Think about Lehi's experience. There were really two options: Jerusalem or wilderness, preach or flee, sail or not. Similarly, Lehi describes spiritual options as clear choices: Savior or devil, joy or misery, life or death.

2 NEPHI 2:16-18—THE DEVIL FELL FROM HEAVEN AND ENTICES MEN TO SIN

Lehi surmised that an angel had fallen from heaven, became miserable forever, and "sought also the misery of all mankind" (2:18). Some people think that the source of Lucifer's misery is that he was cast out of the presence of God and cannot go back. No, Satan opposes God. Satan is not miserable out of a longing to return to God's presence. Satan's misery is that he can never become *like* God. He is miserable because he is stopped in his progress. He can never have a physical body, he can never be a husband, or have children, or posterity. In his misery, he does everything possible to turn God's children against their God.

In verse 16, notice that for God's purpose to be accomplished, man should be enticed by a choice or its opposite. I like that word *entice*; it's a little different than the word *tempt*. There is opposition so that we might be *enticed*—drawn to things—and because of that enticement, we can then make choices which lead to greater enticements as our desires ripen

2 NEPHI 2:21—THE DAYS OF MANKIND WERE PROLONGED

Lehi teaches here that we are in a state of *probation*. The word *probe* is identical philologically to *prove*. It's a time when we can prove ourselves, not only to God but also to ourselves. We learn by our experiences, and in our *probation,* we learn the difference between good and evil.

Since God is *just,* He could have created a world in which any transgression brought on an immediate punishment or a consequence. God knows all things. He doesn't need further evidence or witnesses. There's no risk that He would judge improperly. So why doesn't He just go ahead?

One way to extend mercy is to withhold judgment and allow time for the person to learn for themselves the results of their actions. In verse 21 we learn that the "days of the children of men were prolonged . . . and their time was lengthened." While we live in mortality, we are granted a period of probation. We have time on earth to make choices, have experiences, learn, repent, and prepare to meet God.

2 NEPHI 2:23-25–ADAM FELL THAT MEN MIGHT BE; JOY IS LINKED WITH FAMILIES

The Fall was a planned event; it was a noble thing for Adam and Eve to fall, otherwise they would have remained in the garden. In their state of innocence, they would have had no children or posterity. We would have remained in the premortal existence, waiting, rather than progressing through mortality. There was no way for the great family of God to receive bodies until after the Fall of Adam. I suspect that I was chanting, *eat the fruit! eat the fruit!* in order for the plan to take effect.

Adam fell that men *might* be. The word *might* is the important operative word in this famous saying, not the resultant word *joy.* The great purposes of God would have been frustrated without the Fall of Adam. Yet, Adam and Eve did not know all things—they did not know exactly how to multiply and replenish the earth once they were cast out of the garden. It took tremendous faith for Adam and Eve to choose to fall. And then Lehi says, "Men are that they might have joy." Initially, Adam says in Moses 5:10: "For because of my transgression my eyes are opened, and in this life I shall have joy." In verse 11, Eve more specifically details aspects of that joy: "Were it not for our transgression we never should have had seed [children], and never should have known good and evil, and the joy of our redemption, and the eternal life which God giveth unto all the obedient."

Lehi knows from his vision of the tree of life that a joyous outcome is not guaranteed but must be chosen. It must be deliberately chosen again and again over a lifetime of progressing along the covenant path, despite opposing voices, sneers, or enticing mirages.

For further reading, see Book of Mormon Central, *"Why Did Lehi Teach That the Fall Was Necessary? (2 Nephi 2:22–25)," KnoWhy* 269 (February 1, 2017).

2 NEPHI 2:26-27–CHRIST IS THE ONE WHO SETS US FREE TO CHOOSE

We have freedom to choose, and that is because the redemption of Christ allows us to choose either life or death. Without that redemption, we could not have that choice. However, it doesn't mean that we are free to do whatever we want. We are not free to do things and not suffer the natural consequences. It means we are free to make a choice between Christ and life or Satan and death.

Lehi goes on to explain how this will happen. First of all, you are free to make a choice, and in order to make that choice, you must know good from evil. You are then free to act for yourselves and not to be acted upon. That is crucial—you aren't being compelled, and you aren't being driven. So, we have here the Creation, the Fall, and now we have the Atonement—three grand pillars of eternity.

Every mortal has the opportunity to act and not just be acted upon, to choose between right and wrong, between Christ's way of life and Satan's way of death (2 Nephi 2:25–27). Making that choice, and hopefully making it to our eternal joy, is our primary purpose in this existence.

TAKEAWAYS

- **How does understanding that "all things must needs be a compound," or have an opposite, help you endure?**
- **What are the sources of Satan's misery?**
- **Why is our joy linked with our families?**
- **What is the significance of calling the Creation, the Fall, and the Atonement the three grand pillars of eternity? What is the function of a pillar?**

7: 2 NEPHI 3-5

2 NEPHI 3:1-2—LEHI BLESSES HIS SON JOSEPH

Joseph was probably less than ten years old when Lehi gave him this blessing, perhaps just barely old enough to fully understand what was being said. Lehi quoted heavily from the scriptures as he spoke to his son. Perhaps Joseph, who was ordained as a teacher, is being mentored. Lehi is teaching him how to teach: you read the scriptures and you apply them to your situation, which relates to the need for establishing and maintaining their traditions.

2 NEPHI 3:3-4—JOSEPH'S SEED WILL NOT BE UTTERLY DESTROYED

In 2 Nephi 3:4, Lehi says, "I am a descendant of Joseph [of Egypt]" and throughout the remainder of the chapter he quotes some ancient texts from the brass plates concerning Joseph and his seed. Similar texts are found in the Joseph Smith Translation of Genesis 48:7–11 and 50:24–38. Lehi promises his son Joseph four times in this chapter that his seed will not be destroyed. How can Lehi be so confident? Because such a promise was part of the covenant God made to Joseph of Egypt and his seed: "Thus prophesied Joseph: I am sure of this thing, . . . for the Lord hath said unto me, I will preserve thy seed forever" (3:16; compare. Joseph Smith Translation Genesis 50:34).

2 NEPHI 3:5-18—JOSEPH IN EGYPT PROPHESIED OF JOSEPH SMITH

Who is this seer that Joseph of Egypt saw? Joseph Smith was the choice seer raised up by the Lord. Verse 7 states that "he [the seer Joseph Smith] shall be esteemed highly among the fruit of thy loins . . . [and] he shall do a work for the fruit of thy loins." Indeed, many who have come into the restored Church of Jesus Christ have discovered through their patriarchal blessings that they are the fruit of the loins of Joseph, as was Joseph Smith.

In 2 Nephi 3:9, we read, "He shall be great like unto Moses." Doctrine and Covenants 28:2 states that "no one shall be appointed to receive commandments and revelations in this church excepting my servant Joseph Smith, Jun., for he receiveth them even as Moses." Then in Doctrine and Covenants 107:91 we read, "And again, the duty of the President of the office of the High Priesthood is to preside over the whole church, and to be like unto Moses." By fulfilling these priesthood responsibilities, Joseph Smith fulfilled the Lord's promise to Joseph of Egypt. In 2 Nephi 3:11, the Lord also promised Joseph of Egypt that this seer will "bring forth my word unto the seed of thy loins . . . to the convincing them of my word, which shall have already gone forth among them." Thus, the Book of Mormon validates the truths found in the Bible regarding the preservation of the seed of Joseph of Egypt.

2 NEPHI 3:12—THE WRITINGS OF JUDAH AND JOSEPH SHALL GROW TOGETHER

In harmony with the Lord's declaration to Joseph of Egypt, the prophet Ezekiel prophesied that two sticks or records, one for Judah (the Bible) and one for Joseph (the Book of Mormon), would become one in the Lord's hand (see Ezekiel 37:15–17). When we study the Bible and Book of Mormon together, it is beneficial to notice the subtle ways in which these two volumes of scripture complement one another.

Did Lehi know Ezekiel? Quite possibly. Ezekiel would have been a young man at the time Jerusalem was destroyed; he was likely about the same age as Nephi. In that relatively small circle of prophets in Jerusalem, there is no reason why Lehi and Ezekiel should not have known each other or have at least known *of* each other.

Lehi then quotes five reasons given by the Lord as to why these two records need to come together. Carefully consider these five purposes:

- Confounding false doctrines.

- Laying down contentions.

- Establishing "peace among the fruit of thy loins." Notice that it does not say establishing peace in the whole world. But when this book is brought together with scriptures from Judah, it can establish peace in the hearts of those who are of the House of Ephraim and the seed of Joseph, the son of Lehi. Bestowing peace is one of the great purposes the Book of Mormon will serve for all who read it.

- Bringing them to the knowledge of their fathers in the latter days.

- Bringing them to the knowledge of the Lord's covenants. Moroni reiterates this final purpose on the Title Page of the Book of Mormon ("that they may know the covenants of the Lord"), thus emphasizing the importance of the Book of Mormon in fulfilling these purposes.

2 NEPHI 3:19–20—A VOICE FROM THE DUST

The Book of Mormon contains the voices of those who have long since passed away. "And they shall cry from the dust." From the brass plates, Lehi would have known the words found in Isaiah 29:4, "And thy speech shall be low out of the dust . . . one that hath a familiar spirit." It is the testimony that Jesus is the Christ, that He has risen from the grave, and that He is the Only Begotten Son of God. It is a call to repentance.

2 NEPHI 4:3-7—LEHI'S GRANDCHILDREN ARE FREE FROM THE SINS OF THEIR PARENTS

Lehi promises his grandchildren that they will not suffer in the eyes of God because of the failures of their parents. In Deuteronomy 24:16, a principle of Jewish law was established that prohibited vicarious punishments: "The fathers shall not be put to death for the children, neither shall the children be put to death for the fathers: every man shall be put to death for his own sin." This was not the case in most ancient Near Eastern laws. Under the Code of Hammurabi, for example, if a physician committed malpractice and killed the son of a freeman, then the son of the doctor was to be killed. But as Lehi and hence Joseph Smith knew, everyone will be punished for their own sins, and not for anyone else's transgressions.

2 NEPHI 4:11—SAM IS BLESSED TO BE NUMBERED AMONG THE NEPHITES

In his last will and testament embedded in these four chapters, Lehi arranged his posterity into seven different groups, but he went out of his way to divide his property into eight shares. This was because Laman, as the oldest son, was entitled under Deuteronomy 21:17 to a share twice the size of the other sons' portions of Lehi's estate. Typically, this was the rule because the oldest son had the obligation to take care of his mother and other dependents in the family.

But if that were the case, then Lehi had a problem. God had called Nephi to be the leader of the people, and thus Lehi reaffirms Nephi's call to be his successor. But how can Nephi be Lehi's successor unless he has the resources to manage not only his own family but to lead the whole group? And perhaps Lehi also wanted to keep as much balance and harmony in the family as possible. So, for Nephi and Laman to have equal resources, Lehi gave Laman the "first blessing," while at the same time combining Sam's share with Nephi's, putting the two of them into one tribe. Lehi says to Sam, "thou shalt inherit the land like unto thy brother Nephi. And thy seed shall be numbered with his seed," and the two of you will merge. Undoubtedly, this was clever estate planning. Lehi was doing everything he could to divide his estate fairly but also effectively.

2 NEPHI 4:16-35—NEPHI'S PSALM

The text in 2 Nephi 4:16–35 is often called the Psalm of Nephi. It is among the most eloquent, sublime writings found anywhere in scripture.

Lehi has just died, and Nephi tried to admonish his brothers; but it didn't work. His psalm reflects his lament. He felt that he was weak and had failed. By the end of his psalm, however, his confidence is rebuilt and restored, because he knows in whom he trusts.

There are about thirty different Hebraic literary forms or styles of writing, but the basic one is parallelism. And there are different kinds of parallelism, such as *synonymous* parallelisms, *synthetic* parallelisms, or *antithetic* parallelisms. All these types of parallelisms are present in

Nephi's Psalm. It is a masterful work in the highest tradition of the Hebrew lament. There are about twenty psalms in the Old Testament that fall within the form of the lament. In the formal lament, there are five stages:

- Stage 1 is an invocation, where the petitioner invokes or addresses God.

- Stage 2 is a complaint, where you then register some kind of complaint.

- Stage 3 is where you confess and profess your trust, reassuring God that you will trust in Him.

- Stage 4 is the actual petition—where you ask for something.

- Stage 5 is where you make a vow of praise.

It is not hard to see that Nephi's Psalm follows the ancient lament pattern precisely.

The word *Lord* (the translation for the name *Jehovah* or YHWH) is spoken ten times in this psalm. Under Jewish law and ritual practice, that could only happen once every year, on the Day of Atonement. On that day, the high priest offered a prayer of repentance and other prayers on behalf of the people. Two goats were offered: one would be sacrificed, and another—the scapegoat—would be sent out into the wilderness to bear the sins of the people away from the city. During these prayers and rites, the high priest alone could speak the name of Jehovah ten times aloud. And each time the people heard the name, the Jewish texts say they had to fall on their face, to be completely reduced to the dust of the earth, acknowledging the great presence of the goodness of God.

The Psalm of Nephi makes a perfect Day of Atonement text. It is possible that Nephi composed it on the first Day of Atonement after the death of Lehi. It shows how we are ultimately dependent upon the Lord, not just for guidance and strength, but for His forgiveness, that we might become one again with Him, to be encircled in the robes of His righteousness. Then we can go forward trusting in Him.

2 NEPHI 4:18-25—NEPHI TRUSTS IN THE LORD

Nephi leads us through a series of statements of what the Lord has done for him.

- He hath led me through mine afflictions in the wilderness.

- He hath preserved me upon the waters of the great deep.

- He hath filled me with his love, even unto the consuming of my flesh.

- He hath confounded mine enemies, and unto the causing of them to quake before me.

- He hath heard my cry by day, and he hath given me knowledge by visions in the night-time. Upon the wings of his Spirit hath my body been carried away upon exceedingly high mountains. And mine eyes have beheld great things, yea, even too great for man.

Each of these statements represents personal events in Nephi's life, which he has recounted in 1 Nephi. So, this psalm is not simply a lyrical poem of abstract experiences. It offers a template for meaningful and successful prayer. When we remember all that God has done for us, we should not just merely say "Thanks." We would do well to remember and rehearse in detail the specific ways God has blessed us in our personal lives.

2 NEPHI 5:4-7—FOLLOWING LEHI'S EXAMPLE, NEPHI DEPARTS

Consider the many ways in which Nephi's departure from the land of first inheritance echoes Lehi's departure from Jerusalem (5:4–7). Both Lehi and Nephi left under threats of death (5:2, 4) because of their words (5:3); both were warned by the Lord to depart and flee into the wilderness (5:5); both took their families, took their tents, journeyed for many days, and pitched their tents (5:6–7). Might Nephi's mentioning of these detailed similarities be significant in reflecting and fulfilling Nephi's need to establish himself as Lehi's legitimate successor? How might this pattern of obedient and organized response to serious threats help anyone in following the Lord's prophet in fleeing from spiritual dangers?

2 NEPHI 5:10-11—THE PROMINENCE OF THE LAW AMONG THE NEPHITES

Nephi specifically affirmed that they kept the law of Moses "in all things." What would this involve? Nephi testified that his people "did prosper exceedingly" in the land, as their crops and herds flourished (5:11), just as the law in Deuteronomy 28:2–6, with its seven-fold blessing, had assured the covenant people. How does striving to observe the requirements of the Lord with exactness help promote righteousness and spirituality?

2 NEPHI 5:12-14—NEPHI'S THREE SYMBOLS OF AUTHORITY

Nephi mentioned three symbols of authority that he took with him: (1) the plates of brass, (2) the Liahona, and (3) the sword of Laban. In many kingships throughout history, three elements have dignified royal authority, namely the book of the law, the orb or world sphere, and the sword of defensive power and justice. What can these three symbols represent in our lives and in the world today, as we strive to make righteous judgments and to become kings and queens unto the Most High God?

2 NEPHI 5:15-17—THE TEMPLE'S IMPORTANCE TO THE NEPHITES

Certainly, the temple was central in Lehi's and Nephi's world. It was the place where people gathered to be taught the law of the Lord, to express their loyalty to God and to their leaders, to make purifying sacrifices, to pray, and to experience and express joy. Life in Nephi's world would have been almost unthinkable without a temple. And so, one of the very first things Nephi did when he established his new city was to construct a temple. Having been taught many useful building skills and being hard workers, Nephi and his people, at great sacrifice, built a glorious temple, modeled after the temple of Solomon. Although not as opulent, it was no less the House of the Lord. It was the center of life, devotion, and happiness for Nephi and his people. The temple is just as important in the world today, and maybe even more so.

2 NEPHI 5:18—NEPHI'S RIGHTEOUS KINGSHIP

Why might Nephi have been reluctant to become a king? He certainly knew the Lord told him he would become a ruler and teacher over his brothers. But becoming a king would have been something else! Nephi had not been raised in the royal household. He was not of the tribe of Judah, let alone in the bloodline of King David. Kings were anointed and consecrated in coronation ceremonies (see Psalms 2), but who would have enthroned Nephi? Only the voice of God Himself, elevating the new monarch to this high and holy office. Reading in Deuteronomy 17:14–20, Nephi would have learned the Lord's scriptural handbook of instructions for his kings, in which he requires that they read the law all the days of their life; and do not multiply wives, gold, silver, or possessions (including horses) unto yourself. Considering Nephi's humble example and the guidelines found in Deuteronomy, what qualities should still be found in the character of good leaders of all kinds today?

2 NEPHI 5:20-23—MAINTAINING MEMBERSHIP MARKERS

As their leader, Nephi did all that was within his power to help his people, and he needed to deter members of his small and fragile group from defecting back to their cousins. Especially because those family members who would not obey Nephi's words were "cut off from the presence of the Lord"—which would have meant that they could not enter the temple of Nephi nor intermarry with the people of Nephi (compare Exodus 34:16; Deuteronomy 7:1). It was important to the survival of that fragile society that those dissenters should "not be enticing" unto the people of Nephi. Their hearts were hard as flint; their hands were impure; but these social problems were not indelible. They were not innate. These defects could be overcome simply if those dissenters would "repent of their iniquities." This concern, especially in antiquity, was not about any modern construct of the idea of race but was rather about ensuring generational obedience to the first commandment to have no other god before the Lord (Exodus 34:14–16).

2 NEPHI 5:30-32—THE ACUTE NEED FOR ACCURATE RECORDS

Nephi gladly reports that his people "lived after the manner of happiness" (5:27), and he was told by the Lord to begin keeping a second set of records "for the profit of thy people" (5:30). In modern times, the first instruction given to the Church upon its organization on April 6, 1830, only ten days after the Book of Mormon had come off the press, was that "there shall be a record kept among you" (Doctrine and Covenants 21:1). And it has always been thus among the faithful. In addition to their religious purposes (1 Nephi 6:4–5; 9:5), accurate records also enhance our memory, provide wisdom in addressing social and political challenges, and will be one of the bases on which we will be judged according to our knowledge and accountability (see, for example, Mosiah 3:24).

TAKEAWAYS

- Ponder the blessings Lehi lists from having both the Bible and Book of Mormon (3:12). How can you better use both to claim those blessings in your life?
- "The cursing" in 5:21 seems to refer to the previous verse. According to that verse, what exactly was the cursing of the Lamanites? How does this better explain the outcomes in v. 24 and the relevance of these verses to all people?
- Which family or personal records have blessed you? How might you improve your record-keeping?

8: 2 NEPHI 6-10

2 NEPHI 6:1-10—WHY IS JACOB'S SERMON IN NEPHI'S RECORD?

Many of the themes that show up in 2 Nephi 6–10 have been identified as typical of the New Year, Day of Atonement, or the Feast of Tabernacles on the regular Jewish calendar. During those annual festivals, ancient Israelites typically held coronations and the renewal or re-enthronement of the king as well as a covenant renewal of the people's loyalty to obey the king of Israel. Jacob's speech is likely a covenant renewal speech given at such a time of traditional celebration.

We know covenant is a central theme because in 2 Nephi 9:1, Jacob states his purpose as follows: "And now, my beloved brethren, I have read these things *that ye might know concerning the covenants of the Lord* that he has covenanted with all the House of Israel." Several parts of Jacob's speech follow old traditions that the Nephites continued. For example, several scholars, both those who are and are not Latter-day Saints, have identified in the Old Testament a covenant treaty pattern, though this pattern was not just limited to the Hebrews. Such "treaty-covenants" (1) had a preamble, (2) gave a historical overview, (3) stated stipulations of the covenant, (4) extended blessings and curses structured as "if you do this, this will happen; if you do not do it, such and such will happen." Then there was (5) a witness formula, and (6) a recording of the covenant. Jacob's words in 2 Nephi 6–10 can be read well in the context of the treaty-covenant pattern, similar to King Benjamin's covenant speech given in the context of Mosiah's coronation.

One might get the impression that this was Nephi's inauguration or coronation as king. However, 2 Nephi 5:28 tells how the Nephites built a temple, and thirty years passed away, and then Nephi made the record, and then another ten years had passed away (5:34). It is not certain when Jacob's speech occurred, but it may have been during one of Nephi's royal anniversaries for which the Feast of Tabernacles was known.

2 NEPHI 6:17-18—WHAT DREW JACOB TO THESE WORDS OF ISAIAH?

In his speech, Jacob quoted Isaiah 49:22 to Isaiah 52:2. What was it that drew Jacob to these particular words of Isaiah?

First, Jacob was told by Nephi to read these selected words to the assembled people of Nephi (6:4). As prophet and king, Nephi surely wanted to reassure his people that God would protect his people: "the Mighty God shall deliver his *covenant* people" (6:17; Isaiah 49:25). This fledgling community must have worried and needed this reassurance.

Second, all the people were to know that "all flesh shall know that I the Lord am thy Savior and thy *Redeemer*, the *Mighty* One of Jacob" (6:18; compare Isaiah 49:26). Jacob, the priest of the temple in the city of Nephi, would have been especially desirous that his people would find redemption and deliverance through Jehovah, their Redeemer (Jacob used the word *"deliver"* or "deliverance" 12 times in 2 Nephi 9). Despite their being more alone than ever before, the Lord had not abandoned them in the wilderness. Thus, this block of text suited their needs perfectly.

Third, from these words, Jacob hoped that the people were to "learn and glorify the *name* of your God" (6:4). Previously, Jesus Christ had been called several names, such as "Messiah," "the Lamb of God," "the Lord [Jehovah]," and others. Now, in order that they might "learn . . . the name" of their God, to be used in glorifying Him, Jacob disclosed to his people that His holy name, when He would come among the Jews in the flesh, would be "Christ." That name had been spoken to Jacob by the angel of the Lord during the night (10:3) in the interval between the two days of this coronation and covenant-renewal celebration. Because the word "Christ" literally means "anointed," raising that name when renewing the people's covenant to God and loyalty to His anointed king (as kings in Israel were called, Psalms 2:2) would have been especially appropriate.

2 NEPHI 7:1-10—THE LORD HAS NOT PUT AWAY HIS PEOPLE

Isaiah likens our covenant with God to a marriage covenant. Under the law of Moses, a man could find some offense in his wife and say, "I divorce thee" and give her a paper of divorcement, which would end the marriage. If a person had huge debts, they would sometimes sell their children into slavery to the creditors. But the Lord has not, and will not, do any of those things.

2 NEPHI 7:11—WHAT DOES IT MEAN TO "WALK IN THE LIGHT OF YOUR OWN FIRE"?

Joseph F. Smith warned against those who falsely teach, using their own light, preaching false doctrines disguised as gospel truths. He said they are "proud and self-vaunting ones, who read by the lamps of their own conceit; who interpret by rules of their own contriving; who have become a law unto themselves, and so pose as the sole judges of their own doings" (Joseph F. Smith. *Gospel Doctrine* [Salt Lake City: Deseret Book, 1939], 373).

2 NEPHI 8:1—THE ROCK FROM WHENCE YE ARE HEWN

Isaiah's words continue by telling people to "look unto the rock from whence ye are hewn." But from what rock are we hewn? Consider the rock of Abraham and Sarah's bond (the covenant promise), the priesthood that Peter would be entrusted with when he was called the Rock (the power), the eternal nature of the covenants made in the temple also called the dome of the rock (the place), in other words, the rock of our Redeemer.

The words of Isaiah paved the way for Jacob's main words to his people. Seven times Isaiah used the emphatic opening expression, "O . . ." in Isaiah 51–52 (2 Nephi 8): O my nation, O arm of the Lord, O Jerusalem, O Zion, O Jerusalem, O Jerusalem, O captive.

Jacob will continue this pattern throughout these chapters, beginning fourteen of his powerful exclamations this same way: O the wisdom, O how great the goodness, O how great the plan, O the greatness and justice, O the greatness of the mercy, O how great the holiness, O that cunning plan, O the vainness, O my beloved brethren (five times), and O Lord God Almighty. Not just stylistically, but thematically, Jacob's words elaborated and personalized many of the main themes found in the words of Isaiah that Nephi assigned Jacob to read and teach (6:4).

2 NEPHI 8:24—MODERN-DAY REVELATION CLARIFIES

In Doctrine and Covenants 113:7, a very thoughtful man named Elias Higbee asked, "What is meant by the command in Isaiah, 52d chapter, 1st verse, which saith: Put on thy strength, O Zion—and what people had Isaiah reference to?" (Of course, Isaiah 52 and 2 Nephi 8 are the same.) Joseph Smith explained,

> [Isaiah] had reference to those whom God should call in the last days, who should hold the power of priesthood to bring again Zion, and the redemption of Israel; and to put on her strength is to put on the authority of the priesthood, which she, Zion, has a right to by lineage; also to return to that power which she had lost (Doctrine and Covenants 113:8).

And then Higbee asked about the meaning of the "bands around the neck," and Joseph Smith said,

> We are to understand that the scattered remnants are exhorted to return to the Lord from whence they have fallen; which if they do, the promise of the Lord is that he will speak to them, or give them revelation. . . . The bands of her neck are the curses of God upon her, or the remnants of Israel in their scattered condition among the Gentiles (Doctrine and Covenants 113:10).

2 NEPHI 9:1-7—JACOB ON THE ATONEMENT

The Atonement is the first theme of redemption that Jacob addresses in this chapter (expressly in 9:7, 25, 26). What are some of the powers of the Atonement that Jacob mentioned here? The power of resurrection, the power to bring one back into the presence of God, and the power to make what was corrupted incorrupt.

Although ancient people did not use the term *entropy,* the basic principle of this law was understood as a form of chaos. Everything in nature disintegrates. As you look around, you will see decay everywhere. But the power of the Atonement arrests that entropy and reverses it, restoring each corrupted thing to its most perfect state—physically *and* spiritually. Beyond restoration, Christ will permanently stop the process of entropy and corruption. "If it were not so, this flesh must be laid down to rot and to crumble to its mother earth and rise no more" (9:7).

Elder Jeffery R. Holland wrote,

Jacob's testimony was that "the Mighty God" will always deliver "his covenant people," and that the Mighty God is, by his own divine declaration, the Lord God Jesus Christ, the "Savior . . . and Redeemer, the Mighty One of Jacob."

Jacob reflected on such teachings—especially those contained in the writings of Isaiah—so that his current audience and future readers "might know concerning the covenants of the Lord that he has covenanted with all the House of Israel," giving the parents of every generation cause to "rejoice" and to "lift up [their] heads forever, because of the blessings which the Lord God shall bestow upon [their]children."

Elder Holland adds something that is key to chapter 9: "At the heart of the covenant and the reason for such rejoicing is the atoning sacrifice of that 'Mighty God' who is the Savior and Redeemer of the world" (*Christ and the New Covenant* [Salt Lake City: Deseret Book, 1997], 66–67).

2 NEPHI 9:14–A PERFECT KNOWLEDGE OF OUR MISTAKES

For Jacob, it was important that we recognize our sins. True repentance comes from a bright recollection and a genuine confidence that the Lord has provided everything essential for us, pending our acceptance. President Gordon B. Hinckley often taught that a daily recommitment to accepting the Atonement of Christ and an honest willingness to change *is* daily repentance. It is not the Lord's intent that we read these things and say, "O how wretched am I?" and cry all night.

2 NEPHI 9:27-38–JACOB'S TEN WOES

After assuring his people that the Atonement would satisfy the demands of God's justice "upon all those who have *not* the law given to them" (9:26), people who know better will be held accountable. As a warning, Jacob then pronounced a set of ten woes upon those (1) who set aside the counsel of God, (2) who despise the poor, (3) who will not hear and obey, (4) the blind who will not see, (5) whose hearts are impure or uncircumcised, (6) who tell lies, (7) who deliberately kill, (8) who commit whoredoms, (9) who worship idols, and (10) all who die in their sins (27–38). In a covenant setting, this list of woes functions much like the list of twelve curses found near the end of the book of Deuteronomy (27:15–26).

Several of Jacob's woes are consequential warnings related to several of the Ten Commandments, which served as the basis of the Lord's covenant with the children of Israel at Mount Sinai. Covenants come with commitments, and failing to keep one's righteous commitments leads to unhappiness. Such ten-fold structures signal to listeners the completeness or perfection of the Lord's covenant teachings and promises (see Figure 1, on page 173 of the John W. Welch Notes, 2 Nephi 6–10).

2 NEPHI 9:41–CHRIST KEEPS WATCH OVER THE GATE TO SALVATION

As the high priest, Jacob would have stood guard over the gates and the holiness of the House of the Lord. Entering the temple can cast our minds forward to the time when we will come to the gate that is kept by the Holy One.

2 NEPHI 9:44-45–JACOB SHAKES HIS GARMENTS

Visualize Jacob as he took off his high priestly robes and shook them saying, "I shake them before you . . . I am rid of your blood" (9:44). Why would he do that? This is a symbolic action signifying that he has performed his priestly duty to teach and administer the covenant of the Lord to them; therefore, he is avoiding being judged of priestly neglect, and is no longer responsible for the sins they may commit (compare Jacob 1:19).

Jacob wanted to absolutely impress upon his people the importance of holiness. God wants His people to be holy. Several keywords are used by Jacob in this chapter, including "judgment" (seven times), "remember" (eight times), and "deliver" (twelve times). But the dominant key word in this temple covenant speech is "holy." It appears twenty-three times, and "holiness" two times more. The dominant name used by Jacob here for the Lord is "the Holy One of Israel," which appears thirteen times. One may well conclude that the main theme of Jacob's temple speech here is holiness: "Holiness to the Lord."

2 NEPHI 10:1-2–THE NEPHITE BRANCH WILL BE RESTORED

The next morning, Jacob resumed his speech where he left off, by assuring his people that they are a "righteous branch" (9:53; 10:1). Zenos and Isaiah and Nephi had spoken about branches of the House of Israel, righteous or evil (for example, 1 Nephi 15:12; 19:24; 2 Nephi 14:2; 21). Jacob thus assured his audience: You too are a branch of that tree, and you still belong to that tree, and you will be grafted back in when their posterity comes to a knowledge of their Redeemer (10:2). They will be preserved. That image, of course, will reappear in Jacob 5, when Jacob recited to the people Zenos's lengthy Allegory of the Olive Tree.

2 NEPHI 10:3-7–JESUS WILL BE REJECTED BECAUSE OF PRIESTCRAFTS

Just as the leaders of the people had killed prophets like Urijah and were prepared to kill Lehi and Jeremiah, the descendants of those leaders will likewise kill the anointed Holy Christ. Jacob rightly does not blame all the people in Jerusalem, but primarily those priests involved with priestcrafts and iniquity (10:5). Nephi called them wicked shepherds. "Because of the wickedness of the pastors of my people," those who have been driven out have been broken off (1 Nephi 21:1). Years later, people like those wicked priests will reject Jesus in spite of—and perhaps because of—the "mighty miracles" (2 Nephi 10:4) He would perform. Those powerful signs and wonders would understandably have terrified people who did not think Jesus was the Son of God, figuring that His miracles were powered by the Evil One. Likely the same angelic being who spoke along these lines to Jacob (10:3) later explained further to King Benjamin that Jesus's opponents would condemn Him, declaring Him to have "a devil" (Mosiah 3:9).

From their point of view, death was the required legal penalty for performing miracles, signs, or wonders that led people away to follow other paths or to worship in unauthorized ways (see Deuteronomy 13:1–5), and the mode of execution for such an offense was crucifixion or "hanging on a tree" (Deuteronomy 21:22). And, indeed, as Jacob knew, no other nation had such laws as are found in Deuteronomy. For these reasons, Jacob could well have foreseen that in no other nation would a group of priestly leaders react with such awful fear and hostility against such beneficial miracles, signs, and wonders. But nevertheless, and amazingly, on the cross the Lord had the strength to forgive the soldiers who knew not what they were doing. In addition, it would seem, Jesus also would have soon held out forgiveness to all who were involved in any way in bringing about His death. They too must not have really known what they were doing. Evidence of Jesus's continued extension of mercy and willingness to forgive can be found in Jacob's declaration that Christ has "covenanted with their fathers that [these people] shall [still] be restored in the flesh, upon the earth [when they] shall believe in me, that I am Christ" (10:7). He has not thrown them away or cast anyone off.

2 NEPHI 10:8-19—ISRAEL WILL BE REMEMBERED IN ALL LANDS

To prepare the way for that to happen, the Jews and Israel who will be scattered among the nations will be remembered and gathered from "the isles of the sea" (see 2 Nephi 10:8). Jacob and his people would have been relieved to hear this promise. They would have been comforted not only in their being remembered, but also in the knowledge that there would be others like them scattered about amidst the nations of the world. When we hear the word *gentiles*, we often think of people who are not members of the Church. But the word *gentiles* in ancient times literally meant the *nations* or birth lines. We get our word *genealogy* from that root word. The Lord was saying that He will work through all kindreds and nations, their kings and queens (10:9, see 2 Nephi 6:6), to restore His people.

In this prophetic connection, Jacob also spoke concerning the future of his people's posterity in their land of promise, which will be a "protected" and "consecrated" land of liberty, where no kings "shall raise up unto the Gentiles" (10:11, 19). Secret works of darkness will be destroyed (10:15), those who fight against Zion must needs perish (10:16), the hearts of the Gentiles will be softened, and they will be "like a father to them" (10:18; compare 2 Nephi 6:6). These are wonderful promises of the Lord that surely gave great assurance to Jacob and his people.

2 NEPHI 10:20-25—JACOB COMFORTS THE NEPHITES

In closing, Jacob reassured his people that they will not be forgotten. They will receive the promises of the Lord, including the ultimate promises of a resurrection and eternal kingdom. Jacob's plea that people will choose the way of life over the way of death echoes Lehi's words regarding choice and accountability spoken to Jacob and his brothers in 2 Nephi 2:27. And those words align with Joshua's ancient covenant-renewal charge: "Choose ye this day whom you will serve," either the Lord or other gods (Joshua 24:15).

TAKEAWAYS

- In what ways can chapter 7 give you strength to endure difficulties and trials, especially those caused by sin?
- Can we be guilty of other people's sins? What does Jacob teach in 9:44 (cf. Jacob 1:19) about why we can and about how to rid ourselves of others' iniquities?
- How does Christ's Atonement give you reason to rejoice?

9: 2 NEPHI 11-19

2 NEPHI 11:1-3—NEPHI ESTABLISHES HIS WORD IN THE MOUTH OF THREE WITNESSES

Nephi begins this long section, in which he quotes from Isaiah 2–14, by testifying that his "soul delights in the words of Isaiah." He says that he will liken those words unto his own people and call them forth because Isaiah "verily saw my Redeemer, even as I have seen him, and my brother, Jacob, also has seen him as I have seen him." Nephi thus produces three witnesses of this most important eternal truth, namely Isaiah, Jacob, and himself. Nephi is probably thinking of Deuteronomy 17:6 or 19:15, which requires that by the words "of three witnesses, shall the matter be established."

We too can be strengthened by three witnesses in important ways: by the testimony of the Three Witnesses of the Book of Mormon, by the harmony of the three members of the First Presidency, and by the unity of other presidencies or bishoprics in the Church. These triads find their model in the Godhead. As Jesus taught, He and Heavenly Father and the Holy Ghost "bear record" of each other (3 Nephi 11:36). Nephi invites all people to receive blessings by hearkening to (hearing and obeying) these righteous witnesses.

2 NEPHI 11-25—INTRODUCTION: THE NEPHITE PROPHETIC VIEW

Here in these chapters, Nephi will follow the same basic prophetic pattern that he introduced in 1 Nephi 11–14 and used in 1 Nephi 19–22. Now, in 2 Nephi 12–24, Nephi quotes many chapters from Isaiah as a further witness to the visions of the future that he had also received from the Lord. Nephi will then interpret these Isaiah passages in 2 Nephi 25–30, using his four-stage pattern to help readers understand these Isaiah chapters.

Throughout this block of Isaiah chapters, elements of all four of these stages are scattered. This is because Isaiah's writings were recorded as somewhat of a scrapbook of prophecies given at different times. Isaiah did not sit down and write the book of Isaiah at one time. Each prophetic saying was a separate prophecy, like a piece in a large prophetic puzzle. We do not know when all those prophetic pieces were gathered. An old Jewish tradition says they were collected in the days of King Hezekiah (about forty years after Isaiah died), but no one knows who put them into their present order as the book of Isaiah.

Nephi first quotes Isaiah 2–14 in 2 Nephi 12–24. Note that the chapter numbers of these thirteen Book of Mormon chapters are exactly ten chapter numbers greater than their numbers in the Bible. After including those chapters in his small plates, Nephi explains in 2 Nephi 25–30 the main topics in those chapters from his perspective, especially considering what he has established as the four stages of his Nephite prophetic view of God's plan for the future of the world.

Readers can use Nephi's four prophetic stages (as explained above) to unpack and clarify the meanings behind many of Isaiah's key words.

For example, Stage 1 is about the coming of Jesus Christ among the Jews and His rejection because of priestcrafts, and thus, in 2 Nephi 17:10–16 (or Isaiah 7) one reads that Isaiah foresaw that a sign would be given of the coming of Jesus, which Isaiah speaks of as the birth of Immanuel. And in 2 Nephi 19:17–25 (or Isaiah 9), Isaiah prophesies that the land of Judah will be forsaken and will become desolate. In 2 Nephi 19:6, Isaiah says that a great light will shine and "unto us a son is given." But in 19:16 their leaders will unfortunately "cause them [the people] to err."

In Stage 2, Nephi prophesies that the Jews will be scattered, and yet the Lord will not forget them. Regarding this stage, see 2 Nephi 13:1–14:1; 15:13; 15:25–26; 19:21 (or those same verses in Isaiah 3, 5, 9).

In Stage 3, in the day of the Gentiles, a remnant of the House of Israel will be called and gathered again from the islands of the sea and all nations. See 2 Nephi 15:26–30; 16:13; 20:20–23; 21:10-16 (or those same verses in Isaiah 5, 6, 10, 11).

And finally, in Nephi's Stage 4, in the day of judgment the wicked will be destroyed (see 12:11–22; 20:1–19; 23:1–22; 24:9–28), and the righteous will be blessed (see 12:1–5; 21:1–9; 24:1–8, 29–32; and the corresponding verses in Isaiah).

Nephi's prophetic worldview offers a plain, four-stage framework within which to understand the otherwise complicated words of Isaiah, as the following comments further illustrate. Equipped with this spirit of prophecy, Nephi rejoices in the "plainness" of the words of Isaiah (2 Nephi 25:4), whose meanings are not otherwise plain.

2 NEPHI 11:2-8—ISAIAH'S INFLUENCE ON NEPHI'S WORLD

Because Isaiah was active as a prophet of Judah living in Jerusalem from 740–701 BC, only 100 years later, Lehi and Nephi thought of Isaiah as "The Prophet," much as we think of Joseph Smith as our founding Prophet.

2 NEPHI 15:1-7—ISAIAH SAW THE GREAT APOSTASY

Isaiah saw there would be a falling away after the Lord would come and establish His church. We see in Isaiah's allegory of the vineyard that the Lord did all he could to save the choice vine, but it brought forth wild grapes. He built a wine press, perhaps an allusion to the Garden of Gethsemane (or the Olive Press), the press of the Atonement. Moreover, he took all the bad stones out of the vineyard. He gave it every possible chance, but it still produced wild fruit.

2 NEPHI 15:26—THE LORD WILL CALL HIS PEOPLE BACK

The Lord will remember the covenants He has made with His people. Verse 26 says that He will lift up an ensign. He will hiss (or whistle) to them to call them back. The ensign (or flag) will mark a gathering point and a rallying post that will bring people back together in victory.

2 NEPHI 16:1—ISAIAH RECEIVES HIS PROPHETIC CALL

Isaiah recorded his experience in receiving his prophetic call. Isaiah was in the temple, in the sacred backroom called the Holy of Holies. There he saw the Lord, who likely explained to Isaiah the foreordained plan of salvation, what the Lord would do, and how Isaiah should invite all to love and obey the Lord.

2 NEPHI 16:5-7—ISAIAH AFFIRMS THAT HE IS "A MAN OF UNCLEAN LIPS"

Isaiah felt self-conscious about speech, that his voice was unclean or inadequate. In comparison to God's words, even the words of a mighty prophet seem impure. Likewise, if our lips and thoughts are not pure, we will feel uncomfortable in the presence of God. We need to be clean—in every way. To clean Isaiah's lips, the Lord used a hot coal from the altar. Similarly, here's how people in ancient times determined if a witness was telling the truth. According to some ancient Near Eastern texts, a witness whose honesty was in doubt could be required to submit to an "ordeal." Something very hot (such as a hot spatula or a coal) was put on the witness's tongue. If it hurt, that was evidence that he was lying, because someone lying normally has a dry mouth and cannot tolerate something burning hot on his tongue. However, if the witness was telling the truth, his tongue would be coated with saliva to prevent the heat from hurting his tongue. This operated like a type of primitive lie-detector test. We might wonder if Isaiah was thus affirming that he was telling the truth, having passed this ordeal of the hot coal.

2 NEPHI 16:8-10—THE LORD CALLS ISAIAH TO BE A PROPHET

The Lord asked, "Whom shall I send, and who will go for us?" Isaiah answered the call, "Here am I; send me." As recorded in Abraham 3:27, these are also the words spoken by the Savior in the premortal council as He accepted the call to perform the Atonement as Savior of mankind. The Lord explained that the people in Jerusalem were not ready or worthy to be told everything in plain language, so Isaiah would need to speak in ways those people wouldn't completely understand. But, as Nephi will later explain, Isaiah's prophecies are clear to those who have a willing mind and have "ears to hear."

2 NEPHI 17:3—THE MEANING BEHIND THE NAME OF ISAIAH'S SON

Isaiah gave his son the name of "Shearjashub," which may mean "a remnant shall return." Through the Son of God, a remnant of Israel would indeed return.

2 NEPHI 17:14—A VIRGIN WILL CONCEIVE

The word in Greek describing this woman is *parthenon*. This is normally interpreted as "a virgin" but can also mean "a young girl." However, the meaning of Isaiah here in Hebrew, which Nephi understood, clearly indicated virginity. Isaiah was prophesying that there was going to be something unusual about this birth, even more than other miraculous births in ancient scripture, such as a very old woman giving birth (e.g., Sarah, wife of Abraham; or Elizabeth, wife of Zacharias). This child would become the Mighty Counselor and Prince of Peace.

TAKEAWAYS

- Compare the things that delight you to the things that delight Nephi in chapter 11.
- In what ways has the Lord fulfilled 14:5-6 in your life today?
- Are there other scriptures that can help you determine what the following items of Isaiah's song-parable in chapter 15 represent? 1) vineyard, 2) fruitful hill, 3) fence/hedge/wall, 4) stones, 5) choicest vine, 6) tower, 7) winepress, and 8) grapes.
- Why would the Lord through Isaiah choose the birth of a child to be the sign that Judah's enemies will no longer be a threat (2 Nephi 17)? What does this teach us about the birth of Christ?

10: 2 NEPHI 20-25

2 NEPHI 21:1-5—THE STEM AND ROOT OF JESSE

Isaiah continued to prophesy about the coming of Christ in 2 Nephi 21:1–5. Among the many biblical prophecies Moroni quoted to Joseph Smith in 1823, words in Isaiah 11 (appearing here as 2 Nephi 21) were declared in particular as "about to be fulfilled." Isaiah 11 speaks of "the stem of Jesse," "a rod [or branch] that will come out of the stem of Jesse," and a "root of Jesse." Doctrine and Covenants 113:1–6 explains that the stem of Jesse refers to Jesus Christ. Who was Jesse? He was a descendant of Judah and the father of King David. Isaiah was prophesying that the Savior would come through this royal line, as indeed Jesus did, whether one looks at the genealogy given by Matthew (see 1:6) or the genealogy given by Luke (see Luke 3:31).

Isaiah also spoke of a rod or branch, as well as of roots, that would come from the central stem. The rod and the roots are described in Doctrine and Covenants 113:3–6 as being two different people who would both descend from the tribe of Joseph as well as from the tribe of Judah. Might Joseph Smith be either the "rod" or the "root" of Jesse, with Jesus Christ being the "stem"? Was Joseph Smith a descendant of Jesse? He might be, through a collateral ancestral line. We don't know that for sure, but we do know that he is of the tribe of Ephraim and thus a descendant of Joseph, a son of the Old Testament Jacob. Even though the prophecy of Isaiah may not be clear on this or every detail, the symbolism of the "stem" is clear—the stem refers to the coming of Christ.

2 NEPHI 21:11—THE LORD WILL GATHER HIS PEOPLE A SECOND TIME

The important words in this verse are "the second time." There would be a gathering, as Nephi said, when a remnant of Israel would be brought back from the first exile in Babylon. Nephi explains in 2 Nephi 25 that they would be brought back so that the Lord could appear to them in Jerusalem. However, the House of Israel would be scattered again because of the hardness of their hearts and their rejection of Jesus. Here, Isaiah knew that the Lord would have to set His hand a *second time* to gather them "from Assyria, and from Egypt, and from Pathros, and from Cush, and from Elam, and from Shinar, and from Hamath, and from the islands of the sea." Nephi spoke of this second gathering of Israel both in physical and in spiritual terms.

2 NEPHI 25:1-11—NEPHI'S COMMENTARY ON ISAIAH'S TEACHINGS

After quoting from Isaiah 2–14 (2 Nephi 12–24), Nephi provided six additional chapters of his own interpretation of Isaiah (see 2 Nephi 25–30). Nephi wanted his people to understand what

Isaiah meant, which Nephi could understand since he had lived in Jerusalem and understood the manner of speech, language, and culture there. Nephi illuminates these chapters in light of the four main elements in his prophetic worldview mentioned in the previous chapter (chapter 9), beginning with the mortal ministry of Christ.

2 NEPHI 25:12-17—JESUS'S DEATH AND PASSOVER

The three days of darkness surrounding the death of Jesus in 3 Nephi 9–10 correlate with the three days of darkness and death that prevailed in Egypt at the time of the first Passover. The latter foreshadowed the three days of darkness when Jesus would be crucified, would shed His blood like a lamb, would die, and would lie in the tomb. As in the Passover, those who were among the "more righteous" were "spared" (3 Nephi 9:13).

2 NEPHI 25:18-19—ONE TRUE MESSIAH

Nephi said to his people that they should not look for another Messiah. There would be no other Messiah, "for there is save one Messiah spoken of by the prophets, and that Messiah is he who should be rejected of the Jews." The word *mashiach* in Hebrew means "anointed" or "anointed one." In ancient times, the high priest was anointed. So, in a way, every high priest was a "mashiach"—a messiah. In 1 Nephi 10:5, Lehi said that *a* messiah would come. Lehi did not say *the* Messiah, so Nephi clarified all this by revealing the name of the Messiah, namely "Jesus Christ, the Son of God." These words were used in introducing the resurrected Lord to the Nephites (3 Nephi 11:7, 10). Nephi did not pin the date down precisely, but he did say that Jesus would come "six hundred years from the time that [Lehi and his family] left Jerusalem." Christ's birth was close enough to 600 years that people recognized that Jesus was indeed the Messiah, and they had no need to look for another.

2 NEPHI 25:23-24—AFTER ALL WE CAN DO

Nephi says that "we are saved by grace *after all we can do*." What does that mean? Some, including the German translators in the 1960s, have thought it is saying "in spite of all we can do," meaning that anything we do is inconsequential. That translation, however, was soon corrected to say, "after all that we can do." What we do in truly accepting the gift of grace matters.

Verse 24 continues: "Notwithstanding [even though we are saved by grace], we believe in Christ, we keep the law of Moses, and look forward with steadfastness unto Christ, until the law shall be fulfilled." Thus, all of us must rely on grace—the Atonement, the Resurrection, and the sustaining influence of Jesus Christ—to be made perfect. But through our faith and faithfulness we are made alive in Christ, being willing to do what He has commanded. Keeping the commandments is part of "all we can do."

The story of the Ammonites, who buried their weapons of war to have their sins remitted, bears out this understanding. They state that this was "*all that we could do* (as we were the most lost of all mankind) to repent of all our sins and the many murders which we have committed, to get God to take them away from our hearts, for it was *all we could do to repent sufficiently* before God that he would take away our stain" (Alma 24:11). Likewise, all that we can do includes turning to Christ, renouncing our sinful ways, and making a covenant, and He will be there for us. So completely did the Ammonites understand this that many of them offered to give up their lives rather than fight.

2 NEPHI 25:26—NEPHI WRITES THE PROPHECIES OF CHRIST FOR HIS POSTERITY

No other prophets in the scriptures tell what they taught their children. For Nephi, it was important to mention his children. He taught them about Christ. He put this at the top of his list of important things to do.

2 NEPHI 25:29-30—LIVING THE LAW OF MOSES

Soon after Nephi and his people settled in the land they eventually called Nephi, they built a temple. Because Nephi's people were still living the law of Moses, they needed that temple in order to obey many parts of that law. However, Nephi understood and taught that the ordinances under the law of Moses pointed to Christ.

TAKEAWAYS

- **What things does Nephi say in chapter 25 that can help define what it means to have the "spirit of prophecy"?**
- **How can Nephi's use of the word "sufficient" in 25:28 give confidence to parents, teachers, or anyone who is trying to guide others?**
- **How do we truly accept the Savior's gift of grace?**

11: 2 NEPHI 26-30

These chapters would have reassured Nephi's people that, even though they would live in isolation and their civilization would not last, their efforts were not unimportant. The Lord would come to them (2 Nephi 26), they would leave a record that would come forth miraculously (2 Nephi 27), and even though the devil would seek in many ways to impede the progress of that book (2 Nephi 28), it will figure prominently in the last days (2 Nephi 29), when many covenant people shall be restored with rejoicing unto the blessings of the Lord (2 Nephi 30).

2 NEPHI 26:4-7, 9—WICKED AND RIGHTEOUS NEPHITE POSTERITY WHEN CHRIST APPEARS

Nephi identified among his posterity those who will be destroyed, namely the proud and those who do wickedly, particularly in reviling the prophets. He specifically warned of thunderings, lightnings, and earthquakes that would occur. Can you imagine Nephi's feelings as he was shown the awful destruction of his own people? Despite that inexpressible agony, however, what was his response? Did he curse God and object to what would happen? No. He said, "I must cry unto my God: thy ways are just" (26:7). What a remarkable example for responding to current calamities and problems.

Nephi also saw that those people who hearkened to the prophets would not be destroyed. The "Son of righteousness" (26:9) would appear to them, heal them, and they would have continual peace for three generations. All who personally interacted with Christ became eyewitnesses of the Savior, and throughout their lives they could relate their firsthand experience to others. Have you thought about the direct impact your influence could have over three or four generations?

2 NEPHI 26:24-27, 33—EVERYTHING IS FOR OUR BENEFIT, ALL ARE ALIKE UNTO GOD

"He doeth not anything save it be for the benefit of the world; for he loveth the world" (26:24). That is an absolute statement—*everything* Jesus does is for the benefit of the world. Think of it: creating, healing, revealing, delegating, forgiving, encouraging, teaching, commanding, atoning, redeeming. All His efforts are for our benefit. When we help others to repent, we assist Him. Christ commands us to "persuade all men to repentance" (26:27). There is no intellectual challenge greater than figuring out what you can say or do to help someone else repent. This is a quintessential Christlike endeavor.

The love Nephi is speaking of is a welcoming love. Christlike people invite others into their life and into the Kingdom of God. "[H]e inviteth them all to come unto him and partake of his goodness" (26:33). We are all children of the same Heavenly Father, and we are all loved by Him and by our Savior. That makes us alike in the ways that really matter. What a wonderful, universal message Christ's Atonement extends to all people throughout the world.

2 NEPHI 27:6-8—THE NEPHITE RECORD WILL COME FORTH

Think of how disoriented and isolated Nephi must have felt. He had lived much of his adult life in wilderness lands under harsh conditions, first fleeing Jerusalem and then leaving the original family settlement in the promised land. Now, Nephi was a king trying to run a city. Administratively, he worked to reestablish a society and bring order to his people. For their spiritual growth, they had built a temple. Given Nephi's foreknowledge of great wars that would lead to Nephite extinction, he may have sometimes wondered if all his efforts were futile. Yet, Nephi also understood that their record would speak to the whole house of Israel. This must have given him hope.

Nephi saw that these writings would be witnessed and sealed, meaning that the record would not just be closed, but that it would be preserved with authority. Anciently, when a scribe wrote an official document, he would bind up the written record, put a lump of clay or wax on the knot, and imprint his seal to indicate that the record was an official, correct document. We can learn something from the fact that the record of the Nephites was witnessed and sealed. It is important to ascertain the attestation of those who influence us.

2 NEPHI 27:26—WHAT IS SIGNIFICANT ABOUT A MARVELOUS WORK AND A WONDER?

Isaiah's prophetic phrase regarding the Book of Mormon coming forth is translated into English as "*a marvelous work and a wonder.*" Isaiah actually wrote that this record would be a *miraculous work and a miracle.* In many ancient languages, especially Hebrew, repetition was considered a good writing style; it enhanced importance. When Lehi stated, "I dreamed a dream," for example, he was using this same form, termed "cognate accusative." It was not enough for Isaiah to simply say, "It is going to be miraculous." By using the cognate accusative form, Isaiah suggests that the book would be a double miracle, or a miracle squared.

The Book of Mormon is a miracle of gigantic proportions! It simultaneously manifests simplicity, complexity, spirituality, artistry, subtlety, accuracy, consistency, reliability, sanctity, and more. Rendering a complete list of its qualities is impossible. Elements within the record also manifest its antiquity; the use of cognate accusatives is one of these elements.

2 NEPHI 28—NEPHI WARNS AGAINST SATAN'S PLANS AND TOOLS

Chapter 28 is dense with warnings alerting us to the many ways in which Satan ensnares an unsuspecting mortal. Knowing how the devil works and recognizing his tactics can help us avoid being taken captive by him who leads people "carefully," using his influence and powers (28:21). Nephi's treatise on Satan's tools is truly remarkable. It is full of phrases that encapsulate Satan's false doctrines and wrong attitudes. The digital format of these notes contains an exhaustive list of Nephi's phrases paired with their equivalent ideology. A few examples will suffice here.

2 NEPHI 28:3-6—MANY FALSE CHURCHES WILL RISE IN THE LAST DAYS

"I am the Lord's" (28:3) may be called exclusivism. This statement manifests a sense of pride and selfish privilege that excludes others. The truth is, "all are alike unto God" (26:25).

"They shall contend one with another" (28:4) is disputation. Contention is not of the Lord. It drives away the Spirit, it drives out love, and the devil knows that. We most certainly live in a time of contention, and we deceive ourselves when we believe that disputes reveal the truth.

People will "deny the power of God" (28:5). This is secularism—a belief that God is not active in the world today and that He doesn't have the will or the power to affect things. Individuals, not God, decide what is right or wrong. This philosophy can be subtle. A person may say that the power of God exists, yet deny that power by not allowing it to work within them, instead pushing God away. Nephi had seen that the Lord is involved in the affairs of man, he knew that the Lord was a God of miracles, and he testified that these facts will never change.

2 NEPHI 28:7-9, 19-30—THE DEVIL'S TACTICS

Nephi lived in a society that was ripening for destruction. He focused next on social attitudes that lead people away from the Holy Spirit. In the last days, sinners' attitudes will be reflected in the following statements: "[God] will justify in committing a little sin"; "God will beat us with a few stripes"; and "at last we shall be saved in the kingdom of God" (28:8). This is justification and rationalization at its worst. Believing that we will somehow be saved in the kingdom of God in our sinful state is gross self-deception.

It is apparent that Nephi had particular concern for how Satan's tactics would unfold. According to him, the wicked will continue their acts of sin, but say, "nevertheless, fear God" (28:8). Here, Nephi warns that the wicked will continue their immoral behavior, all the while feigning that what they are doing is good.

Nephi described the dangers when a society tolerates, or even encourages, those who lay traps to ensnare others and ruin their reputations or livelihoods. Such a tactic is the incubator for deception, criticism, cold-heartedness, and persecution, relying on others to believe or accept the lies. This is the atmosphere described by the phrases, "lie a little," "take advantage of one because of his words," and "dig a pit for thy neighbor" (28:8).

Nephi further warned that some may take a legalist approach, reasoning that if there is no legally enforceable damage, then it can't be a problem. This assumes too much about the goodness and completeness of public law. How can someone get away with teaching false, vain, and foolish doctrines? They do it by preaching their gospel to a society living in moral relativism, where what is right and what is wrong is determined exclusively by the individual—without consideration for God's laws or for one's duties to society. The phrase "puffed up" (see 28:9, 12, 13, 15) sums up this condition quite nicely, depicting that which looks substantive (e.g., a marshmallow or balloon), but which really consists mostly of air (and some of it hot air).

Nephi concludes chapter 28 by describing additional unacceptable and even dangerous behaviors and attitudes: complacency (28:24–25), denying the power of God and the gift of the Holy Ghost (28:26), refusing to receive more of the word of God (28:29–30), trusting in the precepts of men more than in God (28:31). Nephi knew by revelation that within such a society, Satan would "rage in the hearts of men" (28:20). He affirms that ultimately there will be only two choices: follow God or follow the ways of Satan. The Savior mercifully waits for the repentant sinner with open and outstretched arms (28:32).

2 NEPHI 29: 1-14—WORDS HISS FORTH FOR A STANDARD

This prophetic chapter emphasizes the Lord's intention to speak unto all mankind "henceforth and forever" (29:9). From Nephi's remote vantage point, the Lord makes it clear that He will reach all people by inspiring the production and distribution of sacred records. This process will begin by our remembering those who will bring forth the Bible. Then it promises that the Jews will receive the Nephite record. Testimonies from both Jew and Nephite "shall run together" (29:8), affirming that God is over all the earth and speaks "according to [his] own pleasure" (29:9). All this is done "to show unto them that fight against my word . . . that I am God," and that He will "remember his seed forever" (29:14; compare Ezekiel 37:15–23).

2 NEPHI 30:5-6, 17-18—LEHI'S POSTERITY RECEIVE THE GOSPEL, ALL THINGS ARE REVEALED

Nephi prophesies that after many years, Lehi's posterity will receive the gospel again and be "restored unto the knowledge of their fathers" (30:5). Thus, they will become "a delightsome people" (30:6). The Lord promises that when we repent, He will "remember [the sin] no more" (Doctrine and Covenants 58:42). Repentance provides for an omniscient God to forget something—a promise that is both comforting and miraculous. Nephi describes the conditions that will prevail when righteousness and restoration triumph (see 29:11–15). To the unrepentant, however, Nephi declares that every work of darkness will "be made manifest in the light" (30:17).

TAKEAWAYS

- **What does Nephi say about the importance of continuing revelation in chapter 28 and 29? In what ways can you make that more important in your own life?**
- **According to 30:1-2 what is the expected destiny of Gentiles generally? Why do you think that is the case?**
- **In contrast, what does Nephi say can happen to Gentiles (and to Jews) individually? Who then are "the covenant people of the Lord"?**

12: 2 NEPHI 31-33

As an inspired leader with a prophetic worldview, Nephi wrote his final message in chapters 31, 32, and 33, a total of 45 verses. He chose his words carefully, addressing the core doctrine of Christ. The basic outline deals with baptism, the Holy Ghost, enduring to the end on the way to eternal life, praying always, and giving Christ a place in our souls. One can almost imagine flashing lights around these chapters, asking a reader to pay close attention.

I love this man, Nephi. He is one of the great souls, positioned to stand at the head of these Israelites who had been led out of Jerusalem, protected, and brought to the New World. Theirs was a unique and important mission: to produce a written record witnessing of Jesus Christ, indeed the main tool for gathering Israel in the last days. To get to know Nephi, we must read between the lines. As we do, the depth of his admirable character emerges. His final words are words of faith and optimism. He is realistic and straight-forward, and he instructs clearly on certain things we must do. If we obey, he remains confident that we will live together in the kingdom of God.

2 NEPHI 31:5, 10, 13-14—THE COVENANT OF BAPTISM, BEING WILLING TO OBEY

Baptism is often casually taught as the means of washing away sins when this ordinance is really about committing to obey God's commandments. It witnesses to Heavenly Father a willingness to keep our covenants with Him. Latter-day Saint scholar Noel B. Reynolds found that the Book of Mormon never mentions baptism *washing* away our sins. The Holy Ghost purges (or washes) away impurities, as the baptism of fire that brings forth the remission of sins. Baptism is a voluntary commitment, a way of witnessing to God that we are willing to keep His commandments by covenant. It is a symbolic reenactment of the atoning death and Resurrection of Jesus, while also symbolizing our own spiritual rebirth.

In ancient Israel, to be immersed for purification purposes, the water had to be *living water*—moving water. Standing water was, by definition, impure. Yet, entering a river could be a frightening act. Most people in ancient times did not know how to swim well, and there was a universal belief that evil spirits lived under the water. With this understanding, the ordinance of baptism by immersion signified a great willingness to obey while also trusting in the power of Christ to save and raise a person from evil.

Nephi very clearly teaches about baptism as a covenant. He frames baptism at the center of the gospel of Christ as an important gateway. Baptism is a *covenant* of admittance and entrance. In 2 Nephi 31:13, Nephi says that people must act, "with real intent, . . . witnessing unto the Father that [they] are willing to take upon [them] the name of Christ." This does not require perfect obedience to the commandments, but rather a willingness to give it an honest try each day. God wants a *willing heart*.

2 NEPHI 31:11-18—THE FATHER AND SON COMMAND US TO MAKE A BAPTISMAL COVENANT

Nephi often refers to Jesus as a very devoted, beloved Son. Nephi's own identity as the loyal son, doing the will of his father and his God, was a very important element of his character. Nephi was the quintessential obedient son. It is not surprising that he would see Jesus's submission to the will of His Father in much the same way.

Nephi anchors his teachings to the source of all truth. He quotes both the Father and the Son speaking to him, "The voice of the Son came unto me" (31:12), and later, "I heard a voice from the Father" (31:15). And what do They say? They command people to repent and be baptized in the name of the Son, They promise the gift of the Holy Ghost, They list anticipated blessings, and They include a caution. They end with the Father attesting to the truth of what the Son said. Marvelous lessons are contained in those few verses.

2 NEPHI 31:19-20—NEPHI TELLS US WHAT WE NEED TO DO TO GAIN ETERNAL LIFE

Nephi urges us to "press forward with a steadfastness in Christ" (31:20), being, as Lehi said, "steadfast and immovable" (1 Nephi 2:10). In addition to obeying the commandments, we must also feast upon the word of Christ (31:20). We give place to Jesus in our lives when we spend time with Him in the scriptures. Nephi promises that there is a "perfect brightness of hope" along this journey. The phrase recalls his reflective comment in 1 Nephi 1:1, "Having seen many afflictions in the course of my days, nevertheless, having been highly favored of the Lord in all my days." Seeing the hand of the Lord sustaining you throughout trials and troubles is the essence of a brightness of hope. It is not divorced from reality but is fully grounded in it. "The process of spiritual growth . . . seems to be one of climbing, *pausing* for rest and refreshment and reassurance, *and then resuming* the climb, on and on to the top. . . . If we will seriously call upon the Lord and ask Him regularly to bless us . . . we will sense the divine hand upon our shoulder, nudging us *onward* and *upward* all the days of our lives" (Robert L. Millet, *Coming to Know Christ* [Salt Lake City: Deseret Book, 2012], 49, emphasis added). No matter how rough things are, we do our best to maintain optimism. The Lord will help us on our journey; that is part of our covenant relationship with Him.

2 NEPHI 31:21—WHAT IS THE DIFFERENCE BETWEEN THE DOCTRINE AND GOSPEL OF CHRIST?

The doctrine of Christ and the gospel of Christ are similar but evoke somewhat different aspects of our Father's great eternal plan. The *doctrine* is faith in the Lord Jesus Christ, repentance, baptism, receiving the gift of the Holy Ghost, and enduring to the end—those five elements. The Savior says, "And there will be no more doctrine." In other words, that is the *doctrine* of Christ. (See 3 Nephi 11:28–39.)

In 3 Nephi 27:13–14, the Savior says, "This is the *gospel* which I have given unto you—that I came into the world to do the will of my Father, because my Father sent me. And my Father sent me that I might be lifted up upon the cross." So, one might say that when Book of Mormon writers use the word *gospel,* they may be speaking more broadly, referring to something we would more often call the plan of salvation. The specific *doctrine* of Christ is part of that plan

2 NEPHI 32:2-3—WHAT DOES IT MEAN TO SPEAK WITH THE TONGUE OF ANGELS?

The word for angel in Greek or Hebrew means *messenger.* Angels are God's messengers. They deliver His message with utmost accuracy, so that others correctly understand God's will. As we live righteously, through the gift of the Holy Ghost we may speak with the tongue of angels. We do not want to desecrate that gift by saying things that are unworthy of the Lord.

In his April 2007 general conference talk titled "The Tongue of Angels," Elder Jeffrey R. Holland emphasized a dimension that is not often considered. Referencing Nephi, he said:

> May we try to be "perfect" men and women in at least this one way now—by offending not in word, or more positively put, by speaking with a new tongue, the tongue of angels. Our words, like our deeds, should be filled with faith and hope and charity, the three great Christian imperatives so desperately needed in the world today. With such words, spoken under the influence of the Spirit, tears can be dried, hearts can be healed, lives can be elevated, hope can return, confidence can prevail.

I think it is a very specific and marvelous gift to have the tongue of an angel. Nephi is teaching us that this is what the gift of the Holy Ghost affords.

2 NEPHI 32:3-4, 7-9—FEASTING UPON THE WORDS OF CHRIST AND PRAYING ALWAYS

Nephi implores, "Feast upon the words of Christ; for behold, the words of Christ will tell you all things what ye should do" (32:3). When we make scripture study an important part of our lives, we do more than just nibble at them. We ask how to move forward, we seek what to do, and we learn how to apply the principles they teach. Feasting begins with entreating, "What should I be doing next?" Nephi learned this lesson while still very young. He sought to learn, and when he understood, he acted.

Nephi was not a wishy-washy person. His life was filled with bold choices and decisive action. We get a sense of his frustration with lazy attitudes which result in "unbelief" and "ignorance" (32:7). His clear solution in verse 8 is to pray, "For if ye would hearken unto the Spirit which teacheth a man to pray ye would know that ye must pray; for the evil spirit teacheth . . . him that he must not pray."

Next, Nephi emphasizes that we must pray before performing anything to the Lord. Otherwise, our actions cannot be elevated to the level of being consecrated to the Lord. They will not have the same effect or yield the same results. In this final message, Nephi teaches that we have an immediate duty to get to work using powers and gifts when they are given to us.

2 NEPHI 33:6—NEPHI GLORIES IN THAT WHICH BRINGS HIM CLOSER TO JESUS

Part of the sacrament process is to identify things that trip us up spiritually and ask for the Lord's help to get rid of them. This is the grace of Christ; it is the divine, enabling power with us as we struggle. Our accountability is to be vigilant, to constantly evaluate and eliminate as necessary. As Elder David A. Bednar said, in April general conference, 2006, in his talk titled "May We Always Have His Spirit to Be with Us," "The standard is clear: If something distances us from the Holy Ghost, then we should stop thinking, seeing, hearing, or doing that thing as our own 'I glory in plainness' moment."

2 NEPHI 33:12-15—NEPHI MAKES HIS FINAL FAREWELL AND SEALS HIS RECORD

Nephi's farewell fits his personality. He encourages faith, testifies to the truth, and places on us the responsibility to act. In his clear and direct way, Nephi witnesses to all the world that Jesus is the Christ. To those who will not partake, he forthrightly states, "I bid you an everlasting farewell" (33:14). With his final sentence, Nephi puts his seal on the truthfulness of his words, "For what I seal on earth, shall be brought against you at the judgment bar." He grasped all that was at stake and made us accountable. "For thus hath the Lord commanded me, and I must obey. Amen." That is typical "go and do" Nephi. From the very beginning to the very end, Nephi is steadfastly obedient. He magnified his calling, and we are the beneficiaries.

TAKEAWAYS

- **According to 31:17, when and by what means exactly does one obtain a "remission of sins"? How might this affect what you seek each day?**
- **In 31:18, what exactly does God promise to those who "entered in" by the gate of repentance and baptism? Why would He make such a promise so early in one's spiritual journey and what does He provide to get us all they way to the end (see v. 19-21)?**
- **Why does Nephi assume that he will meet "many souls spotless" at God's judgment (33:7)? How can we look at others in the same way that Nephi does?**

13: EASTER WITH THE NEPHITES

At Easter time, the entire Christian world celebrates the Resurrection of Jesus Christ, which shows His divine power over mortality and death. The New Testament provides several wondrous examples of people seeing and touching the resurrected Lord. At the same time, the Book of Mormon gives even greater assurances of the Resurrection of Jesus Christ and of all people ever born. Through the lengthy account of Christ's joyous visit reported in 3 Nephi, people everywhere can come to know and speak with greater detail and conviction about Jesus's post-resurrection ministry. The sorrows felt at Golgotha are here sublimely transformed by divine affirmations, by God's loving kindness, by Jesus's gentle instructions and commands, by the Savior's generous healings, and by the unspeakable blessings given to parents and their children at the temple in Bountiful. The Book of Mormon prophets bear strong testimonies that every human being on this planet Earth will be resurrected. They give incomparable assurances that the sting of death has indeed been swallowed up by the overwhelming joys of the Resurrection. Greater still is the additional witness that every human will be resurrected. Easter time is indeed a perfect time to celebrate the Book of Mormon's most brightly shining season.

3 NEPHI 11:1-7—THE FATHER INTRODUCES HIS BELOVED SON

Early on an appointed morning after the three days of horrific devastations in the land Bountiful, a sizable group of survivors—men, women, and children—gathered at their temple in Bountiful. This day was close enough to the tragic ordeal of destruction, death, and darkness that the shockwaves had not worn off. People were still "marveling and wondering one with another, and were showing one to another the great and marvelous change which had taken place" (11:1). Yet, it also appears that the date was far enough removed from those cataclysmic events that daily life had somewhat stabilized beyond the immediate concerns about personal safety and survival that naturally prevail following massive disasters. Roads had apparently been cleared enough to accommodate traveling to the temple, and people felt safe enough to go. Still, being at the temple that morning would have required much family and personal effort.

The record also states that in addition to conversing about the change in landscape and demolished cities, the people were also intently talking "about this Jesus Christ, of whom the sign had been given concerning his death" (11:2). At that very moment, a particular voice from up above got their attention. The sound was not harsh and was not loud. Though they did not understand it at first, this small voice "did pierce them to the very soul, and did cause their hearts to burn" (11:3). That tone of voice had deep effects. Everyone there, of course, had recently heard the voice of Jesus Christ, the Son of God, speaking out of the darkness and destruction (3 Nephi 9:2–22; 10:3–7). But this time, the heavenly voice was different, and the whole crowd "did look steadfastly toward heaven, from whence the sound came" (3 Nephi

11:5), as they heard God the Father say of His resurrected Son, "Behold my Beloved Son, in whom I am well pleased, in whom I have glorified my name" (11:7).

God's kind and reassuring introduction came to these people as they were ready and open to receive it. Their thoughts had already shifted from mundane concerns to spiritual matters. It was then that they turned their attention toward heaven and opened their ears to comprehend the words of that day. Similarly, the Holy Spirit works on all people at multiple levels as well, depending on our attentiveness. Understanding the message also required concerted effort. It took three attempts for them to understand the words being spoken as the Father said, by way of commandment and invitation, "Hear ye him" (11:7). Someday, as each of us will be received by our Eternal Father, He will know us individually, loving us as a beloved son or daughter. As He does here, He will no doubt gladly express His pleasure at every word or deed we have spoken or performed to glorify His name.

3 NEPHI 11:8-11—JESUS CHRIST BEARS HIS TESTIMONY OF HIS LIFE AND MISSION

The "Man descending out of heaven" (11:8) stood in their midst, immediately "stretched forth his hand and spake," testifying that "I am Jesus Christ, whom the prophets testified shall come into the world" (11:9–10). In this initial statement, any doubt or confusion as to His identity was dismissed. Moreover, He validated the teachings of the many prophets regarding His coming, dying, and rising. Such biblical prophets would have included Isaiah (25:8), David (Psalms 22), as well as Neum (see 1 Nephi 19:10) and Book of Mormon prophets Nephi (2 Nephi 25:13), Benjamin (Mosiah 3:10), Abinadi (Mosiah 15:8), and Samuel the Lamanite (Helaman 14:20).

Jesus then testified of His position: "I am the light . . . of the world," and of His accomplished mission, "I have drunk out of that bitter cup . . . and have glorified the Father" (11:11). At that point, everyone was so struck that they could no longer stand. They "fell to the earth." One can easily imagine that we would react that way too. These people were the first in the western hemisphere to witness a resurrected being. Jesus Christ Himself, the Savior and Redeemer of the entire world, had arrived as promised. This was an Easter experience never to be forgotten.

3 NEPHI 11:14—"ARISE AND COME FORTH THAT YE MAY KNOW"

The Lord then invited all the people to gain their own personal testimony of Him in His resurrected state: "Arise and come forth . . . feel the prints . . . that ye may know" (11:14). Our Savior wants all to come unto Him and to gain an understanding of the truth of His love and power directly from Him. On one occasion in the biblical world, more than 500 of the brethren "saw" the resurrected Lord (see 1 Cor. 15:6). But here at the temple in Bountiful, well over 500 families (men, women, and children, totaling 2,500 people) not only saw Him but touched the signs and tokens of his wounded, but now resurrected, hands, feet, and side.

While we all live by faith, the promise is that, eventually, true faith and faithfulness will be rewarded and replaced by sure knowledge. For these faithful people at Bountiful, that day had come. After years of waiting, hoping, experiencing persecutions and death threats, and then surviving natural disasters and assisting with the cleanup, they had come to the temple early that day. Their reward was sure knowledge through personal experience that the Lord Jesus Christ lived as a resurrected being after suffering death on the cross. Such an opportunity is too precious to be passed over lightly. Imagine how a person might have felt, who decided, for no specific reason, not to go to the temple that morning, or on the next day (see 3 Nephi 19).

Each person was granted time to touch the Savior's body to know for themselves the reality of the Resurrection. This knowledge was not just given to them for their personal pleasure, but also so they could know "and bear record" (11:15) of that experience for the rest of their lives. Their testimonies resounded throughout the four generations of peace and righteousness that then prevailed in 4 Nephi. Many of their grandchildren and great-grandchildren could say, years later, that they remembered hearing these people testify personally to what they had experienced, even as children, on this grand occasion. The era of Nephite peace in 4 Nephi was surely the living legacy of those witnesses.

3 NEPHI 11:14–15—JESUS GAINED A RESURRECTED BODY

Jesus gets right to work teaching His doctrine and organizing His church among the Nephites. He doesn't spend time talking about His resurrected state, as far as we know. But we can put together the clear doctrine of the Resurrection from clues found in the scriptures. For example, having a physical body is important, and having a human body is needed in immortality as well as in mortality. Housing a spirit within a perfected, resurrected, physical body is necessary for eternal progression and becoming like God the Father, who Himself has a body "as tangible as man's" (D&C 130:22).

Also, a resurrected body retains its physical abilities to see, speak, gesture, move, feel, understand, and communicate. As Alma the Younger taught, in the resurrection "all things shall be restored to their proper and perfect frame" (Alma 40:23). Moreover, knowledge, memories, emotions, and personal relationships are retained in the resurrection. The resurrected Jesus called Nephi by name. He requested certain objects, such as bread and wine. He was aware of past disputations and events. He recited scripture. He wept for joy. Apparently, some resurrected and heavenly beings can defy gravity, descending and ascending at will (see Genesis 28:12; 3 Nephi 11:8, 18:29). The Nephites watched Jesus descend slowly from heaven, and the disciples watched Him ascend at the end of the first day of His visit (3 Nephi 18:39). Such knowledge dispels any doubt of life after death. It also gives expanded assurance of the continuation of a person's personal identity and state of mind beyond physical death.

3 NEPHI 11, 15:4–9—THE STING OF DEATH IS SWALLOWED UP

Seven hundred years before the birth of Christ, Isaiah prophesied that the Lord of Hosts "will swallow up death *in victory*" (Isaiah 25:8; emphasis added), words used by Abinadi in the second century before Christ: "Therefore the grave hath no victory, and the sting of death is swallowed up *in Christ*" (Mosiah 16:8; emphasis added). Then, when teaching gospel truths to King Lamoni's father, Aaron summed it all up: "And since man had fallen he could not merit anything of himself; but the sufferings and death of Christ atone for their sins, through faith and repentance, and so forth; and that he breaketh the bands of death, that the grave shall have no victory, and that the sting of death should be swallowed up *in the hopes* of glory" (Alma 22:14; emphasis added). Interestingly, the Hebrew word *netzach,* which usually means "victory," can also refer, as in these cases, to "the victor" as well as to "the hopes of victory." All three of these prophets spoke with an eye of faith, looking forward to the day of salvation experienced by the people at Bountiful. They came forward, one by one, to know the actuality of Jesus's Resurrection, with His body bearing the marks of His death. They all could testify with certainty that He had indeed swallowed up suffering and death, and now they had hope that this eternal blessing would someday be theirs. This foreknowledge remained a strong theme clear to the end of the Nephite civilization, as Mormon testified at the end of his record that Jesus Christ "hath gained the victory over the grave; and also in him is the sting of death swallowed up" (Mormon 7:5).

3 NEPHI 23—ALL MANKIND WILL BE RESURRECTED IN DUE TIME

At Easter we celebrate the hope of a universal resurrection. We have much to look forward to. The Book of Mormon clearly teaches that resurrection is a vital part of the Father's plan of redemption and salvation. With Christ, the Exemplar, standing before them, the Nephites surely knew that the same resurrection would come to each of them, as Jacob had taught 400 years previously, "For as death hath passed upon all men, to fulfill the *merciful plan* of the great Creator, there must needs be a power of resurrection" (2 Nephi 9:6; emphasis added). Likewise, Alma taught that "it is *requisite and just,* according to the power and resurrection of Christ, that the soul of man should be restored to its body, and that every part of the body should be restored to itself" (Alma 41:2; emphasis added).

While all mankind can look forward to being resurrected, the Book of Mormon (see Alma 40) and modern-day scriptures further inform us of the stages and timing of the resurrection. The first resurrection began with Christ and continues. All will not rise at the same time; and from an infinite, timeless perspective, that does not ultimately matter. The resurrection happens in stages, depending, one can assume, on the needs and will of the Father.

3 NEPHI 11–28—RESURRECTION IS NECESSARY TO AVOID BECOMING SUBJECT TO THE DEVIL

By its physical nature, resurrection provides an important degree of separation from the devil in his unembodied state of being. Satan's progression is permanently halted. Through the Atonement of Jesus Christ our progress can continue. Jacob taught: "O the wisdom of God, his mercy and grace! For behold, if the flesh should rise no more our spirits must become subject to that angel who fell from before the presence of the Eternal God, and became the devil, to rise no more" (2 Nephi 9:8). Without the Resurrection, our progress would also be halted. We would remain in a state like Satan. Thus, we can share Jacob's sense of relief. Even in our mortal condition, we have more power than the unembodied spirits. In contrast, God dwells eternally in a glorified body of flesh and bones. Physical resurrection is an essential element of godhood. To be like Him, we must receive glorified, immortal bodies, which is something Satan will never have. A glorious gift and promise indeed!

TAKEAWAYS

- **How has the Book of Mormon strengthened your testimony of the Resurrection of Jesus Christ? What does the Book of Mormon contribute to the world's understanding of the resurrection?**
- **Find or create a way to share and discuss with someone you know two or three details about the experiences of the people at the temple in Bountiful that enhance the celebration of Easter.**

14: JACOB 1-4

JACOB 1:1-4—KEEPING THE SMALL PLATES

At the beginning of his book, Jacob states the essence of the commandment that Nephi gave to him pertaining to writing on the small plates. He was told to touch only lightly on the history, to record sacred preaching, to summarize great prophecies, and do this all for Christ's sake. And Jacob does exactly that. We don't get much history in the book of Jacob. His preaching in Jacob 2–3 deals with sacred matters, including chastity and consecration. His summations in Jacob 4 and 6 of the prophecy of Zenos in chapter 5 help focus the allegory of the olive tree on Christ. And the episode with Sherem in Jacob 7 affirms the legitimacy of prophesying about the coming Christ, of teaching the people to worship Christ, and of calling Christ a Divine Being.

JACOB 1:15-16—THE NEPHITES BEGAN TO COMMIT MANY SINS

Jacob doesn't jump right out of the starting block and hit his audience over the head by saying, "You people are all awful." Instead, he says, "I know you're beginning to . . ." He is trying to help his people see their problems.

JACOB 1:17-19—JACOB, THE HIGH PRIEST, MAGNIFIES HIS CALLING

Without question, the high priest in ancient Israel had to be especially assiduous about his worthiness and purity. If the Lord was going to be able to bless His people and reveal His will, he had to be able to speak to a worthy high priest. We read in Jewish literature about the great lengths the Jews anciently went to in order to be sure that that high priest was pure, and a lot of it had to do with the family of the high priest. He had to be married, and he had to be living in a righteous home. A similar attitude is reflected in Jacob's writings.

He is likewise concerned about righteousness, purity, avoiding abominations, and having a righteous family and home. These themes recur throughout his writings. It is also worth noting how fragile Jacob's people probably were at this time. After Lehi's death, they must have felt deeply concerned when the group split into different factions. They likely worried that the Lamanites, Lemuelites, and Ishmaelites would either attack them militarily or weaken them morally through marriages or other social interactions. He clearly felt a great sense of responsibility, and I think we can learn a lesson from his diligent concern for his people at that crucial time in their existence.

Jacob and his brother Joseph were set apart by Nephi and consecrated as priests. They were given the responsibility of preaching the gospel to their people, and we see them doing that at the temple. We also see their understanding that if they didn't preach with all diligence, the sins of the people would be on *their* heads. So, they are extremely serious about their calling, and my guess is that when they were set apart, they were given clear instructions about their responsibilities.

When a leader knows that the people under his stewardship have a problem, he indeed has a responsibility to address it. The right way to give reproof is modeled very well here by Jacob. He approached the problem forthrightly, and not only were his people warned, but we get the same warning today because Jacob recorded this important sermon.

JACOB 2:1—WHAT WERE THE CIRCUMSTANCES OF JACOB'S SERMON?

According to Deuteronomy 31:9–13, the Levitical priests were required to read the law so that the people could hear the word of the Lord. They were to be taught the same thing over and over, much like we are taught today. But here there is also a sense that this is a sort of general conference, and that Jacob was inspired to deliver a particular message to the people, based on their needs.

JACOB 2:4-5—THE NEPHITES BEGIN TO LABOR IN SIN

Jacob said, "For behold, as yet, ye have been obedient unto the word of the Lord, which I have given unto you" (2:4). Apparently, they were at least outwardly performing the ordinances of the temple, whatever those were.

Repeatedly, the authors of these small plates tell us that the Nephites were strict in observing the law of Moses, and several centuries later, at this same temple, King Noah will perform daily sacrifices. However, the people generally were prone to obey the outward ordinances (the letter of the law) but failed to live up to the other commandments and standards of the Lord (the spirit of the law).

Jacob's language indicates that this is just a preliminary happening—the people are only now just "beginning to labor in sin" (2:5). This is interesting because Jacob focuses on the wickedness of their "hearts." There are several other occasions during the speech where he similarly emphasizes thoughts and intentions. It is by entertaining sinful thoughts and desires in our hearts that the seeds of disobedient or rebellious actions are planted within us.

JACOB 2:17-19—WHEN IS IT APPROPRIATE TO SEEK FOR MONEY?

In these verses, Jacob issues one of the most trenchant sayings in scripture regarding wealth. Placing God ahead of seeking worldly things and using riches or knowledge to bless those in need were consistent and persistent admonitions of Jacob. Never in Jacob's young life had he had opportunities to obtain either higher education or worldly fortunes. But he had seen the corrosive influence these things can have on people if they seek them for the wrong reasons.

Jacob taught that we must be free with our substance so that others may have what they need, "that they may be rich like unto you" (2:17). This kind of equality is important within a covenant community. Fundamentally, what Jacob is teaching is economically sound as well as morally and religiously desirable. True riches come from having satisfaction of the heart, knowing that you have done what is good, righteous, and socially justifiable.

JACOB 2:22-23—THE NEPHITES BEGIN TO COMMIT WHOREDOMS

An article in the *Deseret News* reported a study in Holland which showed a direct correlation between power and promiscuity. Power tends to go to people's heads, and when they get power, they think they are immune to punishment and above the law and can get away with behaviors that are risky. Thus, it is important that we warn people, especially our young people who have their whole lives ahead of them, about the temptations that accompany any acquisition of worldly power.

Jacob used the word "crime" three times in this discourse (2:9, 22, 23). This is interesting because Jacob is the high priest. I would have expected a high priest to use the word "sin," since a king or another political official would be more likely to use the word "crime." But Jacob's usage can probably be explained by the fact that under the law of Moses, religious sins and civil laws were not distinguished in the polarized way we generally think about church and state today. There was no separation of church and state in the ancient world. When a law was established by God, then breaking it was just as much a crime under the law as it was a sin against God, which accounts for Jacob's use of this word here.

JACOB 2:27-32—THE LORD FORBIDS THE NEPHITES TO ENTER INTO POLYGAMY

In verse 27, Jacob declares, "Hear me, and hearken to the word of the Lord." So, this is apparently a new law that Jacob is giving them. And what is that law? It is that "there shall not any man among you have save it be one wife; and concubines he shall have none" (2:27). Concubines included secondary wives (not prostitutes, as some readers might assume). As secondary wives they usually did not have inheritance and other such family rights. So, Jacob here is saying that his people should not have multiple wives of any kind. He explains why in the next two verses: "For I, the Lord God, delight in the chastity of women. And whoredoms are an abomination before me; thus saith the Lord of Hosts. Wherefore, this people shall keep my commandments, saith the Lord of Hosts, or cursed be the land for their sakes" (2:28–29).

Then, in the third verse, the Lord clarifies the matter further: "For if I will, saith the Lord of Hosts, raise up seed unto me, I will command my people; otherwise they shall hearken unto these things" (2:30). So, there is an exception to this restriction. Polygamy can be permitted, but only when the Lord commands for the purpose of raising up a righteous people. That is what happened with Abraham, Isaac, and Jacob, in order to fulfill the promises that they would have posterity that would be able to bless the entire earth. But Lehi's family was not in that situation.

Particularly, under ancient laws, fathers normally negotiated the prenuptial agreement for their sons, and usually these agreements contained a provision where the father of the bride has control over whether the groom can take a second wife. Therefore, there may well have been an agreement disallowing plural wives that was entered into by Lehi and Ishmael when Ishmael's daughters married Lehi's sons. Notice that it says here that Lehi forbade any of his sons—including Jacob and Joseph—to engage in plural marriage (2:34). That was a right that he as a father could normally exercise over his family. What I see going on here is that Jacob is taking this matter one step further. Not only was this what their father Lehi did for their generation, but this is now to be the rule of the Lord for all these people. Apparently, as they negotiated the terms of these marriage contracts, some of the fathers were saying, "Well, allowing polygamous relationships would be okay with me." And Jacob is saying, "No, that's not going to work because it is against the commandments of the Lord for our people."

JACOB 3:1-2—JACOB ADDRESSES THE PURE IN HEART

It is noteworthy that in chapter 2, Jacob also talked repeatedly about the thoughts and hearts of those who are setting out to do the wrong things, and then in chapter 3:1–2, Jacob followed up by addressing the hearts and minds of the righteous. I love the expression "firmness of mind." It takes considerable moral courage to stand for the right when no one else around you is doing so. Righteous resolve begins with firmness of mind. And the promises here are great. You can just feel the Lord's love and strengthening power that is available to the righteous. What did Jacob tell them to do?

- "Look unto God with firmness of mind" (3:1)
- "Pray unto him with exceeding faith" (3:1)
- "Lift up your heads" (3:2)
- "Receive the pleasing word of God" (3:2)
- "Feast upon his love" (3:2)

In essence, Jacob's message is that sin is real, and we should call it what it is. But his message is also that the Lord can heal those wounds caused by sin and bring reconciliation between those who have caused or received harm.

Do we sometimes unnecessarily separate our daily choices from our covenantal commitments? Perhaps we place our covenants on a separate shelf, when they really apply to our everyday choices throughout every day of our lives. I love temple-recommend interviews for that reason. They give us an opportunity to connect those dots. Every one of those questions points toward a covenant. Live this way, keep these covenants, and blessings will naturally follow.

JACOB 3:5-7—JACOB USES THE LAMANITES AS AN EXAMPLE OF RIGHTEOUSNESS

In a way, the problem faced by Jacob's people was like the plague of pornography in our day. Pornography denigrates women by treating them as commodities or as mere objects of lust. Concerning pornography, you can't just say to kids, "Don't do it, don't do it, don't do it." It is crucial that they understand *why* it is wrong.

The Nephites apparently saw themselves as the righteous lineage, and because of this they were probably tempted to excuse their own sins. They failed to recognize that the Lamanites whom they despised for their apostasy were in fact more righteous in keeping this most sacred of commandments regarding sexual purity. In their smug self-righteousness, the Nephites may not have even recognized their own spiritual decline. We need to be careful that we don't ever feel that personal righteousness can be inherited or that it is a product of culture or upbringing or of any other factor except personal agency.

JACOB 3:11—JACOB INVITES THE PEOPLE TO REPENT

When I came to BYU in the 1960s, we were just beginning to worry about environmental pollution. Previous generations had foolishly believed that the oceans could absorb an endless amount of garbage and waste. We learned that pollution doesn't just go away.

I wonder if people aren't just as naïve today when it comes to personal pollution. They foolishly think that the human mind can absorb an endless amount of filth and violence and that somehow, we can just push a delete key in our brain and erase it. Just as it is true that "whatever principle of intelligence we attain unto in this life, it will rise with us in the resurrection" (Doctrine and Covenants 130:18), so, too, whatever degree of unrepented smut or cynicism we attain unto, it will rise with us as well.

The things we choose to participate in, and witness, will be written in our countenances. I think that is what Jacob was saying when he told his people about the "awful consequences" of "fornication and lasciviousness"—any form of sexual misconduct or deviance (3:12). And he pleaded with his people not to go down that path, which he warned would transform them into "angels to the devil" (3:11). That is ultimately where all sin leads.

JACOB 4:3—JACOB HOPES HIS POSTERITY DOESN'T VIEW THEIR FIRST PARENTS WITH CONTEMPT

Jacob hoped that the posterity of his people would read the words that he and others had written upon plates, and that they would "look upon them that they may learn with joy and not with sorrow, neither with contempt, concerning their first parents" (4:3). It is possible that Jacob was trying to help his posterity better understand the purpose and necessity of mortality, and that Lehi and Sariah, just like the human family's first parents, Adam and Eve, willingly chose to leave their comfortable home and embark on a journey through the wilderness—or, in other words, through a lone and dreary world. Jacob, who was Lehi's "first-born in the days of [his] tribulation in the wilderness," knew very well that "afflictions" and "sorrow" were a necessary part of mortal life and that through our faithful endurance the Lord can ultimately "consecrate thine afflictions for thy gain" (2 Nephi 2:1–2).

JACOB 4:4-7—THE PROPHETS KNEW OF CHRIST AND PROPHESIED OF HIS MISSION

Most of all, Jacob wanted his posterity to know that the ancient prophets knew of the coming of Christ. All this sets the stage for his quoting the prophet Zenos in chapter 5. That was a detailed prophecy, one in which Jacob's people could place their confidence because during their day it had already been partially fulfilled. I think Jacob and his people could already see themselves as that branch that had been planted far away (Jacob 5:13) and how the Nephites and Lamanites had indeed separated (5:14). Thus, if they knew that Zenos's allegory had already been partially fulfilled, then they could trust that the remainder of the prophecy would be fulfilled as well.

JACOB 4:10—JACOB TEACHES HIS PEOPLE NOT TO COUNSEL THE LORD

In verse 10, Jacob also wants his people to know that they should seek not to counsel the Lord, but to take counsel from Him. There are some passages in the allegory of the olive tree where the master and servant of the vineyard debate about what to do. The servant pleads for God to be patient, and it works, but only because the Lord knows what to do and when to do it, in pruning and grafting the branches (Jacob 5:22, 52).

JACOB 4:12—JACOB ASKS, "WHY NOT SPEAK OF THE ATONEMENT OF CHRIST?

Jacob's people, who lived the law of Moses (4:5), believed in the atoning sacrifice of the scapegoat on the Day of Atonement. So why not talk about the Atonement of Christ? It is hugely symbolic. In fact, the symbolism of the scapegoat and most aspects of the law of Moses were indeed meant to point people to Christ.

JACOB 4:14-18—THE JEWS IN JERUSALEM WERE A STIFFNECKED PEOPLE, BUT EVENTUALLY THEY WILL BEAR GOOD FRUIT UNTO THE LORD

The Lord knew that the house of Israel would become sinful, so he provided a way for branches to be cut off, transplanted, grafted in, and eventually brought together again. He would even remember those branches—like Lehi's family—that were grafted into trees in the most remote parts of the vineyard (i.e., the world). It would have been comforting to Jacob and his people to know that, despite their physical separation from the land of Israel, they were still important to the Master of the vineyard.

And, most of all, these people would eventually play an important role in the restoration of the house of Israel. Indeed, somehow those Jews who had "looked beyond the mark" (4:14) would again be able to build upon "the only sure foundation" (4:16). How that would happen was a great "mystery" which Jacob now proposed to unfold to his people.

TAKEAWAYS

- **Knowing that Jacob was the high priest, what do you think he sees as the main evils connected with seeking after wealth and engaging in sexual promiscuity?**
- **When is polygamy ever allowable? (See 2:30.) How have you been helped by being shown your weaknesses? (See 4:7.)**

15: JACOB 5-7

Jacob read an allegory of an olive orchard and explained it to his people; but having been born in the wilderness after his family left Jerusalem, he had probably never seen an olive tree. Cultivating an olive tree is a lifetime's work that requires considerable knowledge and expertise; hence, the full allegorical value is appreciated by those who are already familiar with this process. As this allegory unfolds, each detail mentioned is the exact element needed in the process of raising not just wild, bitter olives, but good ones as well. Jacob explained that Zenos wrote these words to all the house of Israel. In reading this complicated and richly meaningful chapter, it helps to have some charts or a roadmap beside you. The digital version of these notes contains three such charts to help visualize the process being described. (See https://archive.bookofmormoncentral.org/content/jacob-5–7.)

JACOB 5:1—THE STICK OF JUDAH AND THE STICK OF JOSEPH WORK TOGETHER

In chapter five we see a particularly strong example of how the sticks of Judah and Joseph work together. There are allusions to this allegory in Exodus, Hosea, and Ezekiel, yet their poetic allusions assumed that their audience understood the whole story. Together, Old Testament allusions to olive trees, as a composite, bear remarkable similarities to the Allegory of the Olive Tree. Although Zenos's writings do not appear in the Old Testament, there is an interesting and compelling argument to be made that many people in ancient Israel, along with Lehi and Nephi, knew this general prophecy.

In an ancient text known as *Biblical Antiquities*, the grandson of Joshua is a prominent figure, and he gives a speech as they are establishing themselves in the newly conquered land of Canaan. His name is *Cenez*, but in some texts his name is *Zenez*. Guess what he talks about? Olive trees, and how Israel is an olive tree. That is interesting especially because the *Biblical Antiquities* text was not discovered until the 1880s, fifty years after the Book of Mormon was in print.

JACOB 5:3—HOW DID THE OLIVE TREE REPRESENT THE HOUSE OF ISRAEL?

Zenos says explicitly, "I will liken thee, O house of Israel, unto a tame olive tree." The tree was a representation of the whole House of Israel. In this image, individuals are but leaves. Ancient Israelites thought of themselves as a collective identity. They were acutely aware of their shared responsibility to see that the whole of Zion succeeded.

Within the orchard, this tree was the one that the lord really counted on to produce the best fruits. It was important enough to plant it in a prominent place. Olive trees are very resistant to infection, rot, and mold. They can be grafted, cut, or moved. They do not need much water, but they do need to be pruned and cared for. Their fruit was precious and valued for its many uses.

JACOB 5:7-8—THE LORD PRESERVES THE FRUIT OF THE TREE

How does this prophecy begin? A planted tree was rotten to the core—so rotten that God had to come and chop off all the branches, scatter them around, preserve them somehow, and keep the roots alive by grafting in branches from a wild tree.

In the allegory, we meet the lord of the vineyard. The lord has a servant who is in some ways equal to and works together with the master. It is his servant who comes and directs all that goes on. It seems logical that the overlord, the owner, is God the Father, and the long-suffering servant is Christ.

What does it mean to preserve? It means to keep something that was yours to begin with. The lord and servant are trying to preserve everything they possibly can, but some little branches are going to have to be cut off and thrown in the fire because they cannot produce the optimal result all of the time. In effect, God is saying, "This is my work and my glory to preserve my children, or my people. In the end, it is the stalk, or covenant lineage that is preserved to bear fruit in a later season.

JACOB 5:11, 34, 41—THE LORD CARES FOR THE OLIVE TREE

If olive trees are not pruned, they become wild; they revert to being worthless and must be burned. If pruned parts are not burned, infestations of bugs can destroy the fruit and sometimes kill the trees. By reporting the diligent clearing and dunging of the vineyard, Zenos and Jacob were warning their people (and us) that if they did not allow themselves to be cultivated by the master and servant of the vineyard, they would not succeed. Notice that all fruit-bearing little branches in this parable can be grafted back up into the central tree where there are long-standing roots. These deep roots, the covenant that He would always remember His people, represent the stability that supports growth over time and produces the best fruit.

Though not customarily done, under certain circumstances, grafting wild branches into a tame tree is useful. According to Wilford Hess, "Due to the vigor and disease resistance of certain wild species, grafting wild stock onto a tame tree can strengthen and revitalize a distressed plant" (Wilford M. Hess, Daniel J. Fairbanks, John W. Welch, and Jonathan K. Diggs, "Botanical Aspects of Olive Culture Relevant to Jacob 5," in *The Allegory of the Olive Tree: The Olive, the Bible, and Jacob 5*, eds. Stephen D. Ricks and John W. Welch [Salt Lake City and Provo, UT: Deseret Book and FARMS, 1994], 507, quoted in *KnoWhy* #71).

This symbolism reveals the extensive effort our Master is willing to exert in order to reach His lost children. Together, the master and servant work tirelessly. We can see the long-suffering nature of the Lord. Despite those efforts, problems remain, and the master considers getting rid of the tree, but the servant intervenes by requesting more time. Divine effort, mercy, and long-suffering constitute the predominant message of this allegory.

JACOB 5:13—WHAT ARE THE NETHERMOST PARTS OF THE VINEYARD?

Nephites would have understood "nethermost parts" as being the farthest away. Another meaning for "nether" is "lower." Lower areas are often more-protected ravines that get more water runoff while being less exposed to high winds. Thus, even though it seems to be an obscure and undesirable place, being located in the nethermost part of the vineyard can be a good thing.

JACOB 5:48—BALANCING THE GROWTH OF ROOTS AND THE LOFTINESS OF BRANCHES

In botany, we learn that we must have a balance between roots and branches. If the roots become too strong, nutrients will not get pulled up into the branches. If the branches are too big, they suck all the strength up from the roots. In this allegory, great effort was expended to keep the roots and branches balanced. As children of Zion, we must always be rooted in the covenant and its foundational elements, being careful lest the branches of our perceived personal wisdom become too lofty. Lofty branches are always lopped off. They can be suckers that never produce anything, yet they still dilute the strength of the roots. Hence the counsel to not run faster than we have strength or look beyond the mark, that mark being Jesus Christ (see Jacob 4:14). Consider the wisdom of this balance when pondering recent Church organizational changes and the motivations behind those decisions.

JACOB 6:8-9—JACOB IMPLORES HIS PEOPLE TO NOT REJECT HIS WORDS

In verse 8, Jacob implored his people to heed his words, to not "reject the words of the prophets . . . which have been spoken concerning Christ, . . . and quench the Holy Spirit, and make a mock of the great plan of redemption." He wanted to be sure they appreciated these sacred teachings and that they did not mock and ridicule the things spoken in that all-important temple. Otherwise, they would have "shame and awful guilt" when they would stand "before the bar of God" (Jacob 6:9).

It is significant that Jacob focused his brief concluding remarks on temple elements. The purpose of the temple, of course, is to bring us into the presence of God, but if we are not pure, we will stand before Him with shame and awful guilt.

"Finally," Jacob says, "I bid you farewell, until I shall meet you before the pleasing bar of God, which bar striketh the wicked with awful dread and fear. Amen" (6:13). It seems that he saw himself as being close to dying. Yet, he would live long enough to withstand Sherem's strong confrontation, which Jacob reports in his final chapter.

JACOB 7:1-4—WHO WAS SHEREM?

We do not know where Sherem came from. Verse 1 simply says, "There came a man *among* the people of Nephi." Whether Sherem was a Lamanite or a Nephite, family relations would still be quite close at this point. Sherem was a "learned" man. In that society, such a description likely meant that he knew the religious traditions in his small world. He may not have known how to read the reformed Egyptian, but he knew the vernacular.

Sherem was a very sophisticated and overconfident challenger. He had a substantial and technical vocabulary; he was a very persuasive person. We read that Sherem "could use much flattery," so he was obviously playing to the crowd. Sherem gets lumped in with the anti-Christs, yet he did not oppose the law of Moses at all. In fact, he thought that Jacob didn't understand it quite correctly. Sherem argued that it was out of order for a prophet to speak of something so far in the future because the truth of any such statement was untestable in their lifetimes. Therefore, he claimed that worship of Christ must be considered illegal, based on false prophecy.

JACOB 7:6-7—SHEREM RAISES A JUDICIAL COMPLAINT AGAINST JACOB

There are clues that we are in the sphere of high-level legal material from the very outset. The word "contend" shows up in the Old Testament (for example, see Proverbs 28, Ecclesiastes 6:10, Isaiah 49:25); it is *rib,* meaning *a lawsuit*. So, when Sherem contends, it means that he was bringing a legal action. Likewise, in this context, if Jacob bore his "testimony," to Sherem here the word would mean "witness" as in a witness in court under oath. Sherem was raising an accusation against Jacob. As the high priest, Jacob would typically have been the chief judge in such matters. However, since Jacob was the accused, all that either of them could do was submit the matter to divine judgment. "The crucial test in this regard is found in Deuteronomy: 'If a false witness rise up against any man to testify against him that *which* is wrong; Then both the men, between whom the controversy is, shall stand before the LORD' (Deuteronomy 19:16–17). Thus, Sherem's conduct requesting Jacob to produce divine evidence was not a casual case of idle sign seeking, but rather followed a significant rule of ancient Israelite jurisprudence'" (Welch, "The Case of Sherem"). This was certainly a very serious legal event, but it was also an important spiritual event for the whole community, because this is a stand-off of cosmic significance. "Are we going to worship Christ? Are we going to look forward to His coming many years in the future?"

Further Reading: John W. Welch, "The Case of Sherem," *The Legal Cases in the Book of Mormon*, 122.

JACOB 7:6-7—A NEPHITE TRIAL WITH JEWISH ROOTS

In the ancient world, trials could take place anywhere, but they typically took place either on the steps of the temple or near the gates to the city. If Jacob and Sherem had simply conversed in private without public witnesses or observers, the pro-Sherem portion of the populace may have suspected foul play when Sherem fell helplessly to the ground. It would seem there were people present who knew that when Sherem fell, the will of God had been manifested. Someone needed to care for him and keep him alive "for many days" after he fell to the ground (7:15). In addition, there would have been less reason for Sherem to have made a public retraction, had he not made a public accusation.

Jacob was wise. He knew that he alone would be unable to persuade Sherem, who was skilled in presenting his argument competently. Sherem accused Jacob of false prophecy; this was a capital offense (see Deuteronomy 18:20). He also accused Jacob of blasphemy, also a capital offense according to Leviticus 24:16. Leading people into apostasy was another accusation that Sherem leveled; it was a capital crime under the law of Moses (see Deuteronomy 13:1–5). Sherem may have felt certain that God would sustain him. The results of this legal case, in many ways, must have become a foundational precedent at the beginning of Nephite legal history which would affect the next 400 or 500 years until the coming of Christ.

JACOB 7:8-12—JACOB ANSWERS SHEREM'S ACCUSATIONS

Under this legal system, once a formal accusation had been raised, silence or failure to respond was a confession of guilt. Thus, Jacob spoke up boldly, having the spirit of the Lord insomuch that "[Jacob] did confound him in all his words." Such a protestation of innocence could be transformed into a legal accusation against the accuser, raising a counterclaim of some kind, and indeed, that was the effect of Jacob's reply.

JACOB 7:13-15—SHEREM REQUESTS A SIGN, THE LORD SMITES HIM TO THE EARTH

Sherem could have retracted his allegations, but the punishment for those who initiated false lawsuits was strict. The punishment for bringing a claim of capital significance and then losing was death for the accuser. Sherem's accusations against Jacob's testimony amounted to a stand-off. The most common method of breaking such a tie was to invoke divine directions. In the case of Jacob and Sherem, it was Sherem who said, "Show me a sign." It appears that Sherem genuinely believed he was right. He was about to learn that he had been deceived.

Given the seriousness of this matter, it is unlikely that Sherem did it as a political or intellectual stunt; he truly thought there was a case to be made against Jacob. Instead, Sherem was struck to the earth. An accuser had to stand up, and now that he was unable to stand, his accusation literally fell flat.

JACOB 7:16-18—SHEREM CONFESSES HIS SINS

Under such circumstances, it would have been clear to everyone that God had cursed such a person, and Sherem also realized this. He confessed his belief in God and in judgment confessing also that he had been deceived by Satan. Earlier, Jacob had spoken of standing before God with shame and awful guilt. Sherem expressed exactly that as part of his confession.

Shortly before his death, Sherem requested that a public assembly be convened so that he could speak to the people. The assembly met so that Sherem could publicly confess his error and retract his previous teachings. He seems to have given a fully acceptable, voluntary confession. Maybe he was hoping that somehow the curse would be lifted; that he would be healed. He may also have been trying to do everything he possibly could to reconcile himself not just with Jacob and Jacob's people, but primarily with God.

JACOB 7:23—PEACE AND GOD'S LOVE ARE RESTORED

When a controversy arose in the ancient world, society was disrupted. The overriding purpose of any lawsuit was not so much to punish someone. Rather, the ultimate objective was to settle the dispute, to restore peace on terms that everyone could accept. Thus, Jacob concludes "that peace and the love of God was restored again among the people" (7:23). They searched the scriptures, gave no more heed to Sherem, and tried to restore the Lamanites to the truth (7:24). Life ended sadly for Jacob ("we did mourn out our days"), but obedient to Nephi's command, he passed on the records, "hoping that many of [his] brethren would read his words" (7:27).

TAKEAWAYS

- **Thinking of the allegory of the Olive Tree, how do you see Heavenly Father and Jesus Christ preserving and caring for you?**
- **What can you do to keep the "roots and branches" of your life in balance with each other?**
- **Look closely at Jacob's testimony to observe how he answered each charge against him. What do you learn about testifying to the truth?**

16: ENOS-WORDS OF MORMON

ENOS 1:1-14—ENOS PRAYS THAT GOD WILL PRESERVE A RECORD OF HIS PEOPLE

Enos was a grandson of Lehi, a son of Jacob, and a nephew of Nephi. He, along with the other Nephites of his time, must have wondered why the Lord had directed them to a place where they were very isolated—a place where it was difficult to converse with and understand the native people of the new land. However, Enos and his direct line of descendants knew that they were serving an important purpose because they had the oral and written history of Lehi, Nephi, and Jacob. They were told that someday their records would serve a crucial function in gathering and reestablishing Israel.

Enos is best known for spending a whole day and well into the night crying unto the Lord to know personally concerning eternal life, the joy of the holy saints, that his sins were forgiven, and that he would be blessed by the Lord (1:5). When he asked how this could be done—perhaps wondering how that atonement could be made when he had not offered any sacrifices in that regard in his father's temple in the city of Nephi—Enos was told, it is "because of thy faith in Christ" (1:8). As soon as he heard those words, he offered an intercessory prayer, first for his people, the Nephites (1:9), and then for the Lamanites (1:11). Being deeply concerned about the eternal welfare of others is profoundly righteous.

ENOS 1:15-17—FOLLOWING NEPHI'S AND JACOB'S INSTRUCTIONS

Nephi issued a commandment to his brother Jacob that was passed along to Enos and this line of recordkeepers. It involved not only a requirement to add a personal record to the small plates, but also included stringent requirements about the content. The verses noted below in parentheses demonstrate that Enos obediently followed each of these requirements. This pattern, however, can easily go unnoticed if a reader is not actively looking for ways in which Nephi's original directive was followed:

- A record is to be kept on the small plates by way of commandment (Jacob 7:27).

- The record must be personally written (Enos 1:1, 11, 17, 19; Jarom 1:1; Omni 1:1, 4, 9, 10, 12).

- The record must be preserved (Enos 1:13–17).

- The record must be handed down within the lineage of Jacob from generation to generation (Jarom 1:1).

- The record is to be added to by each person within the lineage of Jacob to whom the plates are entrusted. Likewise, Enos issued the command to his son Jarom (Jarom 1:1).

- The record is to preserve only (a) precious things, (b) sacred preaching, (c) great revelation, or (d) prophesying. Even at that, only "the heads" or main points of the few precious, sacred, or great utterances should be written (Enos 1:1–17).

- The record is not to cover the history of the people of Nephi "save it were lightly" (Enos 1:20–21, 24).

- The words on the record are to be written "as much as it were possible for Christ's sake, and for the sake of [the people of Nephi]." Enos, as often as possible, referred to the fact that he lived and preached for Christ's sake "because of [his] faith in Christ" (1:8). He preached, prophesied, and declared "according to the truth which is in Christ" (1:26). The final written testimony of Enos was that he "shall rest" in his "Redeemer" (1:27).

Interestingly, this priestly line of recordkeepers gave their sons names of strong and possibly pure Hebrew origins.

- "Enos" is a Hebrew word meaning "Mankind."

- "Jarom" is a Hebrew name likely meaning "Jehovah is exalted."

- "Omni" may relate to Hebrew expressions such as "The Lord is my faith" or "Jehovah is my trust."

- "Amaron" may be derived from roots meaning "The Command of the Lord" or "Jehovah has spoken."

- "Chemish" has several possible etymologies, including the Hebrew ḥameš meaning "five," possibly because he was the fifth generation in the tribe of Jacob.

- "Abinadom" quite readily relates to Hebrew proper names meaning "My father was a wanderer" or "My father was grieved," a feeling expressed by Jacob at the head of this lineage. While the meaning of the name "Amaleki" remains puzzling, it was a name that would likely have been known from the plates of brass.

JAROM 1:1-15—JAROM, THE SON OF ENOS

The text in the book of Jarom manifests his careful attempt to explicitly perpetuate the tradition of keeping the record according to Nephi's command. Jarom wrote only "a few words" (1:1) and wrote "a little" (1:2) to keep "the commandment of [his] father, Enos" (1:1). Specifically, Jarom wrote his record "for the intent of the benefit of [his] brethren the Lamanites" (1:2). Thus, Jarom mentioned many prophets, priests, and teachers who taught the people "to look forward unto the Messiah, and believe in him to come as though he already was" (1:11). The covenant which the Lord made with Enos that the record would survive any Nephite destruction for the benefit of the Lamanites (Enos 1:13, 16) overshadowed Nephi's and Jacob's previously stated purpose of the plates—benefiting "our" people. These are subtle and understandable shifts.

OMNI 1:1-3—OMNI ALSO KEEPS THE RECORD AS PRESCRIBED BY NEPHI

Starting with Omni, the authors' writings on the final sheets of the small plates began to be very brief. Undoubtedly, the plates were almost filled. Indeed, Jarom had remarked that the plates were "small" (Jarom 1:2, 14). Nephi's command to Jacob was for him to write "upon these plates" (Jacob 1:2). The plates were unique—they had been made by the hand of Nephi, as Jacob himself emphasized (Jacob 3:14). Notwithstanding the lack of space, Omni still wrote something to satisfy the requirements of Nephi's template. He stated that he fought "to preserve my people," mentioning some seasons of peace and other times of "serious war and bloodshed" (1:2–3).

OMNI 1:4-8—AMARON TAKES STEWARDSHIP OVER THE RECORD

Like his father, Amaron made a minimal effort in complying with the command to preserve and write on the small plates. Amaron made no reference to revelations, preaching, or prophesying in his lifetime, but reported the destruction of wicked Nephites as fulfillment of the prophecy given by Lehi that they would not prosper in the land if they did not keep the commandments.

OMNI 1:9—CHEMISH, THE BROTHER OF AMARON

Chemish was Amaron's brother. Perhaps for this reason (not wanting to add two records from the same generation), Chemish did not do more than witness the fact that his brother had fulfilled the basic responsibilities and obligations of keeping the record.

OMNI 1:10-11—ABINADOM, THE SON OF CHEMISH

Apparently, Abinadom observed little that was of spiritual value, and though he made an effort to write, he deferred to the "plates which is had by the kings" for the more predominant history.

OMNI 1:12-30—AMALEKI WRITES, THEN PASSES THE PLATES TO KING BENJAMIN

The last person to write upon the small plates was Amaleki, the son of Abinadom. He wrote of the departure of a group of people led by Mosiah from the land of Nephi and of their arrival in the land of Zarahemla. He spoke briefly about the origins of the people of Zarahemla "who had come out from Jerusalem" at around the same time that Lehi and his family had left Jerusalem.

Amaleki then wrote of Mosiah uniting his people with the people of Zarahemla and of Mosiah's appointment as their king.

Continuing with the history, Amaleki wrote that later, his brother left Zarahemla with another group of people with the intention of returning to the land of Nephi. Amaleki had no subsequent knowledge of his brother's whereabouts.

OMNI 1:14—THE MULEKITES REJOICE OVER THE PLATES

Mosiah took the brass plates with him when he traveled down from the land of Nephi into Zarahemla. The king, who was named Zarahemla, was "exceedingly" glad to finally see these plates which had the record of the Jews. The people of Zarahemla had lost their language, but that does not mean they had completely lost all knowledge of their ancestral history.

OMNI 1:15-16—HOW DID MULEK TRAVEL TO THE NEW WORLD?

The name "Melek" is the word for "king" in Hebrew. It is the opinion of some scholars that several passages in the Book of Mormon which reference the "king" should really be translated as "Mulek" and not "king." Mulek was a son of King Zedekiah. After Lehi left Jerusalem, King Zedekiah, along with his other sons, were taken into captivity by the Babylonians and were killed. However, Mulek was able to escape somehow. We do not know how he got to the New World. I like to think that Mulek and his guardians found passage on a Phoenician ship.

Sidon and Tyre were two major shipping centers in Phoenicia, not far from Jerusalem. One of the cities was a trading partner with Egypt and the other a partner with Babylon. Lehi probably traded with one or the other of these large shipping centers.

Hugh Nibley pointed out that there may have been a connection between the name of the large river running through the land of Zarahemla and the old world of Jerusalem and Phoenicia. That river was named "Sidon"—the same name as one of two large shipping centers in Phoenicia. If Mulek was transported to the New World on a ship run by the Phoenicians from Sidon, they may have chosen to name the prominent river in their new land after their place of origin. This fact may be evidence of a Phoenician connection.

CHRONOLOGY OF MORMON'S WRITINGS

Words of Mormon 1:1–11 appear to have been part of Mormon's farewell address and were among the very last of his writings. In the first verse of Words of Mormon, he stated, "And now I, Mormon, being about to deliver up the record into the hands of my son Moroni . . ." Then, in the same verse, Mormon explained that he delivered his abridgment of the plates to Moroni after he, Mormon, had "witnessed almost all the destruction of [his] people, the Nephites." So, Mormon wrote these passages when it was very close to the end of the Nephite nation, about A.D. 385. The text in Words of Mormon 1:1–11 contains the final words that Mormon wrote. Very likely, these eleven verses were also the last words translated by Joseph Smith.

WORDS OF MORMON 1:1–11—MORMON'S FINAL WORDS (PRAYERS FOR THE GRACE OF GOD)

In his farewell address, Mormon chose not to speak to us, but to speak to God. Mormon recorded three of his prayers or pleadings with God.

One of Mormon's last prayers was to express concern for his son, Moroni. Primarily, Mormon pleaded with God to give Moroni time to complete the record and to write more about Christ (1:2).

Mormon's second wish is recorded in verse 8: "And my prayer to God is concerning my brethren." Who were Mormon's brethren? They were the enemies—the Lamanites and Nephites who had defected and were fighting against him. Mormon was expressing forgiveness for those who had turned against him.

The third prayer of Mormon is found in verse 11: "And I, Mormon, pray to God that [these records that have been kept so faithfully by so many people, including myself,] may be preserved from this time henceforth. And I know that they will be preserved."

Mormon was very familiar with the writings of ancient Nephite and Lamanite prophets. He knew that many prophets revealed that we all shall be judged by those things which are written in the books. There is gravity in knowing that this is the last thing that Mormon says.

WORDS OF MORMON 1:1–11—AN OVERLAP OF TWO ABRIDGED HISTORICAL RECORDS

After a simple reading of the eighteen verses that comprise the text of Words of Mormon, one notices that the first eleven verses (1:1–11) are written using only first-person pronouns. There are twenty-two uses of the pronoun "I," another twenty-two uses of the pronoun "we," and one use of the pronoun "us" in these verses. They contain no third-person pronouns. Then, in the remaining verses (1:12–18), only third-person pronouns are used; no first-person pronouns are found in the latter half of the book. There is a significant shift in the narrative halfway through Words of Mormon. It appears that something worthy of attention is happening at the narrative midpoint of Words of Mormon.

Remember that the first book on the large plates was the book of Lehi. However, Lehi's record was lost when Martin Harris lost the first 116 pages that were translated from that record, and it appears that a very small portion of what was originally the beginning translation of Mosiah was not lost with those 116 pages.

It would have been highly unlikely that what was written on the gather (or bundle of sheets from the printer) that Harris took ended exactly at the end of the book of Omni or exactly at the end of Words of Mormon. Therefore, there would have been text from the original translation from the large plates that Martin Harris didn't lose.

Sometime later, after transcribing the original manuscript to create the printer's manuscript, Oliver Cowdery crossed out a Roman numeral III, changed it to a Roman numeral I (Chapter I), and inserted a notation "Book of Mosiah." This likely indicates that at one point, what was initially called Chapter 3 began with the text that is now Mosiah 1:1. And what was originally the last part of the original Mosiah chapter 2 (perhaps on page 117 of what was left when Harris took the 116-page gather) was appended to Words of Mormon by Oliver Cowdery and Joseph Smith after the 116 pages were lost.

Mormon's actual words may thus end at verse 11. Verses 12–18 were then what remained of the large plates translation after Martin Harris took and lost the 116 pages. These seven verses should be read as part of the introductory material initially found in the book of Mosiah.

WORDS OF MORMON 1:12-18—THAT WHICH HAD BEEN TRANSLATED AND RETAINED

The few verses that comprise the text of Words of Mormon give us a bigger picture of the composition of the Book of Mormon. It is quite remarkable that this, like so many other things, ends up being a very strong confirmation of the accuracy of the Book of Mormon, of its miraculous coming forth, and of the way in which the dictation occurred under difficult circumstances. It is difficult enough for us to read the record and figure out what happened. Imagine Joseph Smith simply dictating these segments, putting them all together, and having them make good sense.

WORDS OF MORMON 1:15—FALSE CHRISTS AMONG THE NEPHITES

Verse 15 states that "there had been false Christs." The word "Christ" is equivalent to the word "Messiah" in Hebrew, which means "anointed one." It may have been that King Benjamin had to deal with people claiming that it was their job not just to be a religious leader (a priest or anointed one), but to also be a political leader of some kind.

Under the law of Moses, a person could be severely punished for causing dissension by spreading falsehoods and holding oneself out as a prophet when one didn't have that calling from God. Freedom of religion did not exist in this world—especially when religion was being used for political purposes by sub-groups. Benjamin was able to unify his people by creating a unified pluralist society where two groups of people of different political and historical backgrounds were accommodated and could thrive by making and keeping a centralizing covenant with God, their Heavenly King. The remarkable peace that King Benjamin was able to accomplish under this unique situation stands as a model for governing in a religiously pluralistic society.

TAKEAWAYS

- **What can we learn today from Enos's wrestle with the Lord? What might you ask for if God said that He would grant you anything you desire, because of your faith? (1:12)**
- **What significance can you find in the Hebrew meanings of some of the names in the recordkeepers from Enos down to Amaleki?**

17: MOSIAH 1-3

The book of Mosiah introduces the reader to the large plates of Nephi. Chapters 1-3 of Mosiah contain reports of preparations for Benjamin's solemn assembly, his declarations about his own kingship, his son's coronation, and prophecies about the promised coming of and atoning powers of Jesus Christ, the Heavenly King. These are King Benjamin's words, not an abridgment. This formal and masterful oration can be authoritatively identified simultaneously as a classic farewell speech, a coronation speech, a prophetic speech, a covenant ritual text, and a literary wonder. Markedly, these words were delivered at the temple in Zarahemla. Temple-related words and temple elements run throughout the text. One reader, Paul Hyde, has identified over 100 of its elements that identify it as a temple address.

KING BENJAMIN'S SPEECH: A GREAT ORATION

This speech compares favorably with the greatest orations of world history: many of these impressive ancient orations have been preserved, analyzed, and used as models for great talks. In a chapter entitled "Benjamin's Speech: A Masterful Oration," I identified twelve key qualities that rhetoricians readily agree are commonly found in the greatest orations. While great speeches often have six or seven of these, all twelve are present in King Benjamin's speech.

MOSIAH 2:3-6—WHY ARE THE TENTS IMPORTANT AT KING BENJAMIN'S SPEECH?

Recognizing the customs and requirements of the law of Moses may add insight to what was going on at this event. Mosiah 2:3 explains, "And they also took of the firstlings of their flocks, that they might offer sacrifice and burnt offerings according to the law of Moses."

The Feast of Tabernacles was an important Israelite festival. Every seventh year, all Israelites–including children—were expected to come to the temple in Jerusalem, where each family would sit in a booth—a *sukkah*—that had been created to remind them that their ancestors had dwelt in tents in the wilderness for forty years. Sacrifices would be made, the law would be read, and they would then renew the Mosaic covenant. See, for example, Joshua 24. That was also the traditional time for the coronation of kings when appropriate.

MOSIAH 2:4—WAS THIS A YEAR OF JUBILEE?

In Israel, the observance of the Jubilee year happened regularly, once every fifty years. The Torah mandates that all slaves were set free, debts were forgiven, and all land should return to its original owners.

Based on several phrases that King Benjamin used, many of which can also be seen in the main Jubilee text in Leviticus 24 and 25, one can conclude that Benjamin gave his speech during a Jubilee year. This explains why Benjamin mentioned not allowing slavery and spoke about indebtedness and forgiveness. The observance of a jubilee would be an ideal time for such a solemn and thankful occasion.

MOSIAH 2:12–13—KING BENJAMIN KEPT THE "LAW OF THE KING"

First, Benjamin offers an accounting of his role as king. When he affirms that he has not accumulated gold or silver, he is certifying that he has kept the requirements of Deuteronomy 17:14–20, which limit the power of the king in ancient Israel. A king under the law of Moses was required to read the law, fear the Lord, do all the words of God's law, and not lift his heart up above his brethren. Benjamin stated bluntly that he was no better than anyone else.

He also reported that he had not allowed people to murder, plunder, steal, commit adultery, or any manner of wickedness (2:13). These are a shortened form of the second half of the Ten Commandments. Benjamin's text became a type of constitution for the Nephites. For example, the five crimes established in Mosiah 2:13 are echoed precisely in Alma 30:10. Above all, Benjamin wants to return to God with a clear conscience and with his garments pure, not stained by the blood of his people (2:27–28).

MOSIAH 2:18–19—BENJAMIN TEACHES HIS PEOPLE TO SERVE AND THANK THEIR HEAVENLY KING

He develops the scriptural exhortation to love God "with all our might, mind, and strength" (see, for example, Deuteronomy 6:5; 30:6; Proverbs 2:2) to say, in effect, "I know that I am commanded to love God with all my heart, might, and mind, but I have also loved and served *you* with all my heart, might, and mind." He tells them that the same opportunities are available for them: "And when you are in the service of your fellow beings you are only in the service of your God" (2:17).

King Benjamin wants them to remember that when we serve God, He immediately blesses us, so we are never out of His debt (2:24). Thus, it follows, "if I, whom ye call your king . . . do merit any thanks from you, O how you ought to thank your heavenly King!" (2:19). This is not only logically coherent, but also ethically right and spiritually fulfilling.

MOSIAH 2:11, 28–30—KING BENJAMIN DECLARES MOSIAH TO BE HIS SUCCESSOR

Benjamin ends this first section of his speech as he began—on the subject of the coronation of the king—his own at the beginning, and Mosiah's at the end. He announces, "I have caused that ye should assemble yourselves together, that I might declare unto you this day . . . that my son Mosiah is a king and a ruler over you." A sacred ceremony may have followed, an investiture in which Mosiah would be consecrated (2:11) and perhaps be given the brass plates, or the sword of Laban. King Benjamin provided for an unusually smooth transition from himself to Mosiah, which was uncommon in the rest of the ancient world.

MOSIAH 2:31–41—HOW IS THE NEXT SECTION OF BENJAMIN'S SPEECH ORGANIZED?

In the second part of his speech, King Benjamin pronounces the following:
> He promises his people temporal blessings that will come from obedience (2:31),
> > Condemns willful rebellion against God (2:32–33),
> > > Stresses the accountability of the people (2:34–36),
> > Once again condemns willful rebellion against God (2:37–39),
> And promises his people eternal blessings that come from obedience (2:40–41).

This section marks the end of the installation of Mosiah as the new king. Its central section holds the people accountable, insisting upon their obedience and loyalty to the new king, who stands as an intermediary between the people and their Heavenly King.

MOSIAH 3:2–5—KING BENJAMIN WAS VISITED BY AN ANGEL AND USES HIS WORDS

In section three, many of these teachings come from words that an angel of the Lord spoke to Benjamin regarding the coming of Christ. The angel began with: "For the Lord hath heard thy prayers, and hath judged of thy righteousness, and hath sent me to declare unto thee that thou mayest rejoice; and that thou mayest declare unto thy people, that they may also be filled with joy" (3:4). Benjamin wants all people to know that the Atonement is joyous. In the world, there is misery and sorrow, but the one thing that makes this life bearable and something we can enjoy to the fullest is the knowledge of the Atonement.

MOSIAH 3:5—THE CHRIST WILL BE RECOGNIZED BY HIS MIRACLES

This chapter is about the Atonement and is the doctrinal heart of Benjamin's speech. The angel assures Benjamin that people will know this Redeemer when He comes. He will look like a man and will dwell in a tabernacle of clay, but He will come with powers beyond anything normally seen: "working mighty miracles, such as healing the sick, raising the dead, causing the lame to walk, the blind to receive their sight, and the deaf to hear, and curing all manner of diseases" (3:5). Jesus Himself used similar words to illustrate to John the Baptist's followers that He was indeed the Son of God: "The blind receive their sight, and the lame walk, the lepers are cleansed, and the deaf hear, the dead are raised up, and the poor have the gospel preached to them" (Matthew 11:4–5).

MOSIAH 3:7—FOCUSING ON THE ATONEMENT OF JESUS CHRIST

The Lord shall "suffer temptations, and pain of body, hunger, thirst, and fatigue, even more than man can suffer" (3:7). The angel says that Jesus would suffer so intensely that blood would come from every pore (3:7). Symbolically, His blood is sprinkled from His body onto all the world as He is performing that Atonement, as foreshadowed by the high priest on the Day of Atonement when he sprinkled the cleansing sacrificial blood on the altar and on the people.

The most amazing part of Jesus's accomplishment—on top of all the pain and suffering—is that at any time, even after He said, "Not my will but thine be done," He could have called down the powers of heaven to intervene on His behalf.

MOSIAH 3:8—KING BENJAMIN REVEALS TO HIS PEOPLE A GLORIOUS NAME OF JESUS

One purpose of this assembly is for King Benjamin to give his people a new name within the covenant renewal, by which "they may be distinguished above all the people which the Lord God hath brought out of the land of Jerusalem" (Mosiah 1:11). The name is "Jesus Christ, the Son of God, the Father of heaven and earth, the Creator of all things from the beginning" (3:8). Notice that this important ten-term name will be quoted precisely, over a century later in this same city, by Samuel the Lamanite (see Helaman 14:12).

In this coronation setting, King Benjamin is recognizing the Savior as their Heavenly King. In chapter 5, all his people will enter into a covenant whereby they will take upon themselves this revealed name of Christ (5:8) and become spiritually reborn as His sons and daughters (5:7).

MOSIAH 3:9—JESUS WILL BE CRUCIFIED BECAUSE PEOPLE WILL SAY HE HAS A DEVIL

Benjamin prophecies that some people would try to diminish Jesus's miracle-working. They will "consider him a man," not a god. In order to rationalize His supernatural, miraculous deeds, they will "say that he hath a devil." Under the law of Moses, miracles were viewed with great caution. Judges were required to ask, "By what power or authority was this miracle performed?" (See Matthew 21:23; Mark 3:22.) If these miracles were by the power of the devil or evil forces, the judges were ordered, "Thou shalt not suffer a witch [male or female] to live" (Exodus 22:18). No one was allowed to use magic, miracle-working, or sign-giving to lead people to worship or follow some other god (Deuteronomy 13:1–4). Such conduct in Israel was seen as violating the first and greatest commandment, loving and having only the Lord as God, and the death penalty was to be enforced unequivocally (Deuteronomy 13:5, 8–11).

Roman law also strictly prohibited magic and spellcasting; it was associated with treason, the most serious of all crimes. Benjamin's prophecy explains best why Jesus was rejected and killed. More than any other single text, this passage has informed all my years of study of the trials and death of Jesus.

MOSIAH 3:11–THE ATONEMENT WILL AUTOMATICALLY COVER THREE TYPES OF SINS

Section four of Benjamin's speech (3:11–27) discusses the doctrinal theology and the religious behaviors that are consistent with repentance and the transformation that comes with the Atonement. Earlier, Benjamin had made it clear that people must repent of their own sins, so as to not "remain and die an enemy to God" (2:38). The Atonement allows repentant people to "dwell with God in a state of never-ending happiness" (2:41). After explaining the legal, religious, and practical operations of the atoning blood of Christ, Benjamin now conveys additional important information that certain transgressions or human conditions will be automatically covered by the "infinite and eternal" Atonement (see also Alma 34:10). He first tells them that the Atonement is guaranteed to cover three things:

1.) "The sins of those who have fallen by the transgression of Adam."

2.) "[Those] who have died not knowing the will of God concerning them."

3.) "[Those] who have ignorantly sinned."

The third category of sins mentioned here refers to *specific* things that people have done, yet being unaware that what they were doing was against some point of the law. We no longer think about such accidental matters as sins, but back then, they did (see Exodus 21:13; Numbers 35:11).

MOSIAH 3:18-19–THE NATURAL MAN IS AN ENEMY TO GOD

King Benjamin's speech has an overall chiastic structure. It is organized into seven sections. Section 4 is the middle section, and in the very middle of that middle is this chiastic centerpiece in Mosiah 3:19:

(a) for the natural man
    (b) is an enemy to God, and
        (c) has been from the fall of Adam, and
        (c') will be, forever and ever, unless he
    (b') yields to the enticings of the Holy Spirit, and
(a') putteth off the natural man.

This beautiful, instructive speech is used constantly today as a guide to living the gospel of Jesus Christ. Elder Neal A. Maxwell has seen Benjamin's text as a "manual for discipleship," establishing "the mysteries" by way of covenant (Mosiah 2:9), establishing loyalty to the laws of obedience, submissiveness, meekness, consecration, and loving kindness. (See Maxwell, Neal A. "King Benjamin's Manual of Discipleship." *Ensign* 22, no. 1 [1992]: 8–13, reprinted as Maxwell, Neal A. "King Benjamin's Sermon: A Manual for Discipleship," in *King Benjamin's Speech: "That Ye May Learn Wisdom,"* eds. John W. Welch and Stephen D. Ricks [Provo, UT: Foundation for Ancient Research and Mormon Studies, 1998], 1–21.)

TAKEAWAYS

- Why did King Benjamin desire that his sons "should be taught in all the language of his fathers"? What language, vocabulary, etc. do we need to teach our children? Why? (Mosiah 1:2)
- What name is the king about to bestow on his people? Why is this long name significant? When did you receive the Savior's name upon you? How do you renew that relationship? (Mosiah 3:8)
- What behaviors does Benjamin indicate that God requires in Mosiah 2:17–22? Are there any that you could tune up a little?

18: MOSIAH 4-6

Mosiah chapters 4-6 deal with the response to Benjamin's words as the people express their willingness to enter into a covenant with God. Benjamin instructs them concerning their obligations under that covenant (chapter 4), as they enter into that covenant (chapter 5), and as their names are recorded as being bound under this covenant with God, as well as with their new mortal king (chapter 6). This part of King Benjamin's speech, again, is masterfully organized and literarily unified, as well as ceremoniously cohesive and ritually rich.

MOSIAH 4:1-2—THE PEOPLE FELL TO THE EARTH AND CRIED OUT WITH ONE VOICE

The people fell "to the earth," as the fear (*godly* fear or *reverence*) of the Lord came upon them. It was common to prostrate oneself in awe or reverence. Then they all cried aloud with one voice. The words were probably a coronation-affirmation or covenant-making ritual that required formal responses. In saying "Oh have mercy and apply the atoning blood of Christ," they were reflecting that they wanted that purifying blood to be sprinkled on them, just as the high priest made the atoning sacrifice on the Day of Atonement by sprinkling blood on the altar of the temple (see also Joshua 24:16, 21–26). They now understood that symbolism.

MOSIAH 4:4, 5, AND 11—REMEMBER YOUR NOTHINGNESS COMPARED WITH THE GREAT GOODNESS OF GOD

The fifth section (4:5–12) of this speech begins and ends with a statement for us to remember our "nothingness" (4:5, 11). We are not "nothing" in an absolute or potential sense, but when we are compared in our present condition with the great goodness of our God, we must bow and confess, "O Lord, my God, how great thou art!"

MOSIAH 4:9-10—INSTRUCTIONS TO BELIEVE IN GOD

Benjamin next teaches the requirements "whereby salvation cometh" (4:8). We must believe and trust in the following:

1.) That God exists.

2.) "That he created all things, both in heaven and in earth."

3.) "That he has all wisdom" and that He has a plan for us.

4.) That He has "all power, both in heaven and in earth" to carry out His plan.

5.) That we cannot comprehend all that God comprehends.

Next, King Benjamin provided the "how-to" with five required behaviors. We must:
1.) Believe that we must repent of our sins.
2.) Forsake them and leave them behind.
3.) Humble ourselves.
4.) Ask sincerely for forgiveness for our sins.
5.) If you believe all these things, see that ye *do* them.

Benjamin understood that *belief* without *doing* is pointless.

MOSIAH 4:12, 26—RETAINING A REMISSION OF SINS

After the five "believe" and five "repent" statements (4:9–10), Benjamin added two "knowledge" statements (4:11), and two mentions of the word "remember." We must always *retain* in remembrance what God has done for us (4:11). It is not enough to know. In 4:26, Benjamin returns to retaining a remission of sins with chiasmic closure.

MOSIAH 4:13-30—THE ELEMENTS OF A COVENANT-MAKING CEREMONY

Ancient treaties or covenant-making ceremonies had several common elements. Section six of Benjamin's speech followed this pattern of covenant-making quite strictly. (1) There was a historical preamble, followed by (2) how the people came to where they were, and (3) what the relationship had been between the parties entering into the covenant. These are covered in Mosiah chapter 2. The parties then affirm (4) that God created everything and that He is part of their covenant relationship. (5) The terms of the covenant were then stated in a contract mode. (6) Witnesses recorded the names of those entering into the covenant. (7) Next there were blessings if the parties kept the covenant, and curses if they did not. (8) Finally, the covenant was written and permanently stored.

MOSIAH 4:13, 28—RENDER TO OTHERS WHAT THEY ARE DUE

As a result, as we experience the change of heart, we will have no thought or "mind to injure one another" (4:13); we will "live peaceably" (4:13); and if people have done good to us, we will reciprocate and "render to every man according to that which is his due" (4:13). Benjamin repeats the same theme in Mosiah 4:28, where he specified that the people had to return the very *thing* they had borrowed.

MOSIAH 4:14-15—TEACH THE CHILDREN THE LAWS OF THE COVENANT

The people must agree to teach their children the laws of God, or they would not be worthy to enter into this covenant. This requirement is also found in Deuteronomy 4:9–10, where Moses was promulgating the covenant with Israel. Benjamin was very familiar with Deuteronomy's requirements.

MOSIAH 4:16-26—GIVE FREELY SO THAT YOU CAN BE FREELY FORGIVEN

As a central requirement of this covenant text, Benjamin emphasized the need to give to the poor: Deuteronomy 15:7–8 says, "If there be among you a poor man . . . thou shalt not harden thine heart, nor shut thine hand from thy poor brother." He addresses the problem of people judging the poor to avoid being obligated to give (4:17, 22). Anyone who makes such excuses "perisheth forever, and hath no interest in the kingdom of God" (4:18).

This all makes logical sense as well as conveying theological certitude: For "if God . . . doth grant unto you whatsoever ye ask that is right, in faith, believing that ye shall receive, O then, how ye ought to impart of the substance that ye have one to another" (4:21).

MOSIAH 4:27—DO NOT RUN FASTER THAN WE HAVE STRENGTH

King Benjamin warned that they should not try to do more than they were able. "It is not requisite that a man should run faster than he has strength" (4:27). Benjamin was essentially conveying that there is no need to provide luxuries for the poor, but we do need to be concerned about their essential needs, and that is precisely the goal of the welfare program of the Church.

MOSIAH 5:2—NO MORE DESIRE TO DO EVIL

The people observe that their hearts have indeed been changed: they had no more desire to do evil, which may be the greatest evidence of the "mighty change of heart." This is the difference between resisting sin and forsaking sin. We can ask ourselves how we are doing in not even considering or wanting to commit sins.

MOSIAH 5: 3-4—A TRIBUTE TO A GREAT LEADER

The people's joyous response assured Benjamin that they believed his words, and had, through the Spirit, received a witness of the truth. They had experienced a "mighty change of heart," as he had described. The "exceeding joy whereby we do rejoice" is another consequence.

MOSIAH 5:5—WILLING TO ENTER INTO THE COVENANT

The people were required to avow that they were willing to enter into this covenant and were doing it voluntarily. Willingness and choice are important features of sacred covenants. During the sacrament, *we* also manifest our willingness as we witness unto God the Eternal Father that we "are *willing* to take upon [us] the name of thy Son" (3 Nephi 18:10; Moroni 4:3; Doctrine and Covenants 20:77).

MOSIAH 5:7—THE NEPHITES ALL BECAME THE CHILDREN OF CHRIST WITH THE LAW

Here, Benjamin declared that through the covenant, the people had become sons and daughters of Christ. These people were in transition. They were living the law of Moses, but they were expecting the fulfillment of the prophecies of Christ. In Deuteronomy 17:18–19, we read that a king was required to write himself a copy of the law and read it "all the days of his life." Benjamin had certainly done that! He also gave everybody a copy of his speech so that *they* could read it for the rest of *their* lives. He changed their hearts and lives forever, and this text can change ours.

MOSIAH 5:8-12—IF WE DO NOT SERVE GOD, OUR NAMES WILL BE BLOTTED OUT

Benjamin then spoke about *obedience* "unto the end of your lives" (5:8). "Whosoever doeth this shall be found at the right hand of God, for he shall know the name by which he is called; for he shall be called by the name of Christ" (Mosiah 5:9, compare. 5: 10, 12).

Mosiah 5:10–12 is one of the most famous passages in the Book of Mormon, because of its clear and meaningful chiastic structure. This passage was the very first chiasm that I found in the Book of Mormon. Over 50 years later, that discovery on that morning is unforgettably exciting. It changed me, my focus, my testimony, my life, and my already deep love for the scriptures and the gospel of Jesus Christ, in many creative and productive ways.

It also changed the way that people everywhere read the Book of Mormon. More than ever before, people now approach this sacred record with much greater respect for its deliberate organization, for the elegant composition of its passages, for the meaningful placement of its individual words, for the compelling logic of its coherent messages, for its convincing mode of timeless communication, for the enduring value of its spiritual and practical examples, and for the joy of its attractive manner of persuasion and invitation to come unto Christ and repeatedly find there God's beautiful plan of eternal life and happiness.

MOSIAH 5:13-15—WE MUST SERVE GOD IN ORDER TO KNOW HIM

Benjamin returns to the concept of service at the end of his speech. With the skill of the great orators, he explains *why* we are expected to serve. "For how knoweth a man the master whom he has not served? (5:13)." When we know the master, we belong to Him because we have entered into a covenant with Him. We do not serve God to try to repay Him; we can never get out of his debt (Mosiah 2:21). "When ye are in the service of your fellow beings ye are only [merely, exclusively] in the service of your God" (2:17). Service is about building a relationship with God so He can then exalt us and seal us to be bound together in righteousness. This conclusion to Benjamin's speech is a truly beautiful, prophetic blessing upon all his people, ending with the sealing, the placing of the Lord's seal of approval that binds us to Him. They now belonged to the Lord in that sense, and they were spiritually reborn and begotten into His family. With this formality completed for each of us, life has just begun. A new life lies ahead.

MOSIAH 6:1-2—NAMES WERE TAKEN OF THOSE WHO ENTERED THE COVENANT

Finally, King Benjamin had his priests record the names of all who had entered into the covenant. King Benjamin is again transforming Nephite society and perception. Everyone in his kingdom was numbered among the covenant-makers equally. That numbering brought them together with obligations as members of this covenant house. The keeping of a record was the first commandment that was given to the restored Church when it was organized in Fayette, New York, in 1830. Doctrine and Covenants section 20, the organization of the Church, was approved. Then came Section 21, of which the first verse says, "There shall be a record kept among you." All the names of the people who had become members of the Church were recorded. We can go back to the very earliest days and know when everyone was baptized. This practice has been invaluable to the performing of the Savior's work.

TAKEAWAYS

- **The people did "cry aloud with one voice" (Mosiah 4:1–2). How did the people know what to say and when to say it? When do you accept a covenant simultaneously? What kind of declarations were made in Joshua 24:14–25? Can you sustain them? How?**
- **Does knowing that you are a child of God make a difference for you? What can you do to strengthen that relationship? See also Mosiah 5:8–12.**
- **Benjamin understood that belief without doing is useless. He made two sets of five lists in Mosiah 4:9–10, the "know" and the "do." Review the requirements; are there any that we could do better at?**
- **What are the results of accepting the Savior into our lives?**
- **Why are we expected to serve others? How important is service to our salvation (Mosiah 4:26, 5:8–12)? How is this principle reflected in the new ministering "program"? What happens if we accept Christ, but fail to serve?**

19: MOSIAH 7-10

BONDAGE AND DELIVERANCE

Mosiah 7–10 exemplifies what it takes to be delivered from bondage, physical and spiritual. The Nephites came into bondage through sin and were delivered by turning to the Lord. The *captivity* experienced by these people functions as an allegory for our own spiritual captivity; the Book of Mormon contains these stories to offer guidance on how we can get out of spiritual captivity. The bondage we face today may be different, but the message about how we overcome such challenges is as important now as it was then.

MOSIAH 7:3—TWO AMMONS

There are two Ammons in the Book of Mormon. This one was sent by King Mosiah (7:1–3), to look for those who had left Zarahemla some years earlier with a man named Zeniff to reclaim their inheritance in the land of Lehi-Nephi. This Ammon must have been a trusted member of King Mosiah's court.

The other, $Ammon_2$, was one of the sons of King Mosiah (Mosiah 27:34) who left Zarahemla at the *end* of King Mosiah's reign to become missionaries to the Lamanites in the land of Nephi. $Ammon_2$ may have been born around the time $Ammon_1$ led his group of explorers to the south. $Ammon_2$ may have been named after the highly trusted $Ammon_1$.

MOSIAH 7:9—KING LIMHI IS QUOTED DIRECTLY

King Limhi was "the son of Noah" and the grandson of "Zeniff, who came up out of the land of Zarahemla to inherit [the land of Lehi-Nephi]." Though the son of wicked King Noah, Limhi was a just man who had faith in God.

According to John Gee, "It seems that Limhi had spent a good deal of time studying and memorizing the records of his people" (see Gee, John, "Limhi in the Library," *Journal of Book of Mormon Studies* 1, no. 1 (1992): 54–66, quoted in *KnoWhy* #85).

Thanks to the inspired preservation by Mormon, we can look to Limhi as a righteous example. "We need look no further than Limhi for reasons to be serious about studying our scriptures."

MOSIAH 7:19-21—LIMHI'S PEOPLE WERE IN BONDAGE BECAUSE OF THEIR INIQUITIES

We learn from Limhi that he knew his people were in bondage because they had sinned. After the arrival of Ammon, he gathered his people at the temple and reminded them that God had saved their ancestors, reiterating the miracle of the Israelites crossing the Red Sea on dry ground. But "it is because of our iniquities and abominations that he has brought us into bondage."

MOSIAH 7:25, 32-33—GOD'S COVENANT STILL APPLIES

King Limhi spoke to his people about their status in the covenant. Because of sin, the Lord "will not succor [His] people in the day of their transgression" (7:29), and thus "the promise of the Lord is fulfilled, and ye are smitten and afflicted" (7:32). But then he added the positive promise of the covenant: "But if ye will turn to the Lord with full purpose of heart, and put your trust in him . . . he will . . . deliver you out of bondage" (7:19, 33). Limhi may have had in mind the promise given in Leviticus 26:40–44: "If they shall confess their iniquity, and . . . be humbled . . . [t]hen will I remember my covenant with Jacob, and . . . Isaac, and . . . Abraham."

The law of Moses applied to these Nephites just as it did to other descendants of the patriarchs. Many of the problems faced by Zeniff's community (see Mosiah 9:14–16, and Mosiah 11:13–17) were the same afflictions imposed upon the Israelites when they broke their covenants. Both these events are reminiscent of what the Lord had said, in the law of Moses, would be the dire consequences for those who broke their covenants (see Deuteronomy 28:31). They (the Nephites) were warned that if they refused to repent, they would be in bondage to their enemies, which also corresponds with the warning given to the Israelites in Leviticus 26:25 (war and pestilence).

The Book of Mormon repeatedly demonstrates that the covenant God made with ancient Israel still applied to the Nephites. Likewise, the blessings of God's covenants as well as the consequences for disobedience apply to us today unless we repent and accept His atoning mercy. Verse 33 states three things we must do to obtain the blessings: (1) turn to the Lord, (2) trust Him, and (3) serve Him.

MOSIAH 8:3—KING BENJAMIN'S SPEECH IS SHARED WITH THE PEOPLE OF LIMHI

Ammon either had a copy of King Benjamin's speech, or he knew it from memory, for he repeated it to the people of Limhi and explained it. Ammon and King Limhi likely believed that these people would benefit from knowing the revelations Benjamin had shared with his people. In addition, they would benefit by following Benjamin's public laws, since these statutes and ordinances had already proven to be beneficial to all the people of Zarahemla.

MOSIAH 8:7-12—LIMHI'S SEARCH PARTY DISCOVERS THE JAREDITE REMAINS

Earlier, hoping to deliver his people from bondage, King Limhi had sent a party of forty-three people to Zarahemla to appeal for help. The group never made it to Zarahemla. They became lost and discovered instead the land once populated by the Jaredites, where they found the Jaredite records. Limhi was anxious to know what they contained.

MOSIAH 8:13—A GIFT FROM GOD

We are reminded of Joseph Smith when reading Ammon's response to King Limhi. "I can assuredly tell thee, O king, of a man that can translate the records; for he has wherewith that he can look, and translate all records that are of ancient date; and it is a gift from God."

Joseph's ability to translate ancient records was also a gift from God, and it only worked when God's prophet and seer obeyed His will. Like Joseph Smith and Mosiah, we all have gifts from the Lord that can only be accessed, used, and magnified properly when we seek to build up the kingdom of God.

MOSIAH 8:15-19—GREATER THAN A PROPHET?

King Limhi was impressed that King Mosiah, in Zarahemla, had such a great gift as to be able to translate the twenty-four Jaredite plates. His great joy in knowing this is mentioned twice (8:19; 21:28).

King Limhi repeated an oft-quoted statement: "[A] seer is greater than a prophet" (8:15). Ammon then delineated a distinction between prophethood and seership. He stated that seership is greater than prophethood because a seer unlocks the meanings of what happened in the past as well as in the future (8:17), which would include past mysteries, secrets, obscured teachings, lost scripture, and hidden knowledge.

With the restoration of God's ancient order in our time came the restoration of the gift of seership. Members of the First Presidency and the Quorum of the Twelve Apostles are sustained as prophets, seers, and revelators who direct the Church by means of divine revelation (see Bible Dictionary, "Seer").

MOSIAH 9:1-7—ZENIFF TELLS HOW HE LED A GROUP OF NEPHITES TO THE LAND OF LEHI-NEPHI

The story of Zeniff begins in Omni 1:27–30, where Amaleki mentioned two expeditions to the land of Lehi-Nephi, the first of which ended disastrously as all but fifty of the group were slain due to infighting. Regarding the second expedition, which consisted of a large group of men, Amaleki, whose brother was part of that group, explained that he had no knowledge of what happened to them.

The land of Lehi-Nephi was occupied by Lamanites. In Mosiah chapter 9, Zeniff recorded expanded details regarding the two expeditions that Amaleki briefly mentioned. During the first of these expeditions, Zeniff was sent to scout out the situation so that their army could "destroy" the Lamanites (9:1), but when he "saw that which was good among [the Lamanites]," he recommended making a treaty with the Lamanites rather than trying to conquer them. However, the Lamanite ruler, "being an austere and a blood-thirsty man" (9:2), saw things differently, which caused contention and bloodshed among the expeditioners. All but fifty were slain. The survivors, including Zeniff, returned home to Zarahemla to tell their families the tragic outcome.

Zeniff, "being over-zealous to inherit the land of [his] fathers" (9:3), set out on a second expedition to Lehi-Nephi. This group suffered "famine" and "sore affliction," recognizing that their problems were rooted in their behavior, "for we were slow to remember the Lord our God" (9:3). Zeniff negotiated with and trusted the Lamanite king, and he and his people were given the lands of Lehi-Nephi and Shilom. They began to build and plant, not realizing that the unscrupulous Lamanite king had designs to put them into oppressive servitude (9:10).

MOSIAH 9:14-16—THE LAMANITES GREW UNEASY AND GREEDY

Twelve years later, the Lamanites, who were worried that "they could not overpower [the growing group of settlers]" (9:11), attacked Zeniff's people. The people of Shilom fled into the city of Nephi, seeking protection from Zeniff, who straightway armed them "with all manner of weapons which [they] could invent, . . . and did go forth against the Lamanites to battle" (9:16).

MOSIAH 9:17-18—IN THE STRENGTH OF THE LORD

Zeniff records that as the Nephites went to tackle the Lamanites, they turned to the Lord, remembering the deliverance of their forefathers from Egypt. President Spencer W. Kimball was fond of teaching that one of the most important words in the dictionary is *"remember."* Remembering the goodness of God and the deliverance of their ancestors turned the hearts of these Nephites to the Lord. Their prayers were answered, and they were able to go forth "in his might."

MOSIAH 10:12-17—CAUSES OF LAMANITE ANIMOSITY

Zeniff recorded why the Lamanites, generations later, were hostile toward the Nephites. From the outset, Laman and Lemuel had seen things differently than Nephi, and they perpetuated this tradition of negative perceptions regarding their history and grievances. We can appreciate the efforts of the Nephites to understand the Lamanite perspective, expressed in detail in these verses: wronged in being driven out of Jerusalem; wronged in the wilderness; wronged while crossing the sea (10:12); wronged because Nephi was favored of the Lord, which they could not understand (10:13–14); wronged in the promised land because Nephi took over as ruler (10:15); wronged because Nephi and his people "departed into the wilderness," sneaking off with the brass plates (10:16). This attention to Lamanite grievances will no doubt be helpful in the missionary efforts of people like the sons of Mosiah (Alma 17–26) as they carry the gospel to later generations of the Lamanites.

MOSIAH 10:10, 17-18—SUCCESS COMES ONLY IN THE STRENGTH OF THE LORD

As mentioned in Mosiah 9:17–18, as the Nephites went forth to fight, they all turned to the Lord. This was the key to their success: "We did go up in the strength of the Lord, . . . putting [our] trust in the Lord" (10:10, 19). After declaring that he "did confer the kingdom upon one of [his] sons," even Noah, Zeniff ended his record with one last, heartfelt prayer that undoubtedly had guided him throughout the challenges of his life: "May the Lord bless my people" (10:22).

TAKEAWAYS

- Limhi recalls the history of his people (7:19-20). "Creation accounts" tell the origin or beginnings of a people, country, or business, or the earth, etc. Why are "creation accounts" important?
- Look at Mosiah 7:18-20, 1 Nephi 5:15, 1 Nephi 17:40-41, 2 Nephi 25:20 (and innumerable other examples). What do they have in common, and why? Why do we celebrate Pioneer Day, and the Restoration of the Gospel?
- Are we ever "over-zealous" for things? What problems can this cause for us? (7:21–23, 4:27).
- How did Zeniff stereotype the Lamanites? How did they stereotype the Nephites? What grievances did Zeniff say that the Lamanites held against the Nephites? (10:12-13). How do we stereotype people of other cultures? Why do we do this?
- Many problems faced by Zeniff's community were the same afflictions imposed upon Israel if they broke their covenants (see Mosiah 9:14–16, and Mosiah 11:13–17). How much of this applies to us today? What must we do to stay firmly on the covenant path? According to Mosiah 7:33, what three things we must do to obtain the blessings?

20: MOSIAH 11-17

These chapters report the message, trial, and death of the prophet Abinadi. They are specific and detailed, including legal and doctrinal elements. The record likely began as a legal report, telling of the trial and execution of the prophet Abinadi from a judicial point of view. Striving to understand the trial of Abinadi in light of ancient legal principles makes sense, and this fundamental legal perspective undergirds and informs the reading and interpreting of this powerful scriptural episode. King Noah did not walk in the ways of his righteous father, Zeniff. Along with his priests, his version of keeping the law of Moses was riddled with rationalization. As a result, tragedy befell him.

MOSIAH 11:2-7—ABINADI DISAPPROVED OF NOAH'S CHOICES

Noah and his priests had many wives and concubines. Deuteronomy allowed an Israelite man to have more than one wife, but their problem, under the limitations of the paragraph of the king, Deuteronomy 17:16, was that they had *too many* wives. Noah's immoderation was unacceptable to Abinadi, who was commissioned by the Lord to preach repentance to Noah and his people.

This king-focused text also prohibited a king from amassing too much gold and silver (Deuteronomy 17:17), but what is too much? Noah imposed a twenty percent flat tax on his people. To people in the ancient world, that was enormous, even greedy.

The Nephites, under Noah's influence, became idolatrous. Idolatry is defined in Exodus 20:4, but what constitutes idolatry? Is the making of the image problematic, or is it the worshiping of such images? Clearly, Abinadi believed that Noah and his priests had gone too far.

MOSIAH 12:3—ABINADI PROPHESIED AGAINST NOAH

Abinadi's warning, "It shall come to pass that the life of King Noah shall be valued even as a garment in a hot furnace," constitutes a Hebrew poetic form of prophecy called a *simile curse*. Such statements conveyed serious predictions and severe consequences. The priests reported this prophecy to the king; according to Exodus 22:28 ("Thou shalt not . . . curse the ruler of thy people"), Abinadi's prophecy was illegal.

MOSIAH 12:20-24—THE PRIESTS QUESTIONED ABINADI

The king wanted to get rid of Abinadi, so the priests tried to demonstrate his "false prophecy" by trapping him with questions. They read from Isaiah 52 and asked how he interpreted the passage. Why would the priests think they could prove Abinadi to be a false prophet by quoting that? Perhaps they believed that Isaiah 52 was a prophecy about the city of Nephi and its greatness. From their point of view, they could have thought it was talking about them, so all was well in

Nephi. Would Abinadi falter?

Bear in mind that Abinadi had no advanced legal warning about the charges they were trying to prove; there were no lawyers and no time to prepare an answer. Abinadi was prepared, nevertheless, and answered by reciting the messianic Isaiah chapter 53 (see Mosiah 14). Thus, his real answer was, "If you want to understand Isaiah 52, read Isaiah 53."

MOSIAH 12:33-36, 13:11-24—ABINADI TAUGHT THE BASIC TEN COMMANDMENTS

Abinadi began by reteaching the Ten Commandments. In Israel, the feast of Pentecost celebrated the giving of the law on Mount Sinai. There are several markers and similarities between Moses's experience and this occasion. It would have been very appropriate for Abinadi to quote the Ten Commandments, and, indeed, the face of Abinadi (Mosiah 13:5) shone with luster—as did Moses's—as he began to recite the law for the benefit of the priests.

MOSIAH 14:1-12—ABINADI PRESENTED ISAIAH'S "SUFFERING SERVANT" TEXT MESSIANICALLY

Abinadi recited the chapter in Isaiah that addresses the suffering servant of the Lord and elucidated it as referring to the Messiah. Interestingly the text in Isaiah 52:14 says, "His [the Servant's] visage was . . . *marred*," but in the Isaiah scroll from Qumran, the word for *marred* is absent—one letter had been added, and the word was *anointed*, rather than *marred*. The word for *anointed* in Greek is *Christos*. Abinadi must have used this version because he says, "Even until the resurrection of Christ—for so shall he be called" (Mosiah 15:21).

MOSIAH 15:1-5—AN ANCIENT PERSPECTIVE ON MONOTHEISM

The *Shema* (Deuteronomy 6:4), a priestly blessing recited by Jews even today, says, "Hear, O Israel, our Lord God is one Lord: And thou shalt love the Lord thy God with all thine heart." People tend to view the word "one" as meaning only one God numerically—but the ancient text was understood in terms of there being only *one true and faithful God*. It has more to do with exclusive loyalty than numerical counting.

Abinadi replaced the text in Isaiah 52:7, "Thy God reigneth," with "*The Son* reigneth" (Mosiah 15:20), and thereby emphasized that *the Son* is the Messiah who will come and redeem. Abinadi explained in what sense Christ is *the Son* and *the Father*. Christ is the Son because He will be born to a human mother in a miraculous way. However, He will also be the Father, because He is the Creator of heaven and earth (Mosiah 3:8), and because we are spiritually born again as Christ's sons and daughters (Mosiah 5:7). Christ is the very Eternal Father of heaven and earth, but not of the whole cosmos. That is God the Father.

MOSIAH 15:6-8—ABINADI PROPHESIES OF CHRIST

Isaiah 53 taught that the Savior will have power to intercede for us, and Abinadi explained the nature of that intercession by saying that he will "[stand] betwixt them and justice" (Mosiah 15:9). Mercy is not inconsistent with justice, because justice occurs eventually, but only after an opportunity for intercession.

MOSIAH 15:10-14—ABINADI ASKS, "WHO SHALL DECLARE HIS GENERATION?"

"Who shall declare his generation?" or, in other words, "Who will declare where He came from?" The true genesis of the Messiah began in the premortal council. The priests had asked Abinadi who would "publish peace" (Mosiah 12:20–21). Abinadi's answer was, "The ones who will declare his generation." He added that anyone who accepts the prophecies of the Atonement of Christ can declare his generation, the good news. We can declare it too. "*He* [the Father] shall prolong his days and the pleasure of the Lord shall prosper in his hand" (Mosiah 14:10; Isaiah 53:10). Abinadi applied that couplet to the Resurrection of Christ.

MOSIAH 15:22-28—THE SIGNIFICANCE OF THE LORD MAKING HIS HOLY ARM BARE

According to Abinadi, the way that God will make bare His holy arm is through the redemptive labor of His Son, who will be seen in the eyes of all nations. This explanation also began in Mosiah 12:21–24, when the priests asked what it means to "make bare his arm in the eyes of all nations, and all the ends of the earth shall see the salvation of our God."

Abinadi concludes his extended testimony by declaring: "I say unto you that the time shall come that the salvation of the Lord [the message of the gospel of Jesus Christ] shall be declared to every nation, kindred, tongue, and people . . . and people shall see [God] eye to eye and shall confess before God that his judgments are just" (Mosiah 15:28; 16:1). He had successfully rebutted the priests' accusations that he had prophesied falsely and had implicitly counterclaimed against them of their own wickedness, for "then shall the wicked be cast out, . . . they [who] are carnal and devilish, . . . and persist in the ways of sin" (16:2, 3, 5).

MOSIAH 16:8-12—THE STING OF DEATH WILL BE SWALLOWED UP IN CHRIST

The priests of Noah accepted the writings of Isaiah, especially Isaiah 52. But Isaiah had also prophesied that the Lord of Hosts "will swallow up death *in victory*" (Isaiah 25:8; emphasis added). Thus, Abinadi testified to Noah's court: "But there is a resurrection; therefore the grave hath no victory, and the sting of death is swallowed up *in Christ*" (Mosiah 16:8; emphasis added). Knowing the story of Abinadi, Ammon would then teach King Lamoni that "the sting of death should be swallowed up *in the hopes of glory*" (Alma 22:14; emphasis added). Since the Hebrew word in Isaiah 25:8 is *netzach* and all three of these meanings—victory, victor, and hope of victory—are contained in that word, these texts all together bear a remarkably inspiring testimony of the message of Easter.

MOSIAH 17:2–ALMA THE ELDER WAS CONVERTED: A GREAT LINE OF DESCENDANTS

The conversion of Alma the Elder directed the path of his descendants for the next 450 years. We can trace the record through his faithful posterity all the way to Ammaron, the last of the line, who gave the plates to Mormon. As far as we know, Alma was Abinadi's only direct convert. Although Abinadi may have thought he was a failure, he had little idea how far and wide his influence would extend.

MOSIAH 17:4–ALMA WRITES THE WORDS OF ABINADI

Alma may also have wondered if he was going to die. So, one of his first actions was to record the words of Abinadi. Mormon, when he knew that his people were done for, likewise said, "All I can do is stand as an idle witness, but I will leave a record." Alma may have been driven by the same compelling motive.

MOSIAH 17:8–20–THE CONVICTION AND EXECUTION OF ABINADI

The priests accused Abinadi of yet another crime—that he had spoken blasphemously against God, for which he would be put to death, unless he retracted the curses that he had placed upon the king and the people (17:8). When Abinadi refused and offered to undergo an ordeal "even until death" (17:10) to validate his testimony (17:10), Noah would have withdrawn the accusations (17:11), but the priests advanced a fourth charge—having previously charged him with the offenses of lying, false prophecy, and blasphemy—they now accused Abinadi of having "reviled" against the king (17:12), which was unlawful (Exodus 22:28).

Abinadi aimed his final prophetic judgment against the priests. He predicted that their "seed shall cause many to suffer even . . . death by fire" (17:15), and that they themselves would be "taken by the hand of your enemies, and then . . . shall suffer . . . the pains of death by fire" (17:18), which soon happened.

Regarding Noah's death by fire, see Mosiah 19:20; on the fulfillment of the prophecy that the seed of these priests would cause other believers to be put to death by fire, see Alma 25:7, 12. Regarding the deaths of some of the priests of Noah, see Alma 25:4; and on the continued hunting of the remainder of these priests, see Alma 25:9, 12.

Abinadi was "put to death because he would not deny the commandments of God" (see Mosiah 17:20). This detail and the accurate qualities of this record about Abinadi's faithfulness allow all readers to appreciate him as a true prophet of God and to strengthen our personal testimonies and obedience even in the face of great difficulties.

TAKEAWAYS

- What sins did King Noah commit that were prohibited by the law of Moses? Why did Noah think he could get away with his behavior? (Why do we?)
- What question did the priests ask Abinadi (12:20-22)? Was this an effective approach to the interrogation? What do you think this scripture from Isaiah meant to these priests?
- Abinadi quotes Isaiah 53 (14:1-12). How does Abinadi interpret Isaiah 53, and how does that allow him to answer the priests' first question about the meaning of Isaiah 52 (Mosiah 15-16)? Was this an effective response?
- What kind of missionary may Abinadi have thought he was? What effect did his efforts actually have? List some small acts of service and gospel-sharing you can do. You never know the benefit.

21: MOSIAH 18-24

At the very center of the book of Mosiah (chapters 11–17) stands that singular story of Abinadi's prophecies, trial, and death at the hand of King Noah and his priests, with the aftermath of that martyrdom then playing out here in chapters 18–24. Those seven chapters have balancing counterparts in the chapters and events and content that led up to the Abinadi section as told in chapters 7–10. Indeed, the entire book of Mosiah can be seen as one large chiastic structure. See *BYU Studies,* 10 no. 1 (1969), 82. Chapters 18–24 contain many important doctrinal and consequential lessons to be learned from the account about Abinadi, which include society's need for righteous political leadership, the importance of heeding the words of the prophets of God, making covenants, obeying the commandments, working together in unity and charity, and patiently enduring burdens by trusting in the Lord.

MOSIAH 18:6-17—PRIESTHOOD AUTHORITY

The misuses of authority by King Noah and his priests, and the righteous use of priesthood authority by Alma, stand as clear contrasts. We are not specifically told how Alma the Elder received his priesthood authority, but he was a priest. He agreed with Abinadi, knew what needed to be done, and obtained the direction from God to organize a covenant community (18:13). The Nephites explicitly recognized the importance of having authority from God to baptize and to create a binding covenant relationship (Mosiah 18:10; 21:35). Mosiah 18:13 says, "And when [Alma the Elder] had said these words, the Spirit of the Lord was upon him, and he said: Helam, I baptize thee, *having authority from the Almighty God*" (emphasis added). It was important then, as it is now, that baptism and other ordinances be performed by one having authority from God through a person who holds the appropriate keys.

MOSIAH 18:8-13—LIVING THE COVENANT

The style of these chapters generally is indirect narrative, but in the case of Alma's authoritative words they are quoted directly (see, for example, Mosiah 18:8–10, 12–13; 23:7–14). In the case of his baptisms, his words bear great resemblance to the words the Lord revealed regarding performing the ordinance of baptism in this dispensation (see Doctrine and Covenants 20:73–74). Here, Alma lists eight elements of the baptismal covenant (see Mosiah 18:8–9):

1.) To come into the fold of God,

2.) To be called His people,

3.) To bear one another's burdens,

4.) To mourn with those who mourn,

5.) To comfort those who need comfort,

6.) To stand as a witness of God at all times

7.) To serve God throughout mortality, and

8.) To keep His commandments.

To those who honor their baptismal commitments, the Lord promises to redeem them, number them with those of the First Resurrection, grant them eternal life, and pour out His Spirit more abundantly upon them (Mosiah 18:12–13).

MOSIAH 18:23-29—ALMA'S COMMUNITY IS CALLED THE CHURCH OF CHRIST

Alma the Elder's people built a strong religious community that emphasized five basic practices:
1.) Keeping the Sabbath day holy (18:23),

2.) Meeting for worship and instruction (18:25),

3.) Thanking God every day (18:23),

4.) Freely sharing their substance according to their respective abundance (18:27), and

5.) Having leaders who did not depend on the people for their support (18:26).

As a small, cohesive covenant community, it was natural for Alma's people to embrace the principle of supporting the poor. This may shed light on their escape; they were blessed because they had become charitable and cohesive as a group, working in unity for the common good of all (see Mosiah 24).

MOSIAH 19:20—ABINADI WAS INDEED A PROPHET

Abinadi prophesied that if King Noah did not repent, his life would be "valued even as a garment in a hot furnace" (Mosiah 12:3); thus, his violent end (Mosiah 19:20) was the precise fulfillment of Abinadi's prophecy in Mosiah 17:15–18. Moreover, Noah had wrongly accused Abinadi, and thus it was ironically appropriate that he ended up suffering the same punishment he had decreed for Abinadi, as Deuteronomy 19:16–19 requires to be done to a false accuser or witness: "Then shall ye do unto him, as he had thought to have done unto his brother: so shalt thou put the evil away from among you."

MOSIAH 20:1—THE DAUGHTERS OF THE LAMANITES

The fifteenth of Av had romantic significance to the ancient Israelites. On that day in the fifth month of the Israelite calendar, the maidens of Israel would gather to dance. Following the conclusion of their summer chores in the fields, youth would turn their attention to "bride-hunting," and the dance of the maidens was "designed to meet that end." According to the Talmud, this day featured the dancing of the maidens of Jerusalem in the vineyards. Similarly:

- When Lamanite daughters came particularly to a place in Shemlon to sing, dance and "make themselves merry" (Mosiah 20:1), it may have been at a traditional place and time of celebration and matrimonial selection, as had been done in the vineyards around Jerusalem.
- The priests of Noah clearly saw this as a time to take wives.

According to Jewish tradition, it was on that day that members of the various tribes of Israel were first allowed to fully intermarry among each other. Thus, the priests, who were Nephites, could have rationalized their action, especially since the fifteenth of Av celebrated the right of intermarriage among the tribes of Israel.

MOSIAH 20:18–THE LAMANITES JUMP TO AN INCORRECT CONCLUSION

The abduction of the "daughters of the Lamanites" (20:1) led to an immediate rupture in the treaty that had just been established with the recently conquered Nephites (Mosiah 19:25–29). The Lamanites had incorrectly assumed that the people of Limhi had taken their daughters, and the rupture was so severe that it brought a military reprisal against the Nephites (Mosiah 20:6–11). In this instance, the people of Limhi and the king of the Lamanites solved their problem by talking about it and arriving at the logical conclusion that it was the priests of King Noah (who had fled into the wilderness) who had abducted the Lamanites' daughters (Mosiah 20:14–24). The Nephites chose righteousness as they showed mercy to the seriously wounded Lamanite king, even though he had attacked them (20:13). Together they all honored their previous oath (20:22), and, unarmed, they returned the Lamanite king to his people (20:26). Unfortunately, this treaty only temporarily solved the problems.

MOSIAH 21:6-12–LIMHI'S PEOPLE FIGHT THE LAMANITES THREE TIMES AND FAIL

The Lamanites remained angry, and they mistreated the Nephites severely (21:3), just as Abinadi had prophesied (Mosiah 12:2, 5). The Nephites, in an attempt to free themselves from bondage, went to war three times, and each time they were slain and driven back (21:6–12). Their circumstances only became worse with each failed attempt, resulting in more cause for mourning throughout the land: "And now there was a great mourning and lamentation among the people of Limhi, the widow mourning for her husband, the son and daughter mourning for their father, and the brothers for their brethren" (21:9).

MOSIAH 21:13-17—LIMHI'S PEOPLE BEGAN TO HUMBLE THEMSELVES AND SERVE OTHERS

Fighting had not worked, and the people of Limhi finally turned to the Lord (21:14), rather than relying on their own strength. They trusted God and served Him by serving their fellow man. They took care of the increased number of widows and orphans (21:17; see also Exodus 22:22). Soon they would encounter Ammon and his small party (21:23; see Mosiah 7:6-13), who had come from Zarahemla to share with them the covenantal words of King Benjamin, which the people of Limhi embraced with enthusiasm. They had already begun to live in harmony with several of Benjamin's words by serving one another and imparting their substance to those in need, and they had entered into a general covenant with God to "serve him and to keep his commandments" (21:32), but lacking someone with proper authority to perform baptisms, they decided to wait to be baptized (21:33, 35).

MOSIAH 22:10—KING LIMHI PLANS THE ESCAPE OF HIS PEOPLE

Gideon, the military commander, detected a weakness for strong drink in their Lamanite guards (22:6). A substantial tribute of wine was delivered to them (22:10), and when the guards were drunk in the deep of the night, the people left with their women and children, their flocks and herds and all their "precious things" through a secret pass in a back wall of the city (22:7–12).

The plan succeeded due to careful observations and planning, proper organization, detailed timing and maneuvering, and complete cooperation from everyone involved. Their escape was amazingly well planned and carried out, but there was also no doubt that divine forces were involved to bring their successful escape to fruition. Success comes by doing all we can and leaving the rest to the Lord.

MOSIAH 22:14—KING MOSIAH RECEIVED LIMHI AND HIS PEOPLE WITH JOY

Mosiah, the son of Benjamin, was now the king in Zarahemla. He had been worried about those who had left Zarahemla, so he had allowed Ammon and his party to go to the land of Nephi, looking for his children. What great joy Mosiah felt (22:14) to learn of the success of Ammon's mission! Here we can only imagine the joy that our Heavenly King will feel when any of His children on this earth return to His presence, as was counseled in the premortal life, in which we left the presence of the Heavenly King. We can see the return of the people to Zarahemla as a type of our repenting and returning home. There will always be divine joy in heaven when we, our Heavenly Parents' precious children, finally make it back home to Them.

MOSIAH 23:6-14—ALMA REFUSES TO BE KING

Back now to Alma and his group, who were still stranded between the Land of Nephi and the Land of Zarahemla! Alma's people wanted him to be their king. His polite rejection of this nomination was filled with advice about the need for all of us to esteem one another as equals, rejecting the idea of kings being above normal human beings, and protecting themselves against people like King Noah (23:14). Instead of accepting the title of king, Alma simply continued to serve as their high priest. These directly quoted words of Alma the Elder, declining the elevation to kingship, no doubt influenced his son, Alma the Younger, as well as King Mosiah, when the decision was made for Mosiah to abdicate the kingship and to appoint Alma the Younger as the first chief judge and also the high priest under the new "reign of the judges" at the end of this book (see Mosiah 29:17, 32, 36 and 38).

MOSIAH 23:19-24—ALMA'S PEOPLE WERE BROUGHT INTO BONDAGE

Alma the Elder consecrated preachers and teachers who ministered to the people (23:16–18), and his group flourished in a land they called Helam. However, Alma warned that the Lord desires to "chasten his people; yea, he trieth their patience and their faith" (23:21). He promises that "whosoever putteth his trust in [the Lord] shall be lifted up at the last day" (23:22; compare words in Alma 36:27–28). He also promises to show us that they were in "bondage, and none could deliver them but the Lord their God" (23:23; compare words in Alma 36:2, 27). Notice that these and other similar wordings used by Alma the Elder will be used a generation later by Alma the Younger in telling his son Helaman of his famous conversion (see Alma 36). Here is yet another case where, over a hundred pages later in the Book of Mormon, exact words are being remembered and reused by the one person who could well be expected to use those words.

As Alma the Elder's wise counsel assures us, whatever challenges the Lord has provided us with or has allowed for us, we can turn to the Lord, trust Him, and serve Him. Within His mind and will, everything will work out as it should in His due time.

MOSIAH 23:33—THE LAMANITE DAUGHTERS PLEAD FOR THEIR HUSBANDS.

Meanwhile, Alma's people had submitted themselves to the Lamanites who had overtaken the land of Helam, and Alma and his people had not resisted (23:29). But the priests of Noah, who were also in the area, feared that the Lamanites would kill them, so they sent their Lamanite wives to plead for their lives. Even though those women had been kidnapped, they were now their husbands' devoted wives.

MOSIAH 24:8—AMULON PERSECUTES THE SAINTS

Amulon and the priests of Noah now joined with the Lamanites, and after Alma and his people were taken captive by subterfuge, Amulon recognized Alma as one of Noah's former priests, the one who had believed the words of Abinadi and had defected. "And now it came to pass that Amulon began to exercise authority over Alma and his brethren, and began to persecute him, and cause that his children should persecute their children" (24:8).

MOSIAH 24:10-23—ALMA AND HIS PEOPLE TURN TO THE LORD FOR HELP

The afflictions suffered by the people of Alma were so great that "they began to cry mightily to God" (24:10). The Lamanites forbade their public prayers, threatening death to anyone "whosoever should be found calling upon God" (24:11). But the people continued to pray in their hearts. We can always do that! The Nephites approached this problem by employing the same three principles—to *turn to Him*, *trust Him*, and *serve Him*—as they had done back in Mosiah 23:19–24.

Three times the voice of the Lord then came to Alma and his people, and the three statements of comfort and guidance given by the voice of the Lord are also quoted directly (24:13–14, 16–17, 23). The Lord's words are tender and breathtaking as He tells them to lift up their heads (24:13) and to "be of good comfort," promising them that He would not only ease the feel of their burdens but would give them the strength to bear their burdens and give them the capacity not to feel them, and that He would "deliver them out of bondage" (24:13–17). The third time, the Lord warned Alma to leave quickly for Zarahemla, adding that he would "stop the Lamanites in this valley" (24:23). Twelve days later they arrived safely in Zarahemla and were received joyously by King Mosiah (24:25).

TAKEAWAYS

- **What Hebrew literary device is used throughout the book of Mosiah? How do you know what the climax of these literary sections is? What is the very center of the whole Book of Mosiah? What does it imply? (Hint: Look for chiasmus.)**
- **How do we know that the Nephites were aware that authority was required for baptism (Mosiah 18:13)? Why is it important that baptism be performed by one having authority from God? (Consider Mosiah 18:13, 18; 21:30-35; and 25:17-18.)**
- **What were Alma's eight elements of the baptismal covenant (Mosiah 18:8–10, 12–13)? Which ones are you better at? Which ones could you improve? What can you do to strengthen your baptismal covenants?**
- **Look at the five basic practices that Alma's covenant community emphasized. How do these five practices create and build a strong sense of community? Think of how you could or do apply them (18:18-24, 27-29).**
- **Alma said they should trust no man to be king unless they were a man of God (Mosiah 23:7). Why? What causes trust to be built when a leader keeps God's commandments? How is trust destroyed when a leader does not walk in God's ways?**

22: MOSIAH 25-28

OVERVIEW

The four chapters covered in the lesson can be confusing, and they set the stage for three complicated political and church organizational developments in the Nephite world around 100 B.C. These changes were due to many demographic, political, and religious factors, including especially a growing diversity in the land of Zarahemla among the Mulekites, Nephites, Nehorites, Zoramites, king-men, covenant-makers, and the rising generation. In response to these developments, King Mosiah, the son of King Benjamin, orchestrated three main innovations: (1) The allowance of independent churches within Zarahemla (Mosiah 25:19); (2) the abandonment of kingship, with the consent of the people (29:38; and (3) the establishment of a new political system, called the "reign of the judges" (29:44). Alma the Younger was initially given all three of the highest offices at the same time, there being little precedent in the ancient world for the separation of powers. He was (1) the high priest of the church organized by his father Alma (29:42); (2) he was the chief judge over the legal system (29:42); and (3) he also served as the commander of the army (Alma 2:16). Before long, Alma would shed all his responsibilities except that of being high priest, "[confining] himself wholly to the high priesthood of the holy order of God, to the testimony of the word, according to the spirit of revelation and prophecy" (Alma 4:20).

Prior to this time, in the days of Omni (about 200 B.C.), the people of King Mosiah (from the land of Nephi to the south) had moved in with the people of Zarahemla (the Mulekites). It seems that this was a friendly merger, which was solidified by King Benjamin's victories over Lamanite aggressions as well as his suppression of internal religious dissensions (Words of Mormon 1:12–15). By covenant, Benjamin left his people united as his son Mosiah succeeded him as king over the land of Zarahemla (see Mosiah 1–5). But soon there came the arrival of the "people of Zeniff," ruled by Limhi (22:13; 25:18), which was followed by the coming of the covenant people of Alma the Elder (24:25), and in addition, some of the children of the priests of Amulon who opted to become Nephites (25:12), as seen in the preceding lesson. This diversity led to complications, and the unity began to unravel.

The main religious fabric in Zarahemla also began to be assailed by internal disputation and unbelief. Many of the next generation did not sustain the covenant made by their parents (26:1), and dissensions arose within the Church (26:5), resulting in excommunications. One of Alma's own sons rejected the Church, and he and the four sons of Mosiah secretly worked to destroy the faith of many people (27:10). But an unexpected intervention by the angel of the Lord changed their precarious course. Those five hardened young men repented, were converted, and began "zealously striving" to repair the damage they had caused and to bring many people "to the knowledge of their Redeemer" (27:35–37). The sons of Mosiah were then granted permission to go as missionaries to the land of Nephi (28:8), where they met with great success (see Alma 17–26).

In preparation for stepping down before his impending death, Mosiah consolidated all the records and entrusted them to Alma the Younger and "commanded him that he should keep and preserve them, and also keep a record of the people" (28:20).

In Mosiah 29, King Mosiah gave his final speech, in response to which all his people relinquished their rights to kingship (29:38). Alma the Younger was appointed to be "the first chief judge" over the land and was consecrated by his father to be the high priest over the Church (29:42). Soon after, Alma the Elder and King Mosiah both died (29:45-46), leaving Alma the Younger to face a very challenging situation.

MOSIAH 25:12—FAMILY IN THE BOOK OF MORMON: FICTIVE KINSHIP

The new arrivals opted to be called Nephites. As the groups of Zeniff and Alma were baptized and organized into units within the Church, this step of joining and belonging created for them, as it does in the Church today, a sense of extended family, of caring for one another; a result of being adopted as sons and daughters of Christ.

In addition, some of the children of the priests of Noah who were displeased at the behavior of their fathers also arrived and opted to be numbered among the Nephites. This creation of kinship-like or fictive group relationships served important purposes in both the Old Testament and the Book of Mormon. Newcomers among the ancient Israelites were adopted into one of the twelve tribes, even though they were not technically part of these extended family groups in the Exodus (see Exodus 12:38), and Lehi had left his family organized into seven tribes: Nephites, Jacobites, Josephites, Zoramites, Lamanites, Lemuelites, and Ishmaelites. Jacob then said, "Those who are friendly to Nephi I shall call Nephites," and those who seek to destroy the people of Nephi, Jacob said, "I shall call them Lamanites" (Jacob 1:13–14). We speak of being adopted into the house of Israel, which forges a powerful social bond by which no one is left any longer a stranger or foreigner.

MOSIAH 26:15-32—CHURCH GOVERNANCE AND ADMINISTRATION

As dissensions arose and transgressions occurred within the Church, Alma the Elder, who had been given authority to determine who could remain a member of the Church, received instructions from the Lord that amounted to what we might call a handbook of membership and discipline within the Church. Its revealed words, found in 26:15–32, were given to Alma by the voice of the Lord. Well worth noting is the Lord's repeated willingness to bless His people and their leaders (26:15–19). Alma was to allow all those who misbehaved to confess, for as often as they would repent, the Lord had said He would forgive their trespasses against Him (26:29).

MOSIAH 27:1-3, 8-10, 14—THE NON-BELIEVERS WERE PERSECUTING BELIEVERS

At this time, non-believers increased their persecutions of believers. Mosiah thus issued a command throughout the churches under his authority that there should be no more persecutions.

That was a relief, but it did not entirely solve the problem, because the persecutors were operating "secretly," including even Alma the Younger and the four sons of Mosiah (27:10). Apparently neither Alma the Elder nor King Mosiah realized the full extent of what their sons were up to, but not surprisingly their conduct was suspicious and rebellious enough to alarm their parents. The Lord, therefore, in answer to many prayers intervened to change the situation. The angel of the Lord appeared and said to Alma the Younger, "Behold, the Lord hath heard the prayers of his people and also the prayers of his servant, Alma, who is thy father, for he has prayed with much faith concerning thee, that thou mightest be brought to a knowledge of the truth" (27:14). The angel's words indicated that the prayers of these congregations as well as of Alma the Elder were crucial to this event.

MOSIAH 27:16—THE ANGEL TOLD ALMA TO REMEMBER THE CAPTIVITY OF HIS FATHERS

Though the angel did not explicitly tell the younger Alma to repent, the message is clear in the first half of this verse: Alma was told to "remember the captivity of thy fathers in the land of Helam, and in the land of Nephi" that had been a consequence of disobedience. The angel also said, "Alma, go thy way, and seek to destroy the church no more, . . . and this even if thou wilt of thyself be cast off." He was given a choice of whether to repent or not, but either way, he was to "seek no more to destroy the church of God." He was certainly in spiritual danger. Later, Alma explained that he would have preferred to "become extinct both soul and body" rather than "stand in the presence of my God, to be judged of my deeds" (Alma 36:15).

MOSIAH 27:19–22—FASTING AND PRAYING AS A COMMUNITY

In the restored Church, ward fasts and prayers are held to help people who have health problems. Have you ever had a ward prayer for a young man or young woman who has been losing (or has lost) their testimony? Perhaps that would be appropriate and effective in some cases. After the angel's visitation, Alma the Younger was left unable to walk or speak, so his father asked all the priests to fast with him, and they fasted for two days and two nights. Then at the end of the second day, their prayers were answered.

MOSIAH 27:29—SNATCHED FROM THE DARK ABYSS

When he recovered, Alma referred to being snatched from "the darkest abyss." His beholding the "marvelous light of God" happened very dramatically, but not immediately. It came after "wading through much tribulation, repenting nigh unto death" (27:28). Here and later in Alma 36 and 38, Alma provides a masterful description of how a person feels after a profound conversion.

Not unlike parts of Alma's experience, Elder Bednar has compared the receiving of spiritual light to two physical experiences with light (video "Patterns of Light: Spirit of Revelation,"

David A. Bednar, churchofjesuschrist.org). The first experience occurs as one enters a dark room and turns on a light switch. In an instant, a bright flood of illumination fills the room and causes the darkness to disappear. That was comparable to Alma's initial experience. Most people, however, have the "sunrise" experience of conversion. In either case, one does not let conversion stop at the first bright moment. Alma continued to seek the light.

MOSIAH 27:24-31—SHARED WORDS IN ALMA'S THREE MAIN CONVERSION ACCOUNTS

Significantly, Alma referred to his experience on three main occasions, namely in Mosiah 27, Alma 36, and Alma 38. These three tellings have several words and phrases in common. Seven similar expressions or ideas are found in all three accounts. Eighteen similarities are found in both Mosiah 27 and Alma 36. Twelve expressions overlap between Alma 36 and Alma 38. This remarkable consistency, over time and place, offers circumstantial evidence for the authenticity of the Book of Mormon. In the different settings of these accounts, and despite the textual layers of compilation, abridgment, and translation, Alma's unique, underlying personal voice still comes through loud and clear.

His initial account of his conversion, found in Mosiah 27:7–37, was given spontaneously and is filled with vivid details. Alma's account to his first son, Helaman, in Alma 36, is the longest of these accounts, and it is far more formally and deliberately structured. The pivotal moment in Alma 36:17 of his calling upon Jesus Christ, the Son of God, as his Savior, is expressed as the dramatic turning point at the heart of an extended chiasm, reflecting Alma's repentant turning point at the center of his life.

His final account in Alma 38, spoken to his second son, Shiblon, is shorter, tracking only the first half of the chiastic structure in Alma 36. Alma's concluding words to Shiblon then shift to offer a personally applicable set of exhortations focused on the mercy and truth of Christ.

MOSIAH 27:32—THE AFTERMATH OF ALMA'S REPENTANCE

Alma experienced the principle of repentance and the effects of the Atonement on a powerful level. He was able to teach effectively because his conversion was personal and real. When the Judaic Apostle Paul was converted, he had the same kind of fiery encounter and could speak from the same type of firsthand experience. But no matter how dramatic or gentle one's initial spiritual transformation is, conversion is really a lifetime process. This certainly was the case for both Alma and Paul, and it should be that way for each of us, continually learning and growing in spiritual strength, with a firm determination to endure to the end.

MOSIAH 27:32, 33, 35—THE FRUITS OF REPENTANCE

One effect of repentance is the desire to share what you have experienced with others. As King Benjamin said, to retain a remission of our sins, we must give to others (Mosiah 4:26). Alma and the sons of Mosiah did just that in a remarkable fashion. In Mosiah 27:33, Alma and the sons of Mosiah "impart much consolation to the church," practicing restitution, reconciliation, and repentance. In Mosiah 27:35, they strove to repair the spiritual damage they had caused. They were "confessing all their sins."

They published peace and good tidings; and they declared to the people that the Lord reigns, which reflects one of the questions that Abinadi answered (Mosiah 15:13–18). Who will be the ones to proclaim peace? Abinadi taught that this would include all the holy prophets (15:13) and all those who heed and believe their words. Abinadi had certainly laid the groundwork for these five friends to publish the good tidings.

MOSIAH 28:1-4—THE SONS OF MOSIAH DESIRE TO PREACH TO THE LAMANITES

As a result of their conversion, the sons of Mosiah were given permission to go to the land of Nephi (28:8) as missionaries, "that perhaps they might bring them to know of the plan of redemption" (Alma 17:16). Their leaving may also have been related to the political environment in Zarahemla. The four sons went partly because they knew, since they were the heirs apparent, that people in the city of Zarahemla might desire them to be king if they stayed in Zarahemla. The situation worked out wonderfully, because they did the right things for the right reasons and followed the inspiration of the Lord.

MOSIAH 28:11, 17, 20—MOSIAH PASSES THE RECORDS TO ALMA THE YOUNGER

In a symbolic act of unity, while preparing to step down and rearrange the governmental system, Mosiah translated the plates that had been found by the people of Limhi (28:11, 17) using the Mulekite seer stones (Omni 1:20–21). He also gathered the plates of brass and the plates of Nephi, and he archived "the record of Zeniff" (headnote to Mosiah chapters 9–22), and he included the "account of Alma" (headnote to Mosiah chapters 23–24), and all the other records that he had preserved (28:11).

Mosiah then "conferred them upon Alma [the Younger] and commanded him to keep and preserve them, and also maintain a record of the people" (28:20). Shortly thereafter, Alma the Younger was consecrated by his father to be the high priest (29:42).

In his abdication speech, Mosiah renounced the Nephite right to kingship, and judges were elected. Alma was then appointed to be the first chief judge (29:42), having developed strong personal connections with all sectors of the nation. "And there was continual peace through the land." At least for a brief period.

TAKEAWAYS

- Why were Alma and his people prohibited from praying (24:10-13)? Does God hear our silent prayers? How did he answer the prayers of Alma's people? How has he answered your silent prayers?
- What two things did the Nephite children not believe (26:2)? How can we increase the faith of our children in these two important truths?
- What lessons can we learn from the conversion of Alma the Younger and the four sons of Mosiah? What was it that converted Alma (see Alma 36:17-18)?
- How do you think the translation and messages of the book of Ether tie in with the book of Mosiah's overall themes regarding kingship and concerning deliverance? How do you think it might have changed the Nephites to learn of the fate of the Jaredites (28:17)?

23: MOSIAH 29-ALMA 4

MOSIAH 29:1-10—MOSIAH SHIFTS FROM KINGSHIP TO A "REIGN OF JUDGES"

Chapter 29 contains King Mosiah's farewell speech, transitioning from the old form of Nephite monarchy to a new type of democracy. His four sons were unwilling to succeed him on the throne and left on missions that would last for 14 years. Wanting a peaceful transition to Alma the Younger as his successor, Mosiah weighed the pros and cons of various options. He and his people had recently learned about the collapse of the Jaredite society, which was destroyed by internal fighting over who should be king. That realization probably affected Mosiah's decision to not leave a power vacuum, over which people would fight.

MOSIAH 29:26-27—A WARNING IS GIVEN TO NATIONS THAT DO NOT FOLLOW GOD

Mosiah believed that the "voice of his people" would normally choose well (29:26), but he recognized that the opposite was also possible. He warned, "If . . . the voice of the people doth choose iniquity, then . . . the judgments of God will come upon you" (29:27). Sadly, within a couple of years, the situation in the land of Zarahemla had degenerated into a vicious revolt led by Amlici. This disastrous outcome still stands as a sober warning today, as nations struggle to make it possible for most of the people to choose wisely and then to ensure that public business is conducted consistent with the voice of the people.

MOSIAH 29:5-36—MOSIAH'S RELIANCE ON EARLIER RECORDS

Mosiah's proclamation wisely appealed to each of his main constituencies. For the Nephite and Mulekite populations, he referred to King Benjamin and his wise public laws (29:13). He next appealed to Limhi's group by blaming King Noah and his priests for the failure of Zeniff's colony (29:18). He powerfully appealed to Alma's group by incorporating almost all the key words and inspired ideas spoken by Alma the Elder when he declined the offer of kingship (see Mosiah 23:6–15). Mosiah wisely imported at least fourteen key phrases, almost in the same order, from Alma's substantive text. It is a fun and revealing exercise to find each of Alma's words (in Mosiah 23) that are included in Mosiah's declaration (in Mosiah 29). In addition, Mosiah's declaration contains only three blocks of procedural materials that contain no parallels drawn from Alma's text, namely (1) the need to be wise in appointing judges (29:8–12), (2) the difficulties of removing wicked kings (29:21–24), and (3) the operation of the voice of the people (29: 25–29). Mosiah's manifesto gives clear insights that are useful today in nations and organizations everywhere.

MOSIAH 29:38—"EQUALITY" AMONG THE NEPHITES

The ideal of equality is not self-defining. Governments need to help people achieve equality in certain ways while maintaining individuality in other ways. Under Mosiah's legal reforms, people in Zarahemla were recognized as being equal in five areas:

1.) in status: eliminating the "inequality" of royal as opposed to ordinary status (29:32),

2.) in accountability: giving all an "equal chance" to be held accountable (29:38),

3.) in expression: each having a "voice" in the government (29:2, 25, 26, 27, 29),

4.) in values: being equally protected in freedom of "belief" (Alma 1:17),

5.) in dignity: by removing the "inequality" caused by pride and by not meeting needs, and by being enabling, "liberal to all" (1:30 and 4:12–15).

Alma, the high priest, recognized that these changes increased his responsibility to teach the people the commandments of God and to preach the coming of Christ (Alma 13:2–3), and for that reason he ordained and sent forth faithful men as priests to help. However, the granting of some powers to the priests also permitted the rise of independent groups of priests, for the people were no longer compelled to belong to any particular religion or temple system and "the law could have no power on any man for his belief" (Alma 1:17). This was an important step forward in building Nephite society, but it also produced a difficult new legal question, namely how far can individuals go in expressing or enforcing their beliefs before their words became punishable as a form of action? It is, after all, possible to "do" things with words. Looking ahead, as will be seen in Alma 30, this law would enable not only Nehor (in Alma 1) but also Korihor to argue that, when they preached, they were merely expressing their beliefs (Alma 30:7–12). Korihor learned, however, that there were limits to what forms of public speech were protected under this new rule of law, as he was legally restrained from committing "blasphemy" (30:30) and also from "lying," knowing that what he was saying was false (30:52).

MOSIAH 29:41-45—ALMA WAS APPOINTED AS THE FIRST CHIEF JUDGE

Alma the Younger was appointed chief judge by Mosiah and confirmed by the voice of the people. Now Alma was at the same time (1) the chief judge—a newly created position; (2) the Recorder and official recordkeeper; and (3) the high priest. For obvious reasons, his first few years in office were challenging, to say the least.

Alma was the first person to serve in this newly created position. He undoubtedly had hoped to receive ongoing guidance from his father, who had been the previous high priest, and also from Mosiah, the previous king. Soon, however, both Alma's father and King Mosiah died. Now Alma, with his limited experience, had to assume and fill these positions alone.

Upon assuming office as chief judge, he had to decide, from scratch, how to set up the new government. There were few guidelines to rely on. The new system changed how justice was administered, but it was unclear to what extent it changed the underlying substantive law. Apparently, there were no provisions for changing or amending the traditional law. The newly appointed judges were simply told "to judge [the people] according to the law which had been given them" (Mosiah 29:39); thus, provisions of the law of Moses apparently continued to apply. Soon it was clear that "King Mosiah's decision to implement a form of democracy (elected judges) among the Nephites was a bold and noble effort, but for many reasons it unfortunately did not thrive" (Gregory Steven Dundas, "Kingship, Democracy, and the Message of the Book of Mormon," *BYU Studies Quarterly* 56, no. 2 (2017): 7–58).

ALMA 1:2-10—NEHOR FORCIBLY INTRODUCES PRIESTCRAFT AMONG THE NEPHITES

In his first year as the new chief judge, Alma was faced with a major challenge—what to do about Nehor, who was teaching incorrect doctrine and gathering followers. Nehor's ideology eliminated all individual responsibility, and also swept away accountability. He formed a new church, where he preached what he called "the word of God," and he provided for priests to be supported financially by their church members (Alma 1:3). The Nephites, however, were still following the law of Moses. In Deuteronomy 13, a person who led others into apostasy could be put to death. And the traditional Nephite law also prohibited priestcrafts (2 Nephi 26:29). In addition, the law in 2 Chronicles 19:5, 10 required that an offending person must be warned that he was committing a crime.

With all that as background, one day Nehor encountered Gideon, an elderly Limhite warrior. Gideon probably intended only to warn Nehor that he might be committing certain crimes, but their discussion devolved into a contentious argument. Nehor became angry. Under Israelite law, anger and hatred functioned as the equivalent of what modern law would call premeditation. In Numbers 35, we find a heightened degree of culpability when killing someone in anger. Nehor drew his sword in anger and killed Gideon.

ALMA 1:11-15—NEHOR IS TRIED AND PUT TO DEATH

Alma was the sole judge over Nehor's case. Nehor appealed to the new "freedom of belief" provisions in their law, which would have allowed him to introduce paid priestcraft into the community. When the elderly Gideon then "withstood" Nehor, he became angry ("wroth") and drew his sword and began to smite Gideon and then killed him (1:7, 9). Nehor was brought to court, and while he defended himself "with much boldness" (1:11), Alma found a novel way to decide this explosive case. In the end, Alma did not convict Nehor of murder or homicide, but held that Nehor was guilty of enforcing priestcraft with a sword (Alma 1:12). The legal question of whether exercising priestcraft was merely an expression of Nehor's beliefs was left for another day, but Alma ruled that when Nehor tried to *enforce* his views with the sword, he took action that went beyond the scope of a protected expression of belief. While this ruling concluded the individual case of Nehor, it did not put an end to the order of Nehors. For the coming decade, Nehorites will figure prominently in the Nephite land of Ammonihah (see Alma 16:18), as well as in the Lamanite lands of Jerusalem (see Alma 21:4) and of Helam (see Alma 24:28).

ALMA 1:26-28, 31—ALMA WORKS TO BUILD EQUALITY IN THE CHURCH

In the changeover, people of the Church were to be accorded equal dignity and respect, all in accordance with deeply rooted principles found in ancient Israelite law. The Israelites understood that every person was equal in God's eyes, and under their law, justice was administered equally among the people. Alma similarly emphasized three core values in the church: (1) equal status and standing, (2) the prohibition of slavery, which would have included limitations on debt servitude, as well as (3) equal substance imparted according to need. Members of the Church did not consider themselves better than another, and they took care of one another. This resulted in greater prosperity than was found among those who did not belong to the Church (1:31).

ALMA 1:24-25, 32-33—MANY SAINTS LEAVE THE CHURCH BECAUSE OF THEIR SINS

A faith crisis arose in Alma's early years as high priest. People were defecting: "many withdrew" from the church because of their iniquities. Despite disappointments, Alma's attitude remained positive and exemplary. He chose to count his blessings. But the land became more secular, and Alma responded with appropriate law enforcement. The long law lists found in Alma 1:32 and later in Helaman 4:12 compare fairly closely with the law lists found in the Ten Commandments in Exodus 20 and the legal regulations found in the Code of the Covenant in Exodus 21–22, showing again that Nephite law before the coming of Christ remained consciously grounded in the basics of the law of Moses.

ALMA 2:1-38—AMLICI SEEKS TO BE KING, GOES TO WAR, AND IS KILLED

However, during Alma's fifth year as chief judge, Amlici, a follower of Nehor, convinced many rebels that the institution of kingship should be restored (Alma 2:2). Amlici put himself forward as the choice for king. When he ran for the office of king and lost, instead of accepting the voice of the people as settling the matter, Amlici gathered an army, including Lamanite allies, and made war against the Nephites. Alma and his people were forced into war. Alma himself fought hand-to-hand with Amlici—in hero combat, like David against Goliath, or Hector and Achilles—and Alma killed Amlici (2:31). Then Alma also went one-on-one with the king of the Lamanites, who retreated and sent his guards to fight against Alma and his guards. But Alma likewise slew and drove them back (2:32). In the end, tens of thousands of people were killed, including women and children (Alma 3:2, 26). The spiritual conclusion drawn from everything in these two chapters is that all these people went individually "to the eternal world, that they might reap their rewards according to their works, whether they were good or whether they were bad, to reap eternal happiness or eternal misery, according to the spirit which they listed to obey" (3:26).

ALMA 4:20–EXAMPLES OF RIGHTEOUS MISSIONARIES

In Mosiah 28:1–10, the four sons of Mosiah had given up all their personal power and privilege to preach the gospel. Each of them declined to become the next king and, instead, risked their lives to teach among the Lamanites for fourteen years (see Alma 17–26). Similarly, while serving as the chief judge, Alma now saw that the Church was starting to slip seriously into sin, so he turned the judgment-seat over to Nephihah, and "confined himself" as the high priest "wholly . . . to the testimony of the word, according to the spirit of revelation and prophecy" (Alma 4:18, 20). Alma served primarily as a missionary for the next five years. At first, he served alone, then he was joined by Amulek, his convert companion. These accounts of dedicated missionary service provide important examples of faith and courage. Today's missionaries also make real sacrifices as they respond to the prophet's call to serve. Whatever the sacrifice and wherever the service, the Lord will always bless those who faithfully serve. Members of The Church of Jesus Christ of Latter-day Saints do not choose where they are called to serve. Like Nephi, Alma, the sons of Mosiah, and others, we submit ourselves, not knowing beforehand where we may be sent and what we may be asked to do.

TAKEAWAYS

- **How did the legal system work under the law reforms of Mosiah? (Look at 29:25-29.) Note especially the protection of freedom of belief (Alma 1:17-18; 30:9-11). How does that apply in our century? How is the current prophet handling this? How are you handling this?**
- **Is it true in our day that "it is not common that the voice of the people desireth anything contrary to that which is right"? Is it still true today that "it is common for the lesser part of the people to desire that which is not right" (29:26)?**
- **What can individual citizens do today to see that we "do our business by the voice of the people"? What can we do if "the voice of the people choose iniquity"?**
- **How do we give "every man an equal chance" (29:38)? An equal chance to do what? (See Alma 1:17; 1:30; 4:12-15.)**
- **Do you commit and need to repent of any of the wrongs mentioned in Alma 1:32?**

24: ALMA 5-7

This lesson covers two of Alma's most inspiring and lengthy missionary sermons. First, Alma 5 was given to the members of the church in Zarahemla, asking them fifty questions to help them in their covenant renewal. That amazing discourse offers us a treasure chest of questions we can ask ourselves as we too, each week, renew our covenants with the Lord as we partake of the sacrament. Second, Alma 7 was given to the faithful people in the city of Gideon, who had managed to escape from King Noah's city of Nephi. Believing the prophecies of Abinadi about the coming of Jesus Christ, those people had left all and had suffered many hardships. Alma rewards them with an expanded understanding of the infinite atoning powers of Jesus Christ.

ALMA 5:1—THE HISTORICAL SETTING, AND THE WISDOM OF THE LAWS OF GOD

If you count the years between King Benjamin's speech in Mosiah 2–6 and Alma's speech in Alma 5, there were 42 years. That means that the year of this speech fell on the sixth sabbatical year (42 = 6 x 7) after Benjamin's speech when Mosiah had become king. That memorable coronation occurred at the time of year when the Feast of Tabernacles and the Day of Atonement were celebrated and covenants were renewed under ancient Israelite law. Now, 42 years later, Alma chose to speak about covenant renewal. In addition, Alma gave this speech in Zarahemla, the same place where Benjamin had given his great and final covenant speech. And indeed, many of the themes in Benjamin's speech can be found in Alma 5.

On the Feast of Tabernacles, ancient Israelites evaluated their lives and confessed their sins, and for that purpose Alma asked his people 50 questions in Alma 5. These questions help all people to consider their lives, to be introspective, to repent, and to renew their covenants with God.

ALMA 5:6-9—QUESTIONS 1-5: REMEMBERING HOW GOD HAS BLESSED HIS PEOPLE

Alma's first five questions asked the audience if they could remember God's great acts for His people, their heritage, and God's deliverance. We covenant today to "remember" Christ always.

I like the way Alma asked these questions in a kind of lawyerly way, with some nice qualifiers. He didn't only ask if they had remembered; he asked (three times) if they had "*sufficiently* remembered." Have we remembered enough? Have we remembered sufficiently the captivity, or the problems Joseph Smith faced, or that our ancestors were plagued with as they came to settle the Salt Lake Valley? Thus, each of the first three questions begins with the phrase, "Have you sufficiently retained *in remembrance*." In Hebrew, the word for remember is *zakhar,* and it means more than just *recalling*. It means to remember in the sense of *obeying*. When your mother says, "Remember what I have taught you," she isn't just asking if you can pass a recall test. She means, "Do what I have taught you." Likewise, in the Book of Mormon, the word *remember* means more than just *think about it*, but *to do it*.

ALMA 5:10-11—QUESTIONS 6-12: KNOWING THE ESSENTIAL LOGIC OF THE GOSPEL

In verses 10 and 11, Alma took his audience through his virtual interview questions in an ordered, step by step process, covering some of the most basic principles of the gospel. He asks, "What was *the cause* of your fathers being loosed?" (5:10), inviting us to ponder the conditions and the cause-and-effect relationship of spiritual blessings. Part of the essential logic of the gospel is that there are consequences. Because of that, we can rely on certain outcomes, and we can also have hope. God does not require us to hope for things that are without foundation. True faith is believing in things that are true, and we have a reason for the hope that is in us (see 1 Peter 3:15). On what *grounds* did Alma's people have hope for salvation? That God will come into their lives and will cause them to be loosed "from the bands of death . . . and also the chains of hell" (5:11). They knew that because they believed the words of Abinadi, who was a true and holy prophet.

ALMA 5:14-15—QUESTIONS 13-17: BEING PERSONALLY CONVERTED

Some of Alma's most penetrating questions next ask, "Have you been spiritually born of God?" "Have you received his image in your countenance? and experienced this mighty change of heart?" By exercising faith in Christ's redemption, one can look forward with an eye of faith, knowing our Savior has already accomplished His promised Atonement. As we turn to Him with sincere and lasting repentance along with deep purpose of heart, we become His spiritual sons and daughters.

ALMA 5:15-24—QUESTIONS 18-29: IMAGINING THE DAY OF JUDGMENT

The eleven questions that begin in verse 15 and continue through verse 24 ask, "Can you imagine the judgment day?" What do you imagine it will be like when we stand before God to give a report of our life? Alma's questions here help us run through a practice exam or a dress rehearsal that will motivate us to measure ways we can be better prepared for that day.

On the Feast of Tabernacles, the Israelites and Nephites celebrated God's kingship. The king eventually was the ultimate judge of his people, and on the Feast of Tabernacles—assuming that is when this speech was given—the people would have come expecting to give an accounting of how they had done. In effect, they would have expected to go through a fiery furnace of judgment before God, so that they could repent and renew their covenants. These questions help us to be reconciled with God and to see places where we can still progress.

In these verses, I really like remembering that Alma was a career judge, serving as the chief judge. We do not know how many cases he tried, but probably quite a few. I am sure as he sat on the bench looking down on these people, he probably heard them making up excuses, pleading for mercy, and saying, "Oh I really did not do it." But we do not fool the judge, and we are not going to fool God. We sense here the voice of a person who has been in the judgment seat.

ALMA 5:26-30, 39—QUESTIONS 30-38: ASSESSING OUR SPIRITUAL CONDITION

Here Alma asks about our "singing the song of redeeming love," of "keeping ourselves blameless before God," being "sufficiently humble," "made white through the blood of Christ," and "stripped of pride" and "of envy." Finally, Alma asked, "Is there one among you that doth make a mock of his brother, or that heapeth upon him persecutions?" (5:30). We must be especially careful never to belittle anyone. Why is mocking or belittling such a problem? I remember my professor Robert K. Thomas once saying, "The problem with mocking and laughter is that there is no answer for it." One cannot reply rationally. One cannot even mock back. Ridicule stops conversation, and people who mock know that. Once the damage is done, there is no way to recover from it. Alma very wisely wants his people to stop making fun of one another. As members of the fold of the Good Shepherd, it is a cardinal sin to offend others.

ALMA 5:45-47—QUESTIONS 39-40: OBTAINING SPIRITUAL KNOWLEDGE

The next step is obtaining spiritual knowledge. Here Alma testified, "Do you not suppose that I know of these things myself? How do you suppose that I know of their surety?" Interesting that Alma uses the word *surety* here. He then goes on to explain how this is possible. "Behold, I have fasted and prayed many days that I might know of these things for myself" (5:46). Once we have expended our best efforts to know of a surety, the Lord God will make them manifest unto us by His Holy Spirit (5:46). This wonderful principle comes with a breathtaking promise. In Alma 36, Alma will later say, "For ye ought to know as I do know" (Alma 36:30), assuring us that this promise is true not only for prophets of God, but for every earnest seeker of truth.

ALMA 5:53-59—QUESTIONS 41-50: THE RESPONSIBILITY TO REPENT

Alma concludes his covenant renewal speech by placing the burden of repentance squarely on the shoulders of each of his listeners and readers. He concludes with ten rhetorical questions, to each of which (I imagine) the people answered with a resounding, No! "Can you withstand these sayings?" No! "Can you trample the Holy One under your feet?" No! "Can you be puffed up?" No! "Will you persist?" No! "Will the shepherd [fail to] watch over his many sheep?" No!

APPLYING THIS SPEECH

Now imagine yourself being in the audience listening to Alma's speech in Alma 5; think how this speech would have affected you. How might it have affected you if you were one of the 3,500 recent converts who had just joined the Church (see Alma 4:5)? Or a soldier who had been seriously wounded in the battle against Amlici? Or the widow of a soldier who had fought for Amlici and against Alma? Or an old-time faithful member of the Church organized by Alma the Elder? Or a Mulekite friendly toward Alma but who still felt politically excluded? Or a faithful father and mother with a rebellious teenage son or daughter? Or a righteous teenager wondering about serving a mission? Or a senior citizen who had entered the covenant following King Benjamin's speech 42 years earlier? Alma was addressing all these people. So, you are welcome to put yourself in the audience here too. What resonates most with you personally?

ALMA 7:1–27—A VERY DIFFERENT SPEECH FOR THE PEOPLE OF GIDEON

In Alma 5, Alma asked 50 questions. How many questions can you find here in Alma 7? There is not one! What a shift! Alma knows these two audiences, and he communicates with them in different ways. In Alma 5, Alma was bearing down in pure testimony against the people (4:19). He often did not want to give them the answers because he wanted *them* to ponder and reflect and answer those questions for themselves. In Alma 7, Alma knows the suffering, the losses, the mourning, and the sacrifices of these people, relatively new arrivals in the land of Zarahelma. Alma could relate. A few years earlier, his father and family had also fled from King Noah and the land of Nephi. Here he now focused on the doctrines of the Atonement of Jesus Christ, testifying openly through the spirit that was in him (7:13, 16, 20).

ALMA 7:7–13—ALMA TEACHES OF THE FULLNESS OF THE ATONEMENT

Alma's sermon on this occasion contained a classic statement regarding the coming of Christ and of His Atonement, testifying that the Son of God would "take upon him the pains and the sicknesses of his people" (7:11). It is possible that Alma is paraphrasing Isaiah 53:5, 7: "He was wounded for our transgressions, he was bruised for our iniquities; . . . he was oppressed, and he was afflicted." Here Alma intensifies this prophetic information in several important ways. (1) Alma mentions pains, afflictions, and temptations of *every kind*. This is a stronger statement of the expansive reach of the Atonement than is found anywhere else in scripture. (2) Alma says this will be accomplished so that the prophetic "word might be fulfilled" (7:11). (3) Alma says, "And he will take upon him their infirmities . . . that he may *know* . . . how to succor his people according to their infirmities" (7:12; emphasis added). It is wonderful that He has done this for us. Not only has He absorbed all infirmities, but He learned something in that process. Hebrews 5:8 says that the Son of God *learned obedience* "by the things which he suffered." (4) And in Alma 7 we learn further that He Himself will also learn in this extreme struggle, namely that His bowels may be *filled* with mercy. If He is filled with mercy, there is no room for any criticism or judgment on His part. You do not have to fear that when you come to Christ, He will be judgmental or critical. If you will ask and receive, He will not turn you away or be disappointed that you have done certain things or had certain problems. He is *full* of mercy, having learned mercy somehow by vicariously experiencing all our infirmities, which gives Him a power, force, and connectivity that He otherwise would not have had, that He may succor His people. (5) And what does this word *succor* mean? The root of this word is "-cor" which means "to run," as in the word courier, a runner. And the prefix "suc-" comes from the Latin preposition "sub," meaning from beneath or below, as in the word "sup-port," meaning "to carry" (to "port") from beneath ("sub"). "To succor," then, means to *run* to a person to give strength and help from a foundation below. Having descended below all things, the Savior now is so full of mercy that He knows how to run to us in our moment of need and bear us up. Alma is the only one who emphasizes this aspect of Christ's sustaining power, as Alma himself, in his own conversion, had firsthand experience with Christ's succoring power and thus can truly say, "Now the spirit knoweth all things" (7:13).

Christ experienced it all and has been filled with the knowledge of all things. Alma personally testifies, "And now behold, this is the testimony which is in me" (7:13). Speaking to people in Gideon who had suffered greatly, Alma's testimony is humble, understated, empathic, reassuring, and is most certainly clear, powerful, and true.

ALMA 7:27–ALMA PRONOUNCES A CONCLUDING BLESSING ON THE PEOPLE

In the ancient Israelite sacrificial system, there were different kinds of sacrifices. *Atoning* sacrifices reconciled and brought man and God back together where there had been a separation between them because of sin or impurity. But there was more. The words *sin, guilt, transgression*, and *peace,* are present in Alma 7. Together those words represent all the types of sacrifices in the law of Moses, under which there were sin offerings, guilt offerings, atoning sacrifices, and peace offerings. Alma, as the high priest, who had probably just performed the special sacrifices on the Day of Atonement during the season connected with the Feast of Tabernacles, would have been especially sensitive regarding the great power and purposes of the laws of sacrifice and obedience. As the high priest, Alma had specific duties to keep the temple pure and holy, to cleanse it on the Day of Atonement, so that it could symbolize to the people the complete workings of the laws of God, welcoming Jesus as the one who fulfills all these forms of sacrificial offerings and of atoning reconciliation for us.

At the end of this chapter, Alma concludes with a blessing echoing the peace offering, and what a remarkable blessing it is: "May the peace of God rest upon you, and upon your houses and lands, and upon your flocks and herds, and all that you possess, your women and your children, according to your faith and good works, from this time forth and forever" (7:27). Perhaps you have been present in situations where an apostolic blessing was pronounced upon an audience and have felt, as Alma's people surely must have felt, encouraged, and empowered by it.

TAKEAWAYS

- Alma asks 50 questions in Chapter 5: What were the questions he asked? Why does he ask so many questions? How would you answer each of these questions? How can you apply his questions to your daily life?
- What questions does he ask about remembering God's acts for his people (5:6-9)?
- What questions does he ask about knowing the essentials of the Gospel (5:10-11)?
- What questions does he ask about being personally converted (5:14-15)?
- What questions does he ask about imagining the judgment day (5:15-24)?
- What questions does he ask about assessing one's spiritual condition (5:26-30)?
- What questions does he ask about identifying with one fold or another (5:39)?
- What questions does he ask about obtaining spiritual knowledge (5:45)?
- What questions does he ask about refusing to repent (5:53-59)?
- How had this audience prepared to receive Alma's message (7:3)? How should we prepare to receive a visiting authority in our wards or stake, or prepare for general conference?
- What four things did Alma say that the suffering and atonement of Christ would accomplish (7:11-13)? How do we claim all these benefits of the Atonement?
- What ten qualities are mentioned here that a priesthood holder or leader must manifest (7:23; compare Mosiah 3:19; D&C 121:41-42)?

25: ALMA 8-12

ALMA 8:6—THREE DAYS' JOURNEY

Many small details add greatly to the meaning and credibility of the Book of Mormon. For example, when Alma the Younger left a city called Melek, after very successfully teaching and baptizing many (8:4-5), he traveled for three days and came to the city called Ammonihah. What might those three days have symbolized? Why did the author, the recordkeeper, and the abridger include this detail? Where else do we see the words *three days*? In 1 Nephi 2:6, Lehi traveled three days before building an altar to give thanks. At the time of the Crucifixion and death of the Savior, the Book of Mormon states that there would be darkness in the land of Bountiful for three days when Jesus was in the tomb (3 Nephi 8:3, 23; see also 1 Nephi 19:10; 2 Nephi 25:13; Helaman 14:20, 27). Moreover, in the ancient Hebrew scriptures, the runaway prophet Jonah languished in the depths of the death monster for three days and three nights (Jonah 1:17), which Jesus said was a sign of His own death (Matthew 12:39–40). Thus, from the time of Jonah in the mid-eighth century B.C. (2 Kings 14:25), "three days and three nights" symbolized a complete descent, going as far away into the darkness as possible.

It would thus appear that the Book of Mormon includes this detail here, in Alma 8:6, to emphasize that Alma went down, all alone, into the depths of the inferno of the wickedest city of Ammonihah. He had been reviled and rejected there once already, but the same angel of the Lord (see Alma 8:15) who had first stopped the rebellious young Alma (Mosiah 27:18; Alma 36:8) now commanded the high priest Alma to turn around and go preach repentance to the people in Ammonihah again, warning them with words similar to those in Jonah 1:2 about Nineveh, that "except they repent the Lord God will destroy them" (8:16).

ALMA 8:19-22—A BLESSING FOLLOWING A MEAL

Upon returning to Ammonihah, Alma was met by Amulek, a faithful citizen of the city, who had been instructed by an angel to welcome "a prophet." Amulek "received him into his house . . . and he brought forth bread and meat and set before Alma" (8:21). *After* eating the meal set before him and being "filled," Alma "blessed Amulek and his house, and he gave thanks unto God" (8:22). Whereas generally, Latter-day Saints and other Christians are accustomed to offering a blessing *before* meals, "in Judaism, while a brief blessing is recited before eating, a series of longer blessings . . . follows the meal." It is "a central feature of the liturgical service in the Jewish home" (see *KnoWhy* #115).

This practice is also found in the Mishnah and among the Dead Sea Scrolls. For example, the Jewish book of Jubilees (ca. 161–140 BC) depicts the patriarchs engaging in this practice (see Jubilees 22:4–9); and one story in Mishnah *Sukkah* 2:5 records, "When Rabbi Zadok ate only a *small* portion of food, he did not say the blessing afterward." This was probably because Deuteronomy 8:10 calls for a blessing only if one has eaten and is *full.* This practice anticipated the time when the Savior would administer the sacrament to the people in 3 Nephi 18, and after they were "filled," Jesus "blessed" them (3 Nephi 18:9–10, 14).

ALMA 9:2, 6—THE LAW OF WITNESSES

The Nephites, even those in Ammonihah, were well aware of the two-witness rule (see Alma 10:12). In our legal system, we do not require two witnesses. In biblical and Jewish law, however, they *had to* have at least two witnesses (Deuteronomy 19:15). Today, this principle of two witnesses is observed as Latter-day Saint missionaries travel two-by-two. At baptism, there must be two witnesses. Similarly, in bestowing the gift of the Holy Ghost, and in the marriage sealing ordinance, and so on, two witnesses are required. Even the notion of the presidency of the bishop and two counselors is based on the principle that in the mouth of two or three witnesses shall all things be established. One should not operate as a presidency without the concurrence of both counselors. When you are involved as a married couple, within a missionary companionship, or as a presidency, there is wisdom and strength in this two- or three-witness principle.

ALMA 9:11-13—THE LAW REQUIRED AN APOSTATE CITY TO BE DESTROYED

Deuteronomy 13:12–18 told Alma what he needed to do to an apostate city in his land: "Then shalt thou *enquire,* and make search, and ask *diligently*; and, behold, if it be truth, that such abomination is wrought among you; Thou shalt surely smite the inhabitants of that city with the edge of the *sword, destroying it utterly*, . . . and shalt burn with *fire* the city, and . . . it shall be an heap forever" (emphasis added).

Alma was the Nephite high priest and had the personal responsibility for seeing that no iniquity defiled the land. Under this law, he was required to investigate the situation personally, warn the inhabitants, and if they did not repent, he would consign the inhabitants to being killed by the sword and having the city burned and remain completely destroyed for seven years. The words *utter destruction,* in Hebrew, form a phrase that is quite distinctive, and it means being wiped off the face of the land. Alma used the phrases *utterly destroy,* and *utter destruction* three times in Alma 9:12, 18, and 24. Apparently the people in Ammonihah knew the scriptures well enough to understand what Alma was saying, because their reaction was extreme. Alma gave them practical and religious encouragement, but also legal notice and fair warning that if they did not change and repent, their destruction would be sure and complete. Amulek spoke as the second witness, telling them they would be smitten "by famine, and by pestilence, and by *the sword*" (10:23; emphasis added), as required by Deuteronomy 13:15. Also, it must be remembered that Alma no longer commanded the army, and could not, and would not, call in soldiers to obliterate the city. After offering them a peaceful settlement, Alma left the judgment to God, despite being mistreated terribly. Ultimately, a Lamanite attack would occur in which the invaders "fell upon the people who were in the land of Ammonihah and destroyed them" (see Alma 25:2). This was a compelling sign of divine intervention and prophetic fulfillment.

ALMA 10:6-11—A PASSOVER SETTING

Without saying as much, Alma and Amulek appear to have met at Passover time. Amulek gave the exact day, month, and year for the appearance of the angel to him: It was "the fourth day of this seventh month, which is in the tenth year of the reign of the judges" (10:6). The first month of the year for the pre-exilic Israelite calendar was in September, so the seventh month was in April, and that was the month of Passover, as everyone knew. It is like saying something happened on December 25; everyone knows that was on Christmas. Passover was a time for family gatherings to celebrate the time when the destroying angel passed over the Israelites and prepared the way for them to escape bondage in Egypt. Amulek stated he was on his way to visit "very near kindred" (Alma 10:7). On Passover, families sacrificed a lamb and had the Passover meal. They set a plate for the Prophet Elijah, expecting that one day he would return. Here the angel told Amulek to go home and "feed a prophet of the Lord" (10:7). Amulek did indeed feed the prophet Alma, "an humble servant of God" (8:19), and together with Amulek's women (likely his wife, mother, and maybe sisters) and his whole household, they were tutored by Alma and converted (10:11). By receiving the Lord's prophet, they were led out of spiritual oppression. That was a Passover never to be forgotten.

ALMA 10:12-16—THE PEOPLE OF AMMONIHAH WERE ASTONISHED

As they had previously complained that Alma was only one person, how surprised and crestfallen they were when Amulek added his testimony to Alma's: "When Amulek had spoken these words the people began to be astonished, seeing there was more than one witness who testified of the things whereof they were accused" (10:12). The Lord again provided a tender mercy to aid in His purposes. He does not abandon His servants, but some of their "lawyers" wanted to cross-examine Alma and Amulek to "catch them in their words" (10:13). What might the word *lawyer* have meant to the Nephites? They did not have lawyers as we do: they did not have bar exams, law schools, reported cases, etc. These people were officials who helped with the administration of the law. Ironically, although Alma was no longer the chief judge over this land, he was still every bit as much a "lawyer" as these people were. When the people in Ammonihah tried to catch Amulek in some contradiction, Amulek boldly shot back, accusing them of "laying traps and snares to catch the holy ones of God" (10:17) and declared, "Well doth the Lord judge of your iniquities" (10:20). In anger, they then accused Amulek of the crime of "reviling" against their laws and publicly selected legal administrators (Alma 10:24). Amulek stood his ground and pushed back, until a certain lawyer, named Zeezrom, saw an opportunity to make a name and some money for himself.

ALMA 11—ZEEZROM ATTEMPTS TO BRIBE AMULEK

This chapter begins with an explanation of how judges were paid, according to their time, under the old law of Mosiah. To inform readers of the great value of six *onties*, a detailed chart of the traditional Nephite weights and measures is given. Zeezrom offered a bribe to

Amulek: "Behold, here are six onties of silver, and all these will I give thee if thou wilt deny the existence of a Supreme Being." That was the equivalent of about forty-two days' work, a substantial amount. But, Zeezrom apparently had not done very well in law school. In Exodus 23, there are ten laws that deal with judicial justice. The last law says, "Thou shalt not take a bribe" (Exodus 23:8). Now maybe Zeezrom was thinking, well, the law doesn't say that lawyers cannot *give* a bribe! So, he was safe offering one. But it is more likely that Zeezrom just did not know the law very well. In fact, Exodus 23 gives ten laws, every one of which was violated here in Ammonihah, justifying even more the fate that eventually fell upon them. And Amulek powerfully counters each of Zeezrom's questions and leaves him trembling.

ALMA 12:9-11—HOW CAN WE KNOW THE MYSTERIES OF GOD?

In Alma 12, Alma then teaches Zeezrom logically, accurately, and convincingly. For example, Alma explains, "It is given unto *many* to *know* the mysteries of God" (12:9; emphasis added). He then goes on to explain how they can still be mysteries if they are known to many. They are things which are kept sacred, and only covenant people can be taught about them and understand them. As the Hebrew prophet Amos says, "Surely the Lord God will do nothing, but he revealeth his *secret* unto his servants the prophets" (Amos 3:7; emphasis added). The underlying Hebrew concept translated here as *secret* is the same as the Greek word translated as *mysteries*. In both cases, the sacred will of God is revealed to servants of God, to the prophets, and to the Apostles (Matthew 13:11). These are obedient people who, according to their faith, heed, and diligence, patiently allow sacred truths to be revealed to them incrementally, "until it is given unto [them] to know the mysteries . . . in full" (12:10). In all of scripture, that statement is the best formula for knowing how to understand and appreciate what are called here "the mysteries." And what do the words *heed* and *diligence* mean? *To give heed* means to hear and pay close attention. In 1 Nephi 16:28, Nephi said that the Liahona worked "according to the *faith* and *diligence* and *heed* which [they] did give unto them." We too need to be diligent in order to obtain the mysteries of God, and diligence requires effort.

King Benjamin unfolded mysteries; by that, he meant "sacred revelations." Often these mysteries have a great deal to do with the temple; they are not mysterious in the modern sense of the word but are *sacred revelations*. The temple is a place where many sacred revelations, especially the foreordained plan of God, are all made manifest.

ALMA 12:25-37—GOD'S GREAT PLAN OF REDEMPTION AND MERCY

Alma goes on to explain how the plan of redemption was laid down by God "from the foundation of the world" (12:25), making it possible for *everyone* (beginning with our "first parents") to repent. God's plan of redemption is simple, clear, and comforting, and His promise is sure. "If ye will repent, and harden not your hearts, then will I have mercy upon you through mine Only Begotten Son; Therefore, whosoever repenteth and hardeneth not his heart, he shall have claim on mercy through mine Only Begotten Son, unto a remission of sins; and these shall enter into my rest" (12:33–34). Alma, ever the wise and gentle high priest, concludes his powerful sermon with a positive, heartfelt, and universal plea for his brethren (including all of us) to repent.

TAKEAWAYS

- What happened in the city of Melek? Why is this short episode even mentioned (8:1-6)? What can we do individually to help our wards and cities become more like Melek?
- What kind of reception did Alma get in Ammonihah? How did he handle it? How would you have handled it? How did the angel want him to deal with those people (8:14-14)?
- Who was that angel? Why do you think the angel identified himself?
- What happened to Amulek on the fourth day of the seventh month of the tenth year (10:6)? Were Alma's first words to Amulek coincidental (10:7, compare 8:19)? What impact must those words have had on Amulek?
- How does Amulek describe his conversion? How do you describe your conversion? Is it important to remember and share our conversion stories? Think of them as a type of "creation story."
- Do you think it is fair that people who know should be held to a higher standard (9:15-18, 24)?
- Why did they need to have a system of weights and measures established at the same time they established this reign of judges? Why would that have been important right then? How much did Zeezrom offer Amulek?
- What were Zeezrom's arguments against Amulek (11:26, 30, 32, 34-35)? Why were those particular questions potent? Did his arguments reflect typical Nehorite teachings? Are his questions relevant today? How did Amulek answer them?
- In Alma 12, why does Alma rehearse the creation account in such detail (See also 7-10)?

26: ALMA 13-16

Alma 13 comprises one of the most sublime and sacred messages delivered by Alma. Ironically, however, together with chapter 12 it stands at the heart of Alma and Amulek's impending six-month imprisonment in the city of Ammonihah. The chapters in this lesson will then end with martyrdoms (Alma 14), with the healing and conversion of Zeezrom (Alma 15), and with the utter obliteration of Ammonihah (Alma 16).

ALMA 13:1-12—BEING ORDAINED HIGH PRIESTS AFTER GOD'S HOLY ORDER

After exhorting the people in Ammonihah to "repent" and to "harden not [their] hearts" (12:37)—words that would have fallen on the deaf ears of the Nehorite priests who stood resolutely against the idea of needing to obey God's commandments, let alone needing to repent for breaking them (see Alma 1:4)—Alma now explains the time when "the Lord God ordained *priests,* after his holy *order,* which was after the order of his Son, to teach these things unto the people" (13:1; emphasis added). In Alma 12:33, God *Himself* calls upon man "in the name of his Son"—recognizing the role of the Savior as a mediator and intercessor between God and mankind. Alma now adds that God also ordains priests after this "order of his Son" to mark the way back to God (13:2). The nature of these priesthood ordinations symbolically demonstrates "in what manner" people are "to look forward to God's Son for redemption" (13:2). Because the Nehorites denied that redemption required any particular action on the part of mankind (Alma 1:4), Alma provided an explanation of this "order." First, men were *called,* and an initiatory *preparation* was given, which happened "from the foundation of the world, according to the foreknowledge of God, on account of their exceeding *faith* and *good works,*" being then left "to choose good or evil" (13:3). "And thus, being called by this holy calling," people were then "*ordained* unto the *high priesthood* of the holy order of God, to teach his commandments unto the children of men, that they also might enter into his rest" through their repentance (13:6; emphasis added). By virtue of this ordinance, "many" became high priests (13:10).

ALMA 13:11—SANCTIFICATION IN PRIESTHOOD ORDINANCES

As Alma makes clear, this holy order resulted in sanctification, as those who "could not look upon sin save it were with abhorrence" were made holy, sanctified, and "their garments were washed white through the blood of the Lamb" (13:11). The Nephites understood this as being symbolic of the Savior's blood that would eventually be shed and then used ritually and symbolically to sanctify the people. Sanctification was closely tied to temple worship. As temple priests would go up from one level or room to another, they were ascending symbolically into God's presence in the Holy of Holies.

ALMA 13:13-29—MELCHIZEDEK USED THE PRIESTHOOD TO INDUCE REPENTANCE

In responding to these men who were after the order of Nehor, Alma wisely points to Melchizedek, the ancient king and priest after the order of the Son of God. As the name *Melchi-zedek* means *my king is righteous,* this name easily relates to Christ himself. Drawing on information from the brass plates, Alma emphasizes that when Melchizedek preached with mighty faith to the wicked, "behold, they did repent" (13:18). What a miraculous use of priesthood power! Of course, Alma hoped that his preaching would bring about repentance as he cried "with a mighty voice" unto the people in Ammonihah (13:21), wishing "from the inmost part of [his] heart, yea, with great anxiety even unto pain" that they would repent and become "humble, meek, submissive, patient, full of love and all long-suffering; Having faith on the Lord; having a hope that ye shall receive eternal life" (13:28–29), gently echoing King Benjamin's central words in Mosiah 3:19.

ALMA 14—BELIEVERS ARE KILLED BY FIRE; ALMA AND AMULEK ARE MIRACULOUSLY FREED

Nevertheless, Alma and Amulek were taken and bound, stripped of their clothing, imprisoned, tortured, and starved for several months; and anyone professing faith in the words of Alma and Amulek was cast out and stoned (14:7). Then, as a final act of utmost wickedness, the people of Ammonihah confiscated the believers' sacred writings and their women and children (including Amulek's) and burned them (14:8–13). Amulek pleaded with Alma to exercise priesthood power to save the believers, hoping that Alma would call on the powers of heaven to stop the suffering. Alma replied, "The Spirit constraineth me that I must not stretch forth mine hand" (Alma 14:11). Even in such dire circumstances, the prophet must obey the Spirit and cannot enforce his own will.

Despite his horror, Alma explained that it was necessary for the event to reach its conclusion so that a just judgment could come upon the people "according to the hardness of their hearts," so that "the blood of the innocent [would] stand as a witness against them . . . at the last day" (14:11). Alma and Amulek believed that in the end, these faithful and innocent women and children would be rewarded for their faithfulness.

This event bears strong testimony to the importance of the principle of agency and choice. As Captain Moroni wrote, "For the Lord suffereth the righteous to be slain that his justice and judgment may come upon the wicked; therefore ye need not suppose that the righteous are lost because they are slain; but behold, they do enter into the rest of the Lord their God" (Alma 60:13).

Alma and Amulek called upon the Lord, who "granted unto them power, according to their faith which was in Christ" (14:28), and an earthquake destroyed the prison along with those who had abused Alma and Amulek. (14:27). A Lamanite army invaded, destroying Ammonihah and taking captives (16:2–3). Ammonihah was left as a desolate heap (16:11; see also Deuteronomy 13:16).

ALMA 16:19-20—SOMETIMES "I DO NOT KNOW" IS A GOOD ANSWER

Whether Alma was preaching among hostile opponents or faithful followers, he was asked tough questions. Following the destruction of the people of Ammonihah, as he and Amulek continued to "preach the word throughout all the land" (16:15), he was asked by faithful followers about "*the place* where the Son of God should come." Certainly, Alma knew *that* the Son of God would come, but whether Alma knew His specific birthplace is not clear. Therefore, he answered cautiously that, "He would appear to them [the Nephites] after His [the Savior's] Resurrection" (16:20), and they were satisfied—in fact, "the people did hear [this news] with great joy and gladness" (16:20). What Alma knew for sure and shared freely was enough to satisfy the spiritual needs of his people.

Is there a lesson here for us? We do not always know the answers to gospel questions, whether it is in a Church setting or in our homes. It is better to say we don't know than to speculate beyond the limits of our understanding. At the same time, it is also essential to share what we *do* know. Hopefully, we know enough to testify of central eternal truths that others will hear with "great joy and gladness."

TAKEAWAYS

- Which key words are repeated distinctively and frequently used in Alma 12-13?
- Recognizing that Alma was the high priest, what temple themes did he mention here? Why did Alma teach his opponents about the temple? (See *KnoWhy* #119: Why Did Alma Teach His Opponents about the Temple?)
- What was the most remarkable thing in Alma's mind about Melchizedek (13:17-18)?
- With what words did Alma bless those who had imprisoned him (13:27-30)? How can you apply this to loving your enemies and doing good to them that hate you?
- Whose women and children were burned? What would you have done in Alma and Amuek's position? Why did they not choose to save the family? Why did (or how could) they obey God instead?
- What happened to the city of Ammonihah? How long did it remain a heap (16:1; 49:1)?
- Why did Zoram and his brother consult with Alma before pursuing the Lamanites (16:5)?
- What did Alma and Amulek (the two lions) teach for the next three years (16:12-21)?

27: ALMA 17-22

In reading these chapters, it helps to be mindful of time, place, and purpose. Everything that happens with the four sons of Mosiah in the land southward as reported in Alma 17–20 takes place during the same fourteen years as do Alma's activities in the land northward recorded in Alma 1–16. The four brothers—Ammon, Aaron, Omner, and Himni—left their life of aristocracy to serve anonymously in different cultural settings with no motive other than to cultivate faith in the Lord Jesus Christ. They served for fourteen years (two seven-year sabbaticals). They hoped to break down barriers of violence, misunderstanding, and doctrinal forgetfulness. Through patience and suffering, they facilitated spiritual conversions that led to peace among families and peoples. Many personal and religious lessons can be learned by attentively reading the accounts of these courageous and inspired brothers.

ALMA 17:1-4—ALMA REJOICES IN SEEING THE SONS OF MOSIAH

Seeing the sons of Mosiah again brought great joy to Alma, but what added most to his joy was that "they were still his brethren in the Lord; yea, and they had waxed strong in the knowledge of the truth" (17:2). Ammon's joy is expressed in Alma 26; Alma sings of his joy in Alma 29.

ALMA 17:6—MORMON INSERTS FLASHBACKS

Mormon's abridgments often result in flashbacks as he shifts from one record to another. His compilations flawlessly combine complex chronological and geographical details spanning hundreds of pages. While keeping all these threads straight can be difficult for readers, these flashbacks are strong evidence that Joseph Smith's dictated translations were divinely inspired. For example, Alma 1, Alma 17, and Alma 21 all begin in the first year of the reign of Judges (91 B.C.). These three threads will merge fourteen years later, explaining the Lamanite attack on the city of Jershon, where Ammon's converts had been given a land of inheritance in the north.

ALMA 17:3-4, 10-12—POWER AND AUTHORITY OF GOD, AND HIS BLESSINGS

Righteous use of authority is key to opening hearts and helping people to repent. These four missionaries were called, set apart, and given the appropriate priesthood authority from their father, King Mosiah. They listened carefully to the contents of the blessing they received from the Lord and worked to live worthy of its promises. In the portions of the blessing they recorded were the words, "Be comforted." And, indeed, the sons of Mosiah "were comforted" (17:10). If we do not remember and faithfully accept reassurances, but choose to fret or worry, those blessings can't take full effect in our lives. The biblical word for the Comforter is *parakletos,* meaning one who helps, mediates, advocates, and advises. Being "comforted" includes being encouraged, assured, or accepted, as well as consoled. The sons of Mosiah are great examples of all this. They were instructed to "be patient in long-suffering and afflictions" (17:11). Their blessing did not promise a mission of ease. While counseling them to be diligent in hard times, they were assured that the Lord was always aware of them.

ALMA 17:2-3, 9-12—LET YOUR LIGHT SHINE, THE SPIRIT OF PROPHECY AND OF REVELATION

As faithful missionaries, the sons of Mosiah desired to be "instruments in the hands of God" (17:9) through which His will could be done. Often in our callings, the primary purpose is to be transparent so that the light of Christ—the glory of God—will shine *through* us and not just *on* us. Christ told His disciples to "let your light *so* shine before men" (Matt. 5:16; 3 Nephi 12:16). The word "so" is key. It means, "Let your light shine *in such a way* that, when people see your good works, their reaction will be to glorify your Father which is in Heaven, and not you." This explains how one should be "an instrument in the hands of the Lord."

Moreover, the sons of Mosiah are worthy examples. They spent time reading the scriptures. This helped them become "men of a sound understanding" as they "waxed strong in the knowledge of truth" (17:2). Next, after "much prayer, and fasting," the four missionary brothers received the "spirit of prophecy" and the "spirit of revelation" (17:3). The "spirit of prophecy" is a gift of the Spirit. Anciently, prophecy meant prophesying about the future. At that time, the main future event to which righteous people looked was the coming of Christ. The "spirit of revelation" refers to moments when the veil is taken from our minds, and we understand things a little better, such as when answers to difficult social problems are uncovered, new insights are discovered, or understanding becomes clear. We understand the mysteries of God best through His influence, and not by our own rationalizations or limited perspectives.

ALMA 17:20-25—AMMON IS CAPTURED, CARRIED BEFORE THE KING, AND SET AS A SERVANT

Upon entering the land of Ishmael, Ammon was captured and carried before the king. Tensions rose in the ancient world whenever an unknown person arrived in any area—especially someone from enemy territory. It was then usually up to the king to determine that person's fate. As a son of King Mosiah, Ammon was likely familiar with courtly protocols. Clearly, Ammon impressed King Lamoni and built trust with the king. Three days later he demonstrated his loyalty when he courageously protected the king's flocks. Even today, building new relationships is a delicate reciprocal process.

ALMA 17:36-38—SERVANTS RETURN WITH THE SEVERED ARMS OF THE MARAUDERS

When the marauders attacked, Ammon killed six of them with his sling, and a seventh, their leader, he killed with his sword. The severed arms of all seven (Alma 17:39) were then presented to King Lamoni. Interestingly, in the ancient Near East and in Mesoamerica, soldiers often returned from the battlefield with a designated body part of those they had killed. Soldiers were not necessarily mercenaries, but they expected to be rewarded for each enemy they killed. Such evidence was often the right hand of the victim. Apparently, this practice was traditional among the Lamanites.

ALMA 18:21-24—AMMON DESIRES ONLY TO TEACH LAMONI GOSPEL TRUTHS

Ammon was filled with the Spirit of God as he again stood before Lamoni, who then offered to grant Ammon whatever he desired. He did not ask for riches, power, or status. He simply requested that the king listen to what he had to say about God and His plan of redemption. Starting with the questions, "Is there a God?" and "Does He have a plan?" is a logical and inspiring starting point.

ALMA 19:11-13, 18-36—LAMONI SEES HIS REDEEMER; LAMANITE CONVERSION BEGINS

King Lamoni was blessed with a vision of the premortal Christ. Visions like this come at important historical moments. We believe that the arm of the Lord "is extended to all people who will repent and believe on his name" (19:36). Why might Mormon have started with Lamoni's story? Perhaps because he received such a clear manifestation. Or perhaps because Ammon was the eldest son of Mosiah and was so wise and courageous. Perhaps because the extraordinarily faithful Ammonites came from Lamoni's conversion. But also, perhaps, because Lamoni worked together so well with his wife in love and support. After Lamoni lay still on his bed for two days and two nights, the queen asked to speak with Ammon. Trusting that her husband would rise the next day, she remained at his bedside. When he arose, the first thing Lamoni did was to reach out to his wife and say, "Blessed be the name of God, and blessed art thou" (19:12). Their love for their people is clear in this queen's magnificat: "O blessed Jesus, who has saved me from an awful hell! O blessed God, have mercy on this people!" (19:29).

The queen's servant Abish also played a pivotal role that day. Having been previously but privately converted, now as a member missionary she ran "from house to house" telling of the miraculous experience (19:17). People began assembling at the palace, including family members of men Ammon had killed. No doubt they saw this as a time for revenge. Moreover, because Ammon was a Nephite, public biases would have naturally run against him. Of those gathered, some believed, but many did not. Some converts were baptized, marking the establishment of the Church and the commencement of the work of the Lord among the Lamanites.

ALMA 20:15-26—LAMONI'S FATHER SEEKS TO SMITE HIS SON

In the ancient world, an ordinary father could kill his son with impunity. This right is known as *patria potestas* (the power of a father), which gave the father the right to kill his offspring for any reason and without being punished. If the father also happened to be king of the land, his supremacy was greater still. Additionally, Lamoni's absence from an important kingly feast may have been regarded as dishonor, if not an act of treason. Thus, Lamoni's father raised his sword against his son. But Ammon won him over, and Lamoni's father granted his son independence. Ammon was soon able to arrange for the release of Aaron and others from prison.

ALMA 21:1-11—THE ACCOUNT OF AARON AND HIS BRETHREN

Aaron and his companions fell among more hardened individuals. Aaron first went to the city of Jerusalem, where the Amulonites, descendants of Noah's priests, held great influence. The record points out that these Lamanites were indeed hardened, but "the Amulonites were still harder" (21:3). Aaron and his companions preached from the scriptures in synagogues full of unfriendly people who were "after the order of the Nehors" (21:4), who no doubt associated Aaron with Alma the Younger, who had just recently executed Nehor, their founder. So, it is no wonder Aaron and his brethren suffered greatly. They were cast out from place to place until they arrived in Middoni (Alma 21:12), where they were thrown into prison and treated badly (Alma 21:14) until freed by King Lamoni and Ammon. The contrast between Ammon's mission and that of Aaron is apparent. While serving at the same time in cities situated not too far from each other, these two brothers had very different missionary experiences. An important message here, that Mormon would have been aware of, is that success or tribulation are not the factors by which a faithful mission can be judged. Both brothers were great missionaries. They had committed themselves to the Lord's service fully, and both were valiant and obedient. God has granted agency to all His children who may choose whether to follow His plan.

ALMA 22:1-18—AARON TEACHES LAMONI'S FATHER, WHO THEN DESIRES TO REPENT

When comparing Ammon's words spoken to Lamoni in Alma 18:24–39 with the words Aaron spoke to Lamoni's father in 22:6–14, many similarities are apparent. Both missionaries explain the basic principles of the gospel, though Aaron emphasizes the primary importance of repentance (22:16), where Ammon focused on belief. Fortunately, Lamoni's father pacified his people "toward Aaron" (22:25) and sent a proclamation granting protection and freedom of religious expression to all four sons of Mosiah "throughout all the land" (22:27). This great king twice asked Aaron, "What shall I do that I may . . .?" (22:15). He then offered this wonderful prayer: "O God . . . if there is a God, . . . I will give away all my sins to know thee" (22:18). It is pleasing to the Lord when we offer to give up or change something in order to receive an answer.

TAKEAWAYS

- What lessons can we learn from how the sons of Mosiah approached their mission? What did they do to prepare (17:2-3, 9-12)? For which activities should we prepare the way they did?
- What lessons are learned from the conduct of Ammon in the land of Ishmael? What virtues did he exemplify? Can we behave like Ammon? In what way?
- What points did Ammon cover in his first missionary discussion with Lamoni (18:24-39)? How and why are these points the same or different from Aaron's first ministry to Lamoni's father (22:6-14)?
- What kind of a person was Aaron? Imagine the courage it took to go to the city of Jerusalem or into their synagogues, or to march into the palace of the father of Lamoni (21:1-5; 22:2-3). What takes courage for you? From where may we obtain courage?
- What did Lamoni see in vision while in the spirit? How remarkable was that?
- What was Lamoni's father willing to give up at first to save his life (20:23)? What was he willing to give up to have eternal life (22:15)? What words did he pray (22:18)?

28: ALMA 23-29

ALMA 23:1-3—ROYAL PROTECTION IS GIVEN TO MOSIAH'S SONS (BENJAMIN'S GRANDSONS)

In a remarkable change of perspective, King Lamoni's father extended royal privileges to the four Nephite brothers. Freedom of religion was not part of this decree, but, like most known diplomatic envoys in the ancient world, these four missionaries were absolutely protected. It is noteworthy that the last words in the Lamanite king's proclamation (23:3) repeat almost exactly the same five public prohibitions found in King Benjamin's speech (Mosiah 2:13), namely that people should not (1) murder, (2) plunder, (3) steal, (4) commit adultery, or (5) do any manner of wickedness. The Lamanite king likely learned this list from the four missionary sons of Mosiah, Benjamin's grandsons.

ALMA 23:17-18—BELIEVERS TAKE THE NAME "ANTI-NEPHI-LEHIES"

This name may simply have designated "descendants of Lehi who are not descendants of Nephi," or as we might say "non-Nephite Lehites." While it is common to think of "anti" as a prefix meaning against, a better possibility is that it comes from the Egyptian *nty*, which means "the one who," or "of," or "part of." In other words, these people wanted to be known as descendants of Lehi who were part of the Nephite religious order. This meaning might have provided additional motivation to their attackers.

ALMA 24:7-26—REPENTANT PEOPLE KEEP THEIR COVENANT TOGETHER IN UNITY

The powerful story of the Ammonites offers great instruction on how we can go about the repentance process. Guided by the heartfelt message of their new king, these Anti-Nephi-Lehies (descendants of Lehi who were not descendants of Nephi) began their new lives by being thankful to God for His goodness, His messengers, His power in softening their own hearts, His forgiveness, and His taking away their guilt no matter how great it was (24:7–10). They then sought to distance themselves from everything they might use to commit sin again by burying their weapons. They all took all their implements of violence and buried them deep in the ground.

These converts knew the importance of standing together in unity. They came forth together "vouching and covenanting with God" (24:18) that their repentance was indelible. They then associated with good people, becoming friendly with the Nephites and opening a correspondence with them. They worked hard together and stopped being idolatrous. They faced challenges and oppositions together, whatever the costs. Many were killed rather than take up arms again. Though the resulting scene was horrific, its effect was powerful, and many of their fellow-Lamanite attackers experienced a change of heart. They firmly accepted the truth by verbally and practically applying the principles of the gospel to themselves. This is a stellar example of things we should do when we repent and want to change. We cannot expect to repent without expending effort.

ALMA 24:28-25:12—THE WICKED FIGHT, CAUSING DIVISION

This brief section appears to have been inserted by Mormon to show that the wicked will not support each other, will even turn against one another to everyone's harm, and that the Lord's prophecies will be fulfilled. Mormon, as the leader of a wicked people facing imminent destruction, understood this point keenly. Opponents to the Anti-Nephi-Lehies were of different groups: some were pure Lamanites, others were mixed-race descendants of Amulon and fellow priests of King Noah, still others were Nephite apostates known as Amalekites. Most of the leaders were either Nephites living "after the order of the Nehors" (24:28), or "the seed of Amulon" (25:4). As the Anti-Nephi-Lehi massacre continued, Lamanites grew angry, witnessing their leaders kill "their [Lamanite] brethren" (25:1). The pure Lamanites turned their "vengeance upon the Nephites" (25:1). They specifically chose to attack "the land of Ammonihah" (25:2), not only because it was close, but also because it was the headquarters of the order of Nehors. Amulonites then usurped "power and authority" (25:5), putting to death any Lamanite who considered defecting; but those additional martyrdoms caused "contention in the wilderness" (25:8), and the remaining Amulonites were then hunted and killed, as Abinadi had prophesied (25:7–12).

ALMA 26:1-9, 11-37—JOYOUS CONNECTIONS

In this chapter, Ammon reminisces joyfully over the blessings of their missions. A close reading reveals four interesting verbal connections:

1.) Ammon acknowledges here the *fulfillments* of the blessings that were given to the sons of Mosiah at the outset of their mission, such as the promise of comfort and success (Alma 26:27, compare 17:10–11) and becoming "instruments" in the hands of God (26:3; compare 17:9).

2.) Ammon *echoes* Alma's words here regarding his personal conversion when Ammon describes the Lamanites' conversions. They both mention the "darkest abyss" (Alma 26:3; compare Mosiah 27:29); a "marvelous light" (Alma 26:3; compare Mosiah 27:29); "pains of hell" (Alma 26:13; compare Alma 36:13); being "snatched" (Alma 26:17; compare Mosiah 27:28); and feeling to "sing redeeming love" (26:13; compare Alma 5:9). Obviously, Ammon (as one of Alma's close associates) had heard Alma talk about his miraculous conversion right after it had happened.

3.) Connections to the *foundational* speech of Ammon's grandfather, Benjamin, are found here in Ammon's words in phrases such as "natural man" (Alma 26:21; compare

Mosiah 3:19) and when referring to God's power, wisdom, and comprehension (see Alma 26:35; compare Mosiah 4:9).

4.) The word "joy" appears seven times in the description of Ammon's *fullness* of joy in Alma 27:17–19, and in the seven-fold set of the word "joy" in Alma's *personal soliloquy* in Alma 29:5, 9, 10, 13, 24, 24, 26. Their expressions of effulgent joy, specifically to the seventh power, seem to be far from merely accidental.

ALMA 27:21-24—THE AMMONITES ARE GRANTED LAND

Immigrants and refugees today can certainly feel the challenges that the Ammonites must have faced. They emigrated seeking safety, protection, the free exercise of religion, and, most importantly, to follow the instruction of the Lord. Gratefully, they were well received in their new country. The Nephites gave to them the land of Jershon, and they were "numbered" (or naturalized) among them. The Ammonites were zealous toward God, honest in all things, and firm in the faith of Christ (Alma 27:27). These are the men and women who later become the parents of Helaman's stripling warriors.

ALMA 28—A VERY FIERCE BATTLE

This short chapter speaks of a tremendous battle, greater than any previous conflict in the land of Zarahemla (28:2), as the Lamanites tried to recoup this loss of population. Casualties are reported in the tens of thousands among Lamanites alone. After the slaughter, bodies of defenders and marauders were likely separated, since many thousands were buried "in the earth," while many thousands lay "moldering in heaps upon the face of the earth" (28:11).

Note how survivors mourned. One type of mourning centered on fear that the deceased were consigned to "a state of endless wo" (28:11). The other type lamented the "loss of their kindred," yet the separation was softened in the hope of a loved one being in a "state of never-ending happiness" (28:12). This final state, Alma emphasizes, is the great "inequality of man" (28:13) caused by sin and therefore the greatest motivation for "men to labor in the vineyards of the Lord" (28:14) to lessen this inequality.

ALMA 29—WHAT PROMPTED ALMA TO WRITE THE WORDS IN THIS CHAPTER?

Any careful reader comes away from Alma's soliloquy inspired, sobered, instructed, comforted, reminded, and fulfilled. Whether termed a hymn, a psalm, or a high-priestly benediction, this remarkable composition was the result of service and struggle, great joy and lamentation. While this message was certainly written as part of mourning for so many fallen soldiers, Alma's words also serve as an exquisite Sabbatical text. As high priest, Alma is writing this at the beginning of the 49th year (33 years from Benjamin's speech to the death of Mosiah, and

16 years of judges). Alma 30:5 says that the 16th year of the reign of judges was a year of "continual peace," consistent with Sabbatical expectations. During this traditional time, people celebrated, rejoiced, remembered the past, praised God, and thanked Him for all the things that He has done, just as Alma does here. Indeed, this text may be best understood as a high priestly prayer. All this would fit perfectly if this text was prepared in connection with an important Sabbatical moment.

ALMA 29:1-17—THE QUALITIES OF LANGUAGE IN THIS MAGNIFICENT EXPRESSION

Alma 29 is a beautiful, powerful piece of writing. In reading many of the writings in the Book of Mormon, the best assumption is that every phrase and every word is there for some meaningful reason. To paraphrase the Book of Mormon usually diminishes its beauty. Like a Bach fugue, where every note has its place, every word in Alma 29 is measured and counted. It is truly a beautiful, rewarding masterpiece that always yields new insights. For example, here Alma expresses a devout personal wish to be like the angel who had appeared to him twice (Alma 8:15; 36:6) but confesses his sin in that wish (29:3). He poses deep introspective questions and glories in his fullness of joy. Here he remembers what God has done for him, and he prays for the ultimate blessing of other people. Alma could easily have kept this masterful writing to himself, but he chose to place it among his records where it could be shared with future generations so that we might know the deepest desires of his heart.

TAKEAWAYS

- The royal proclamation in Alma 23 contains some important provisions. Which do you find to be the most interesting? Does the Restored Gospel hold the potential of convincing men everywhere that they are "all brethren" (23:3)?
- Why did the proclamation of the father of Lamoni not succeed (consider 24:1-4)?
- How many things did the Ammonites do that made their repentance and change of lifestyle so indelible and so permanent? Can we follow their pattern and example?
- Explain the obvious and not-so-obvious reasons why the Lamanites attacked the borders of the land of Zarahemla when they destroyed the city of Ammonihah (25:1-2).
- Which prophecies of Abinadi were fulfilled with the death of the Amulonites (25:7-12)?
- How did the rejoicing of Ammon in Alma 26 acknowledge the fulfillment of the blessings given to the sons of Mosiah at the outset of their mission? Was Aaron correct in objecting to Ammon's exuberance? Do we rejoice enough today?

29: ALMA 30-31

Korihor is a pivotal character with an interesting, although tragic, story. Everything we know about him is found in Alma chapter 30. Alma had been the chief judge but now was the high priest. Because of the importance and complex nature of this case, both Alma and the chief judge Giddonah were involved. The case raised important issues, namely whether blasphemy, reviling, denying the signs of the existence of God, and deliberately teaching falsehoods were still legally actionable under the new system of the reign of the judges, or if they were now protected under the new rule that people could not be punished for their beliefs, only for their actions. The full legal analysis of this case goes well beyond the scope of this book, but it is obvious that legal technicalities abound here, especially against the backdrop of ancient Israelite jurisprudence and judicial process. Several procedural matters such as jurisdiction, the use of signs, ordeals, and confessions are woven smoothly into the narrative fabric of this legal proceeding. This account of this case was written by someone who was not only an expert in ancient laws, but also personally familiar with the fine points of Nephite legal practice.

Most importantly, Korihor was identified as being "Anti-Christ" (30:6). He denied that people could "know that there shall be a Christ" or "that he shall be slain for the sins of the world" (30:26). Challenges to Christ's role as the Son of God, Redeemer, or Judge of individuals had been raised previously in Ammonihah (Alma 9:28; 11:42–44; 15:6–10). So, on this key issue of debate, it can be assumed that Korihor was already well informed.

ALMA 30:7-11—THE BASIC LEGAL ISSUE IN THIS CASE

The case of Korihor begins with the opening affirmation that under Nephite law "there was no law against a man's *belief*" (30:7; emphasis added). If a person engaged in some culpable *action,* however, the law of Mosiah provided that he should be "punished according to the crime which he has committed" (Mosiah 29:15). The legal gap remaining here, however, was whether speaking was an action that could be punished, or was it protected as an expression of one's belief? It appears that keeping one's beliefs private, debating issues, and even being critical of public policies or leaders were acceptable. But, when Korihor "went on to *blaspheme*" (30:30), to "*revile* against the priests and teachers" (30:31), and to make *false,* dishonest accusations (30:32–35), he was found to have gone too far.

ALMA 30:12-18, 23-28—WHAT DOCTRINES DID KORIHOR PROMOTE?

Of interest, intellectually and philosophically, are Korihor's assertions and logic. Surely, he was very bright, quite shrewd, and popular. Many of his one-liners match headlines of numerous ideologies today, resonating with philosophies such as rationalism, relativism, sophism, and existentialism (30:13, 17–18). For example, his proposition that "every man fared in this life according to the management of the creature" (30:17) can be found in the Greek sophists ("man is the measure of all things"). And nihilism's foundational precept states, as did Korihor, that "when a man [dies], that [is] the end thereof" (30:18). Atheism was Korihor's trump card. He asserted that God was a being "who never has been seen or known, who never was nor ever will be" (30:28), and he asked for evidence to the contrary. Alma and Korihor jostle over various issues, and finally Korihor demands that Alma show him a sign (30:45).

ALMA 30:46-53, 58-60—KORIHOR IS STRUCK DUMB, CONFESSES IN WRITING, AND DIES

Accordingly, Korihor is struck dumb by the power of God. Fundamental to biblical jurisprudence is the idea that punishments should be tailored to match the crime. Thus, when Korihor's tongue was cursed, that was a clear sign that his tongue had offended. This punishment suited the crime. Also, since God was the one offended by Korihor's blasphemy, leaving judgment to Him was also appropriate.

The high court in Zarahemla then gave Korihor the opportunity to answer four written interrogatories. But, when asked if he had been convinced of the power of God, he blamed the devil for teaching him what he should say, and he took no personal responsibility for the trouble he had caused (30:53). When Nephihah, the chief judge, asked him to avow that he would "dispute no more," Korihor shrugged (30:51). Thus, the curse of speechlessness was not removed, and Korihor left Zarahemla in disgrace and went to Antionum, the city of the Zoramite dissenters. Whether his death there was accidental, or if the citizens there deliberately eliminated him, is unknown. As Chauncy C. Riddle once admonished, the tale of Korihor reminds us that "the most powerful opposition to the work of the Savior on this earth comes from those who know the truth and then deliberately turn from it and seek to destroy others" ("Korihor: The Arguments of Apostasy," *Ensign*, September 1977). Hence—as the Lord Himself has pleaded with us—we must "watch and pray always lest ye enter into temptation; for Satan desireth to have you, that he may sift you as wheat" (3 Nephi 18:18).

ALMA 31:8-13—THE LEADING ZORAMITES HAD DISSENTED FROM THE WAYS OF THE LORD

Chapter 31 next takes us deep into Antionum. The wealthy Zoramites had withdrawn their city from the polity of Zarahemla, objecting to many basic ordinances and practices of the Church. They allowed prayer only one day per week on their Rameumptom (31:12), and they refused to pray "daily, that they might not enter into temptation" (31:10). Compare the Lord's later instruction to pray, "Lead us not into temptation" in 3 Nephi 13:12, or "Suffer us not to be led into temptation" in JST Matthew 6:12. Their prayers were socially and theologically offensive (see 31:27–29).

ALMA 31:24-35—ALMA PRAYED FOR HELP IN RECONVERTING THE ZORAMITES

Alma took with him seven others (three of the four sons of Mosiah, just back from the land of Nephi, his two recent converts Amulek and Zeezrom; and his two younger sons) (31:6) In Alma's urgent prayer for strength, patience, comfort, and success, Alma called out, "O Lord" ten times (31:26, 30, 30, 31, 31, 32, 32, 34, 35, 35). Remembering that Alma was at this time the high priest, it is remarkable that Jewish traditions in the Mishnah describe the ritual on the Day of Atonement and include the point that on that occasion the high priest pronounced, out loud, the otherwise unspeakable name of the Lord ten times. Alma, the high priest, prayed for reconciliation and atonement through Christ, hoping to overcome the "gross wickedness" of the Zoramites. He prayed for success, power, and wisdom to bring them, our brethren, back to the Lord (31:34–35). He and his companions then separated and went out among the Zoramites (32:1). Many Zoramites, especially the poor, came out to the hill Onidah (32:4), where they heard Alma and Amulek speak. Their words (in Alma 32–34) are covered in the next lesson.

TAKEAWAYS

- Who was Korihor? Where and why was he successful among the people (Alma 30:6-12)?
- In his phrases and arguments, modern readers can find parallels to many schools of thought that have come to dominate much of secular philosophy. How many of Korihor's key doctrines can you identify, together with a standard philosophical counterpart?
- What can we learn about the personality and words of Alma from his comments and participation in the trial of Korihor toward the end of Alma 30, and what lessons can we derive from his example?
- When and why did the Zoramites become dissenters from the Nephites? What were the "great errors" committed by the Zoramite aristocracy in Antionum? Why did this pose such a threat to the Nephites?
- Why did Alma go with his companions to teach the Zoramites the gospel (31:5)?
- What can we learn from the prayer that Alma offered in this difficult situation? How can we incorporate and apply the foundations of his petition in our own lives (31:26-35)? How can we apply this principle?

30: ALMA 32-35

OVERVIEW

Alma 32 is often read as a single composition when Alma's words also include chapter 33. In chapter 34, Amulek speaks as a second witness to the truths Alma taught. Here Alma taught five main points:

1.) The importance of being humble, even when compelled through afflictions or mistreatment (32:6–16),

2.) How true faith is obtained, and its eternal fruit enjoyed (32:17–43),

3.) The proper modes of prayer, crying unto God in the wilderness and closet (33:2–11),

4.) Believing on the Son of God (as taught by Zenos, Zenock, and Moses) brings healing through the Son of God (33:12–21), and

5.) The content of "the word" that should be planted in the heart (33:21–23).

Amulek then reviews and enhances these same points, but in reverse order:

5.) Admonishing all to plant "the word" in your hearts (34:4),

4.) Believing in Christ, the Son of God, as testified by Zenos, Zenock, and Moses (34:5–7), and how faith in Christ's infinite atonement affords repentance and salvation (34:8–16),

3.) The proper content of prayer, crying unto God in the wilderness and closet (34:17–26),

2.) Bringing forth fruit unto repentance and righteousness (34:30–36), and

1.) Humbly worshiping God (34:38), even if afflicted and cast out (34:39–41).

Then, in Alma 35, the poor Zoramites who followed Alma are cast out of Antionum and are relocated in Jershon with the Ammonites, while the wealthy Zoramites begin to "mix with the Lamanites and to stir them up also to anger against [the people of Ammon] . . . and . . . began to make preparations for war against the people of Ammon, and also against the Nephites" (35:9–11). This block of chapters shows the causes of the prolonged wars that will play out in Alma 43–62, in which Zoramite leaders take commanding positions over the Lamanites.

ALMA 32:7-16—COMPELLED TO BE HUMBLE, LEARN WISDOM

The poor Zoramites were bereft spiritually at first, but they were not hardhearted. These people had been forced to be humble, and yet Alma assured them, "I behold that ye are lowly in heart; and if so, blessed are ye" (32:8). Alma said that humility was necessary to *learn* wisdom, and that learning wisdom was necessary for salvation. What might this mean?

We must strive to learn *wisdom* in the eyes of our Eternal Judge. Regardless of status or station, God universally reveals His Spirit to all people who humbly seek Him. Distinct from empirical knowledge, that kind of wisdom may be gained only by *the blessings of the Holy Ghost*.

ALMA 32:2-43—DISCOURSE ON FAITH: THE PLANTED SEED BECOMES THE TREE OF LIFE

Alma declares his famous statement, "If ye have faith ye *hope* for things which are not seen, *which are true*" (Alma 32:21; emphasis added). This is not a definition of what faith *is*, but what faith *does*. Alma's view of faith is active. A faithful person actively hopes. Therefore, faith propels us to move toward an unseen goal. Alma goes on to say: "[God] desireth *in the first place,* that ye should believe, yea, even on his *word*" (32:22; emphasis added). Thus, faith specifically in the Lord Jesus Christ is placed *first* in His gospel. Alma wanted to explain the benefits of the gospel to people who had never experienced a testimony. So, he used an inspiring analogy that stressed obtaining a testimony as an experiential matter: "Now, we will compare the word unto a seed" (Alma 32:28). This metaphor likens living the gospel to planting, giving room, and nourishing a seed. Alma taught that "even if ye can no more than *desire* to believe" (32:27), this seed will begin to swell and then sprout. Planting the message of the gospel in our hearts, and not crowding it out, is the first step in growing our testimony.

Alma continues, "*Give place,* that a seed may be planted in your heart" (Alma 32:28; emphasis added). Those two words speak volumes. We must give the gospel *room and nourishment*. Other things tend to crowd out the gospel, and it will shrivel if assigned to less important parts of our lives. Finally, the seed will grow and "*enlarge* [your] soul" (32:28). This is the litmus test for knowing whether something is truly good.

Hearkening back to the words *white* and *sweet* used by Father Lehi to describe the eternal fruit of the tree of life (1 Nephi 8:11), Alma likewise says that the fruit of the tree that will grow from this seed is "most precious," "sweet above all that is sweet, . . . and white above all that is white, yea, and pure above all that is pure" (32:42).

ALMA 33:3-11—ZENOS'S POETIC EXPRESSION ON PRAYER AND FINDING MERCY

Ultimately, the most important thing we can do to strengthen our faith is to *pray*. God will bless our hearts in many ways so that our wisdom will grow. I fear that prayer is too easily discounted as the source of wisdom, and as a result, many are learned but not wise. Alma wanted these poor Zoramites to *find* mercy. He recites a jubilant poem from the prophet Zenos emphasizing mercy through God's Son. We do not just passively receive mercy, and God does not just give it to us; we must actively seek and find it. God will force no person to heaven; He also will not compel anyone to feel joy.

Zenos's poem then flows progressively from the most remote wilderness, through Zenos's field, into his house, and then into his most intimate closet, affirming that a person can pray wherever the need may be. It then concludes beautifully, accentuating Christ's atoning mercy: "It is *because of thy Son* that thou hast been thus merciful unto me, therefore I will cry unto thee in all mine afflictions, for in thee is my joy; for thou hast turned thy judgments away from me, *because of thy Son*" (33:11; emphasis added).

ALMA 33:22-23—PLANTING THE WHOLE "WORD"

Concluding this teaching session, Alma delineates seven truths that everyone should believe. These elements constitute the gospel DNA of "the word" we are to plant in our hearts. We are not free to pick and choose among these elements. All seven elements of this seed must grow together. Alma gives the most complete statement of Nephite beliefs found in the Book of Mormon. Variations of this list are presented in the Book of Mormon, in writings from Nephi to Moroni. Alma promises that this word, if properly cultivated, will "become a tree, springing up in you unto everlasting life" (33:23). The "Word" is the following 7-part creed:

1.) Believe in the Son of God,

2.) That He will come to redeem His people,

3.) That He shall suffer and die to atone for their sins,

4.) That He shall rise again from the dead,

5.) That He will bring about the universal resurrection,

6.) So that all men can stand before Him,

7.) That they will be judged at the last judgment day according to their works.

ALMA 34:4-16—THE ATONEMENT EXPLAINED, INFINITE AND ETERNAL

Amulek then stood to add his testimony of *the word* to that of Alma's. Here, Amulek was standing as a second witness, but as usual, Amulek developed the idea further. Alma had taught what to have faith in; Amulek clarified why there must be an atonement made, and that its purpose is to save man from perishing in a fallen state. At the end of verse 10, he then adds that it must be an infinite and eternal sacrifice. In what ways is the Atonement of Jesus Christ infinite?

First, it was *made by an infinite being* who redeems His people. Then it is infinite in its *universal application;* everyone will be resurrected. It is also infinite in *magnitude* and *coverage,* actual and potential. Moreover, it transcends all boundaries of *time and space,* answering all the demands of justice without regard to when a sin was committed. It is infinite in *mercy,* and in *love*, in terms of our *willingness* and *obedience*, with no reservations or exclusions of any kind.

It is also infinite in terms of *suffering*, and infinite in *scope*, but its application depends upon our repentance. It is also *perfect* in its function. It is sufficient to atone for all breaches of trust and relationship between deity and ourselves. It is infinite in *origin*, being a part of God's eternal plan. We might even say that the Atonement is infinitely infinite. It is infinite in every way possible.

ALMA 34:18-25—AMULEK'S POETIC WRITING ON PRAYER

We know that the Zoramites left Zarahemla because, among other things, they were not willing to observe the performances of the Church of praying daily; the Zoramites prayed only once a week (Alma 31:10, 12). Continuing his comments on prayer, Amulek recites eight lines of poetic language. Laid out in poetic form, pairs of couplets become clear (each of which begins with *yea, cry, cry, yea;* and then *yea, yea, cry, cry*). The center point of this parallelism is that we should cry unto the Lord "both morning, mid-day, and evening" (34:21), one of the big stumbling blocks for the Zoramites.

ALMA 34:18-41—AMULEK'S CONCLUSION

In his final remarks, Amulek circles back around to the second and first points made by Alma at the beginning of their instruction, namely (2) bringing forth fruit unto repentance and righteousness (34:30–36); and (1) humbly worshiping God (34:38), even if afflicted and cast out (34:39–41). To the fruits of repentance, Amulek adds the need to be charitable (34:28–29), and the urgent need to not delay repentance (34:30–36). Notably, the "space between death and the resurrection of the body" (40:21) seems to be included in the full time mercifully granted by God as the probationary period in which "to repent" (42:4–5).

On humbling oneself, Amulek adds the need to "live in thanksgiving daily," to be "watchful unto prayer continually," and to "not revile against" those who treat you badly (34:37–41). Amulek knew from personal experience what it means to be mistreated by people whom he once thought were his friends. The best antidotes for the poison of revenge are feeling grateful, counting blessings, and praying continually for enemies as well as yourself.

Regrettably, conversion efforts among the Zoramites largely failed, as is reported in Alma 35. These Zoramite leaders would go on to become commanders in the armies at war against the Nephites for the remaining years of the book of Alma.

TAKEAWAYS

- When Alma speaks of "preaching the word" (Alma 31:5, 7), what did he mean by "the word"? (Consider Alma 33:23.)
- How can you do a better job of embracing Alma's words as you strive to strengthen your own testimony, as you work to proclaim the gospel more effectively, and as you desire to help others grow in faith and knowledge of the truth?
- In what ways do the words of Amulek in Alma 34 act as a very powerful second witness to the words of Alma in Alma 32-33?
- What impresses you most about Amulek's teachings on such topics as the Atonement, prayer, repentance, urgency, and humility?
- As you read Alma 35, do you think Alma's mission succeeded or failed in Antionum?
- How do the words of Alma and Amulek directly confront the erroneous teachings of the Zoramites? (As you read, keep Alma 31:8-14 in mind.)
- What scriptural sources from the Plates of Brass or Nephite records do Alma and Amulek draw upon? (See especially 32:42; 33:3, 15, 17, 19; 34:7, 26.)
- How effective are the many metaphors (such as seed, light, nourish, tree, etc.) used by Alma and Amulek? What strength is added by the figures of speech or literary structures in these chapters? (Find the chiasm in 34:9. See the eight-part parallelism in 34:18-25.)

31: ALMA 36-38

OVERVIEW OF ALMA 36-42—ALMA AND HIS THREE SONS

Alma knew the needs and characters of each of his sons. While his words to them may not sound like traditional patriarchal blessings, in important ways these chapters preserve this father's blessings given to his boys. His blessings and instructions in chapters 36–42 will soon turn out to be a major part of his legacy to them, as Alma will depart later that same year from their midst and from this life (Alma 45:18).

ALMA 36-42—ALMA'S COUNSEL AND COMMANDMENTS TO HIS SONS

Alma begins his speech to Helaman by saying, "Hear my words and learn of me" (Alma 36:3). The very first thing that Alma taught both Helaman and Shiblon was: "Inasmuch as ye shall keep the commandments of God ye shall prosper in the land" (Alma 36:1). Alma also added the inverse at the end for Helaman: "And ye ought to know also, that inasmuch as ye will not keep the commandments of God ye shall be cut off from his presence" (Alma 36:30). For Shiblon, Alma began with both promises of the covenant at the beginning—clearly his main teaching point to Shiblon: "Inasmuch as ye shall keep the commandments of God ye shall prosper in the land; and inasmuch as ye will not keep the commandments of God ye shall be cut off from his presence" (Alma 38:1). With Corianton, Alma began his speech by sorrowing that his son had not kept the commandments of God (see Alma 39:1).

Alma took great thought and care when he wrote these words to his sons. He worked both with the Spirit and with his literary skills, preparing personalized messages for each son, setting a good example for all parents when communicating with their children.

ALMA 36-42—A POSSIBLE PASSOVER SETTING?

At Passover, Jewish families traditionally celebrate by singing, telling stories, and acting out the story of Israel's deliverance from Egypt. Following the Passover reenactment, the father would then ask three boys in the family one question each, as is implied in texts in the Torah. Of course, the passing over of the destroying angel was the essence of Passover. Alma certainly remembered how the *destroying angel* passed over him. The word "destroy" (or its derivative) is used six times in Alma 36 when speaking to Helaman, then seven more times in Alma 37 as he continues his words to Helaman, and four more times in Alma 42 when speaking to Corianton. Bondage and captivity are also mentioned (36:2, 29; 38:5), along with other obvious Passover themes. This insight was first ascertained in 1984 and published by Gordon

Thomasson ("Sons of the Passover," in John W. Welch, ed., *Reexploring the Book of Mormon* [Salt Lake City: Deseret Book, 1992], 196–98).

ALMA 36—THE AMAZING CHIASTIC STRUCTURE IN ALMA 36

As the 2020 *Come, Follow Me* manual, p. 115, points out: "Alma 36 is a great example of a form of Hebrew poetry called chiasmus, in which words or ideas are presented in a certain order, leading to a central idea, and then repeated in reverse order." This definition is a perfect description of the structure of Alma 36, first published in *BYU Studies* in 1969 and in the *New Era* in 1972. Of all the passages in world literature that have ever been found to be chiastic, Alma 36 is usually regarded as one of the very best examples of this form of composition. It is truly a masterpiece of world religious literature.

The Book of Mormon Central archive contains an extensive discussion of this carefully structured text. It can be easily found. See https://archive.bookofmormoncentral.org/content/chiasmus-alma-36.

Most importantly, everything in Alma 36 builds up to and then retraces its many steps away from the central turning point, namely when Alma remembered that his father had prophesied about the coming of Jesus Christ, and when he cried out, "O Jesus, thou Son of God, have mercy on me" (36:18). This is the submissive plea that sends Alma's life and his story going in the opposite direction. Note also that Alma gave his oldest son, Helaman, a "doubled story" of his conversion, while Shiblon's blessing in Alma 38 will go through only (but almost exactly) the first half of Alma's conversion account. Perhaps this was done by Alma for a subtle purpose. Under biblical and Jewish law, the oldest son, the firstborn son, was entitled to receive what was called the "double blessing"—a double portion of his father's estate (Deuteronomy 21:17). When the father died and his estate was divided, the oldest son (Helaman in this case) would receive twice as much as the other sons would each receive. As noted in earlier chapters, the eldest son received a double portion because it was his responsibility to provide for the women in the family and to keep the affairs of the estate in order.

ALMA 36:22—ALMA'S JOY AND HIS QUOTATION OF LEHI

While Alma spent three days in some kind of spiritual shock or coma, he was cognizant of what was going on. He agonized; his soul was being racked with eternal torment. He felt "the pains of a damned soul" (36:16). But then he remembered his father having spoken "concerning the coming of one Jesus Christ, a Son of God, to atone for the sins of the world" (36:17). He then called out for Jesus Christ to have mercy on him and apply his atoning blood, then felt "joy" and saw "marvelous light" (36:20). Alma explained that his "joy was as exceeding as was [his] pain!" He then stated, "Methought I saw, even as our father Lehi saw, God sitting upon his throne, surrounded by numberless concourses of angels, in the attitude of singing and praising their God" (36:22). Here, Alma is precisely quoting Lehi's words found in 1 Nephi 1:8—truly remarkable when you stop and think about it.

ALMA 37:1-8—THE VALUE OF SACRED RECORDS

After Alma gave the plates to Helaman, he explained Helaman's sacred responsibility and stewardship. The plates of brass contained their genealogy, which was important; however, Alma pointed out that the plates also "contain these engravings, which have the records of the holy scriptures upon them" (37:3). The plates were to be handed down from generation to generation, and "kept and preserved by the hand of the Lord" (37:4). In other words, the plates were of such significance to the Lord that He would directly assist those charged with responsibility over them. The Lord had a plan and purpose for the records. As Alma explained, "They should go forth unto every nation, kindred, tongue, and people, that they shall know of the mysteries contained thereon" (37:4).

Why has the Lord chosen the Book of Mormon as a means of spreading his gospel to the entire world? Alma gave the following explanation as to why the plates would be so valuable and useful: "For behold, they have enlarged the memory of this people, yea, and convinced many of the error of their ways, and brought them to the knowledge of their God unto the salvation of their souls" (37:8). Those three crucial purposes still stand as valid reasons why the world needs the Book of Mormon.

ALMA 37:14-22—ALMA ENCOURAGES HELAMAN IN HIS RESPONSIBILITIES

Alma had given Helaman a heavy load and entrusted him with enormous responsibility. However, this responsibility came with a promise: "And now remember, my son, that God has entrusted you with these things, which are sacred, which he has kept sacred, and also which he will keep and preserve for a wise purpose" (37:14). Alma continued: "For [God] will fulfill all his promises which he shall make unto you, for he has fulfilled his promises which he has made unto our fathers" (37:17).

ALMA 37:25-34—THE LORD USES THE JAREDITE RECORD TO TEACH HIS CHILDREN

Alma then gave another set of plates to Helaman—the 24 gold Jaredite plates. This set of plates was not filled with good news for future generations, but it could be read as a warning. The people of Jared were destroyed and obliterated. They fought to a bitter end, and their civilization fell, was destroyed, and was lost.

Thus, Alma taught Helaman that God had said, "I will bring forth out of darkness unto light all their secret works and their abominations" (37:25). In the face of social, political, and personal injustices and struggles, it is at least of some comfort to know that there is nothing that is hidden that will not eventually be brought to light and to judgment. Trials, troubles, and tribulations are part of our mortal experience, but they will not last forever. If we are faithful, we will eventually be lifted up on the last day.

ALMA 38:2—ALMA HAS JOY IN SHIBLON

I like what Alma does when he talks to his sons. In Alma 38:2, he said to Shiblon, "And now, my son, I trust that I shall have great joy in you," words that are complimentary and encouraging. Alma's entire blessing to Shiblon in this chapter is a tribute to this faithful and praiseworthy son. Our children need to know that we are confident that they are going to give us joy. They need to know they are loved. Alma then described two specific, positive attributes of this young man—"steadiness" and "faithfulness unto God."

ALMA 38:1-8—SHIBLON RECEIVES A SINGLE BLESSING

Alma's words to Shiblon about his conversion follow the same pattern as the conversion story given to Helaman in Alma 36, but Alma gave Shiblon only the first half of it. Each line of both narratives led directly to the central point. However, here Alma ends his conversion story at the center and does not work its way back to the beginning. While the climax of Alma's conversion story is reached essentially at the same point in both speeches, Alma gave Shiblon just half of the account he gave in his blessing to Helaman. And then, as Alma continued in chapter 38, he gave Shiblon a short section of wise, practical advice, whereas in chapter 37 he gave Helaman a long set of administrative instructions. In effect, Helaman got a double blessing, and Shiblon got the single blessing, all of which is consistent with the rule that the oldest son was entitled to the double blessing because of his double family responsibilities. However, it is well to note that much of what is here reveals Shiblon's integrity and innate goodness, which would be very dear to his father's heart.

ALMA 38:9—CHRIST IS THE SOURCE OF TRUE WISDOM

In Alma 38:9–15, Alma pleads with Shiblon to "learn wisdom," reminding him that salvation comes only in and through Christ. "Behold, he is the life and the light of the world. Behold, he is the word of truth and righteousness" (38:9). Alma goes on to share valuable fatherly wisdom and spiritual advice to guide and encourage Shiblon throughout his life.

ALMA 38:10-12—BOLDNESS, NOT OVERBEARANCE

Alma told Shiblon to "continue to teach." Alma obviously knew and appreciated Shiblon's gift for teaching and wisely encouraged him to continue using this precious gift as part of his spiritual endeavors. Shiblon was also told to be diligent and temperate in all things. This couplet strikes a delicate balance. Diligence can become compulsive, and temperance can become too mild; therefore, it is wisdom to avoid either extreme. Avoiding pride is likewise crucial, and Alma cautioned Shiblon against boasting of his own strength and wisdom. Alma encouraged Shiblon to speak with boldness, but not overbearance, meaning that he should be firm and decisive when speaking about his beliefs without coming across as domineering or tyrannical, an important distinction.

ALMA 38:13-14—HOW TO PRAY

As Alma continued advising Shiblon, he gave him—and us—guidance on how to pray. He reminded Shiblon about the Zoramites, who "prayed to be heard of men, and to be praised for their wisdom" (38:13), all the while congratulating themselves on their superior status. Alma's advice about prayer is a timely reminder for us all: to be mindful of our weaknesses and seek the Lord's help in overcoming them, and to remember to ask for mercy for our brothers and sisters (38:14).

ALMA 38:15—WHAT DOES ALMA MEAN BY "SOBER"?

Alma's last word of advice to Shiblon was, "Be sober." Nowadays, the word "sober" (other than in an alcoholic context) means deliberate, thoughtful, in control, serious, sensitive, and solemn, as well as practical, dignified, and restrained. Thus, Alma's admonition to be sober is closely related to his most famous advice given to Shiblon in verse 12, to "see that ye bridle [control] all your passions, that ye may be filled with love." How fitting that Alma's final reminder to his loyal son Shiblon is his tender advice regarding the importance of doing all things in a spirit of love.

TAKEAWAYS

- How do the words in Alma 36 compare with the words in Alma 38:5-8, and what significance and insights do you find in any differences or similarities?
- Which records does Alma entrust to his son Helaman in Alma 37? As Alma hands these records over to him, what advice and duties does Alma give?
- What can we learn today from the counsel that Alma gave to Helaman in connection with his recordkeeping responsibilities?
- The fatherly encouragement given to Helaman in Alma 37:35-37 is wise and wonderful. Compare those words with Deuteronomy 6:3-9. What continuities or departures do you detect between these two scriptures?
- What typology (or "type," verse 45) did Alma see in the Liahona in Alma 37:38-46? What do you find most impressive or useful about Alma's exhortations in this regard?
- In Alma 38:9-15, Alma speaks to Shiblon so that he "may learn wisdom." How do these instructive lines exemplify the wisdom and experiences of Alma the sage? In what ways do you "learn wisdom" from these verses?

32: ALMA 39-42

These four chapters are all addressed to Alma's youngest son, Corianton. Based on Alma's corrections to Corianton, most of Corianton's misunderstandings came from false teachings of Nehor and Korihor, which included: thinking he could hide his crimes from God (39:8); questioning the resurrection (40:1, 2, 17); denying the justice of God (42:30); and refusing to believe that God could punish sinners (42:1). These are big topics, and they called for profound explanations. Alma's life was repeatedly impacted by horrific deaths, perverse sins, and divisive theological speculations, and he sought and received revelations and an angelic visit (40:11) in addressing these issues. In lovingly teaching and reassuring Corianton, Alma used logic, compassion, imperatives, blunt questions, a variety of approaches, and bold statements of incontrovertible truths. This style differs from Alma's regular sermons.

In his counsel, Alma emphasized that the Lord Jesus shall "bring to pass the resurrection" (40:3) and that "all men shall stand before [God], to be judged at the last and judgment day, according to their works" (33:22). The topics covered in chapter 39 include the seriousness of personal sin and the infinite power of Christ's resurrection over all people, whether before or after Christ's coming. Details of the timing of resurrection and judgment are expanded in chapter 40. The contested meaning of the word "restoration" is brilliantly clarified in chapter 41. And the absolute harmony of both God's justice together with His mercy is orchestrated in chapter 42. Here are a few basic notes on Alma's inspired unfolding of this multidimensional doctrinal matrix.

ALMA 39:2-11—SIN IS SERIOUS

All should know the seriousness of sin. While Alma did not go into painful detail about Corianton's poor choices, neither did he minimize Corianton's sins, which included overconfidence leading to a serious sexual transgression (see 39:2–4). Alma warned: "Ye cannot hide your crimes from God" (39:8). Alma is fighting here with great love for Corianton's eternal life. Alma was also distressed about those who had been adversely affected by Corianton's bad behavior and therefore failed to accept the gospel. This illustration of the principle that choices can have far-reaching, eternal consequences helps us emulate Alma's example of kindness and directness in helping others come to repentance.

ALMA 39:15-17—THE PROBLEM WITH DENYING THE RESURRECTION

Alma perceived that Corianton doubted that Christ would come, and thus he emphasized: "It is he that *surely* shall come to take away the sins of the world" (39:15). Korihor had strongly denied the resurrection, and so Corianton could easily have encountered Korihor's false ideologies during his mission to Antionum, where Korihor was trampled. Even today, after the question of Jesus's Resurrection is strongly answered in 3 Nephi 11, we still need to guard against the negative side effect of ignoring the reality of the Resurrection, namely that sin becomes irrelevant.

ALMA 40—TIME, MORTALITY, PRELIMINARY AND FINAL JUDGMENTS

The timing of an individual's resurrection was a subject of interest in Alma's day, particularly to Corianton. Alma assured Corianton that some details are known, but others are not. Importantly, God sees the larger picture: "All is as one day with God, time is measured only unto men" (40:8). Regarding the "state of the soul between death and the resurrection," Alma learned that, through the resurrection of Christ, all people "are taken home to that God who gave them life" (40:11, 21) and our spirits go either to a state called paradise, "a state of rest, a state of peace" (40:12), or into spirit prison or misery (40:15). It is possible that not all people will rise from the dead at the same time (40:5), but our "final judgment" will occur after we are resurrected, when we will stand before God to be judged according to what we have done on earth (40:21). We will know that this judgment is just, and we will have a perfect recollection of all our deeds.

ALMA 41:1–4, 10–15—THE MEANING OF RESTORATION

In Alma's day, the meaning of the word *restoration* was vigorously contested. Nehor and his followers taught that God would automatically "restore" everyone to the original state of purity that existed in the beginning. But as Alma explained to Corianton, the meaning of the word restoration means to bring back good for good, mercy for mercy, as well as just for just, and evil for evil, and devilish for devilish (41:13). Thus, unless we repent, our sins will rise with us, along with the natural consequences of sin. When we disobey the commandments, our lives are less than happy: "Wickedness never was happiness" (41:10). While Nehor believed that all people would be saved, and therefore, "sin" was inapplicable, Alma correctly taught the meaning of the word *restoration,* which recognizes both the positive and negative consequences of our actions. Alma set forth this principle in a uniquely impressive chiasm, which very creatively gives a list of pairs in one order (in 41:13), and then he very strikingly reverses that into a pair of lists in the opposite order (in 41:14).

Indeed, God is assisting us at every stage in His plan. Providing us with a way to return home to Him is crucial. When Adam and Eve transgressed the law, God placed boundaries around the tree of life so they could not lock themselves into an eternally fallen state. He gave laws with blessings and punishments so that Adam and Eve could consider their choices. While God could at any time judge us and find us guilty, He instead gives us time to repent before being brought back to Him to be judged. That gift of time to repent is an essential part of God's mercy. By mercifully allowing us this time to repent, God does not rob justice, for the time of final judgment has not yet arrived. This way, as Alma explains in 42:10–13, God is both just and merciful, as He must be, having all virtues.

THE FATHER'S PLAN IN ALL ITS PHASES

Finally, throughout Alma's words to Corianton, Alma speaks about several aspects of the Father's plan. He calls it the plan of *restoration* (Alma 41:2), the plan of *salvation* (Alma 42:5), the plan of *happiness* (Alma 42:8, 16), the plan of *redemption* (Alma 39:18; 42:11, 13), and the plan of *mercy* (Alma 42:15, 15, 31). These ten occurrences of the word "plan" in Alma 39–42 remarkably highlight the five important aspects of the Father's eternal plan. Alma, of course, as a young man had personally encountered the fullness of God's wisdom, mercy, and justice and had found great joy therein. He learned by practical experience, keen logic, and by revelation. Alma asked, with a sincere heart, with real intent, and with hope in Christ. Elder James Rasband has noted, "A penitent Alma pleaded for Christ's mercy and then felt joy and relief when he realized that Christ had atoned for his sins and paid all that justice required" (James R. Rasband, "Ensuring a Righteous Judgment," *Ensign*, May 2020). With every fiber of his being, Alma bore witness to his youngest son, Corianton, in Alma 39-42 of the fullness of the eternal gospel of Jesus Christ. As Alma deeply hoped, and despite hardships, his three sons, Helaman, Shiblon, and Corianton, each honored their father's inspired counsel given in these three father's blessings. All three of them remained true and faithful throughout their lives, as far as is known.

TAKEAWAYS

- Corianton seems to labor under several false beliefs. How many of Corianton's doctrinal errors can you identify?
- How does Alma correct or rebut each of these erroneous misconceptions? Does he use different approaches for each of these issues?
- Which of Corianton's problems are still with us today?
- What has helped you to recognize and to teach the seriousness of sin?
- How can you help your family members increase their faith in the principle of resurrection and in the reality of the world to come?
- How can one internalize more deeply the very core of Alma's explanation that God can be, and indeed must be, both just and merciful?

33: ALMA 43-52

Nephite history shifts dramatically here in several ways as Helaman, the eldest son of Alma, emerges as the leading high priest of the Church, as seven years of invasions grip the land of Zarahemla, and as Mormon's record becomes more like a chronicle. Lessons of a different kind can be learned here, as the pages are filled with stories of Captain Moroni and of Helaman's stripling warriors. The Book of Mormon would not be a real history if it did not include real-life problems such as these. Looking back on the millennium of Nephite history from his positions as leader of the Church and commander of the Nephite army, Mormon selected episodes that he thought would be useful to people in our day. Mormon especially appreciated the hardships that his valiant forbearers had endured. In shorter snippets, here are experiences that everyone can learn from.

ALMA 43:1-2—ALMA AND HIS SONS PREACHED THE GOSPEL

It is always good to put God first. Mormon begins by telling us that Alma and his sons "preached *the word,* and *the truth,* according to *the spirit* of *prophecy* and *revelation;* and they preached *after the holy order of God* by which they were called." As new challenges arose, they relied upon the word of God, the Holy Spirit, and the holy order of the Church. Today, we likewise go forth to meet the challenges of life, equipped with the word of God in the holy scriptures and in the words of our living prophets. We hear and rejoice at the guidance and direction we receive personally from the Holy Ghost. And we stay on the covenant path of the holy covenants and ordinances afforded to us by the holy order of God's power and authority, as Alma had explained, especially in Alma 12–13. These three sources of guidance can help everyone who wonders where they can turn to find truth and goodness.

ALMA 43:4—THE NEPHITES PREPARE FOR WAR

We all need to prepare. We are promised, "If ye are prepared, ye shall not fear" (Doctrine and Covenants 38:30). Watch for the words "prepare," "prepared," "preparations," and "preparing" in these next twenty chapters. It appears often, reminding us that we should "be prepared." As is wisely said, "If we fail to prepare, we prepare to fail," no matter what we may be doing.

The brewing conflict here goes back to Alma 35, when Alma the Younger went to Antionum to try to convert the apostate Zoramites. Alma feared that the people from the tribe of Zoram had formed an alliance with the Lamanites. They had broken ties with the Nephite government and were now angry because the Nephites had attracted away many of the poor people in the city of Antionum. Alma had hoped that people like Amulek and Zeezrom, who had seen the power of God administered by Alma, might favorably impress them. While many of the ordinary people were converted, the ruling Zoramites were not swayed. This meant that the land of Zarahemla was now flanked by Zoramites on the north and Lamanites in the south.

Fighting a war on two fronts is extremely difficult, as history has often shown. This escalating conflict will soon demand the greatest determination, righteousness, and faithfulness that the Nephites have ever needed to mobilize before. This seven-year war will fill the pages of the rest of the book of Alma.

ALMA 43:5—WHO WAS ZERAHEMNAH?

The Lamanite leader at the beginning of this war was Zerahemnah. His name hints that he had Mulekite connections, perhaps as a descendant of Zarahemla. He seems to have been honorable; he refused to take the oath demanded by Captain Moroni because he knew of an oath's importance, which he knew that they would break (44:8). The Mulekites had been more integrated into the Nephite world, especially by the covenant they had sworn under King Benjamin, and it seems that they valued the importance of solemn oaths. Would that all people did.

ALMA 43:9—DEFENDING LANDS, HOUSES, FAMILIES, RIGHTS, PRIVILEGES, AND LIBERTIES

As for the Nephites, they were fighting defensively to preserve their domestic needs, lands, houses, families, rights and duties, privileges and responsibilities, liberties and generosity. Would that we might stay mindful of these same objectives this day and always.

ALMA 43:17—THE YOUNG CAPTAIN MORONI

Mormon tells us Captain Moroni was only twenty-five years old when he led the forces of the Nephites against this first onslaught. Mormon himself had become a military leader at a young age, so he could especially relate with Captain Moroni. His courage reminds us to cultivate the noble strengths in each rising generation in every nation or organization.

ALMA 43:23—CAPTAIN MORONI WISELY SOUGHT THE PROPHET'S ADVICE

Like Moroni, we should all assess our difficult situations and follow the spirit of honor and inspiration. Moroni used spies to gather information, and he also checked with the prophet Alma, who revealed what was about to happen. We, too, can seek revelation, personally or through our Church leaders, to help us decide our courses of action.

ALMA 44:6-7—WHY WOULD MORONI LET CAPTIVES GO WITH ONLY AN OATH?

These people understood the seriousness of keeping an oath. Most oaths in the ancient world were undertaken in the name of some god or superhuman power. Breaking that oath would offend that god, and people often preferred to die than to alienate a god. In addition, Captain Moroni was willing to give his enemies a chance to rethink their situation and change their ways. Even after all that Zerahemnah and his allies had done, Captain Moroni was still willing to say, "I will give you time. You can fix this. You can change." This was a practical application of the very doctrine that Alma the Younger was teaching—that God gives us time. It is His mercy to us, and we see Captain Moroni putting that principle into practice during a very difficult situation.

ALMA 45:2-18—ALMA INTERVIEWS HELAMAN

This little block of text provides a window into Alma's ecclesiastical administration, giving us a role model to follow in knowing the importance of holding interviews. Alma was interviewing his successor as he prepared to pass on his responsibilities. Helaman received a blessing, was interviewed, and was given a prophecy from his father. Alma gave Helaman good news but ended with the bad news that the people would not remain faithful. Then he departed as if he were going to the city of Melek, but he was never heard of again.

ALMA 46:1-4—WHO WAS AMALICKIAH?

Amalickiah was a Nephite, but in Alma 46:3 it states that he was angry with his brethren. He was a member of the Church, had no doubt listened to Helaman preach, but had rejected his authority. In Alma 54:23, Amalickiah's brother, Ammoron, tells Captain Moroni that he was a descendant of Zoram. Most of the Zoramites had formed an alliance with the Lamanites and gone down to the land of Nephi. When Zerahemnah's attack occurred, Amalickiah was apparently still living in Antionum, in the Land of Zarahemla. He may have been biding his time for a moment when he could conquer Zarahemla from inside. After Alma's departure, the Nephite leadership lost an important, trusted leader. Helaman and his brothers began to regulate the Church in all the land. In each city, they appointed priests and teachers. Some of them may have been new appointees, and some may have been the same priests and teachers reinstated under their new leadership. Such times of transition in power can be times of weakness, opening the way for dissenters or enemies, like Amalickiah, to make their move.

ALMA 46:12—THE COVENANTAL SIGNIFICANCE OF TEARING A COAT

It likely wasn't as large of a piece of cloth as is depicted in popular art, but still, there was something extremely important and personal about a man's coat in the ancient world. Thus, Moroni was making a very powerful personal statement. "I am willing," Moroni was saying, "to fight for these things; I will give my life for this." He tore his personal coat, symbolizing that he himself was willing to be torn. This must have been very dramatic for his people to witness.

ALMA 46:13–15—BELIEVERS IN CHRIST ARE RIDICULED AS "CHRISTIANS"

Amalickiah's followers had dissented from the Church, and generally did not believe that the Messiah (the Anointed One or the Christ) would ever come. It was a fundamental axiom of these dissenters that the believers could not possibly know that He would ever come. Thus, calling them "Christians" was not a compliment, and might even have branded them as targets.

ALMA 46:19–21—THE NEPHITES GATHERED AROUND THE TITLE OF LIBERTY

This was an ancient, traditional signal to report for battle. A brief account in Roland de Vaux's classic, *Ancient Israel,* talks about a group of surveyors who were mapping the hill country in Palestine a century ago. They put their sighting picket on the top of a hill and then were unnerved to see the local men charging up the hill asking, "Where's the battle?" Raising the pole was a signal to report for military duty. Captain Moroni evidently knew of this ancient tradition as well, for the thing that brought the people running with their weapons was the "pole" (mentioned in 46:12–13). Captain Moroni also ran a good public-relations campaign, as he placed the words of the battle cry on similar banners on the walls and towers of the Nephite cities.

ALMA 46:21–22—THE NEPHITES ENTERED INTO A COVENANT WITH MORONI

They threw their coats on the ground in front of Moroni—right at his feet. But why at his feet? "We covenant with our God, that we shall be destroyed, even as our brethren in the land northward, if we shall fall into transgression; yea, he *[God] may cast us at the feet of our enemies,* even as we have cast our garments at thy feet to be trodden under foot, if we shall fall into transgression" (Alma 46:22; emphasis added). This dramatic symbolism of the making of a covenant, either civilly or religiously, and then depicting the punishment that would follow if they did not keep it was a standard part of covenant-making in the ancient world. War in the ancient world was always seen as involving God (or the gods) in many crucial ways.

ALMA 46:23–27—WHY DID MORONI REFER TO JOSEPH IN EGYPT?

Moroni pointed to the time when the Israelite patriarch Jacob observed that a part of his son Joseph's coat had not decayed over the many years, and Jacob saw that as a symbol that a remnant of his seed would be preserved. Using this powerful simile, Moroni said, "Let us preserve our liberty as a remnant of Joseph" (46:24), confident that God would then similarly preserve Moroni's people for many generations.

ALMA 46:29-33—AMALICKIAH FLED FROM MORONI'S ARMY

Because the numbers were not in his favor and because he noted the doubtfulness of his followers' convictions (Alma 46:29), Amalickiah then fled to the land of Nephi, taking only a few men with him and abandoning the rest, disgracing himself, demonstrating his cowardice and his loyalty to only himself.

ALMA 47:10-12—EVIL IS PERSISTENT

The Lamanite soldiers who did not want to fight took shelter at the top of the hill. Amalickiah tried multiple times to get them to come down, finally wearing them down and convincing them to support him in his ambitions, selling out his own troops. Persistence was another of his strategies. We need to take great care about the evil forces arrayed around us. Often, they are persistent, and we may ignore them, but they just keep coming back, and sometimes we give in.

ALMA 47:33-35—WHY DID THE QUEEN ASK AMALICKIAH TO SPARE THE CITY?

In ancient warfare, when a new general captured a land, he could do whatever he wanted. If he felt like the people were not going to play ball (so to speak), it was very common for a captured city to simply be obliterated. The queen knew she was in a very vulnerable position. And by murder, fraud, and deceit, Amalickiah placed himself at the head of the Lamanite armies. Then by marrying the queen, the queen's children were now his children, and he had eliminated the future problems of claims by the heirs of his predecessor who might otherwise arise claiming the right to the throne. The villainy of Amalickiah stands in stark contrast to the virtues of Captain Moroni. There is great value in having honorable heroes and role models set forth for us. Mormon knew that. We should select our heroes carefully.

ALMA 49:8—MORONI FORTIFIES THE CITIES

Again, we see the value of preparation. It is important to keep a step ahead of Satan. If we know we have a particular weakness, we need to pray that the Lord will help us and strengthen us. The more specific we are in our prayers, the more the Lord can help us. The Nephites were always one step ahead of the Lamanites in terms of technology. Moroni's defenses often involved strategies that had never before been employed, and the element of surprise worked to his advantage.

ALMA 50:1-6—THE NEPHITES CONTINUALLY STRENGTHEN THEIR DEFENSES

Once the Nephites had won, one might think they deserved a rest. It is a normal inclination to want to relax once something is going well. However, Moroni put the troops back to work. "And now it came to pass that Moroni did not stop making preparations for war, or to defend his people against the Lamanites," and they "did prepare strongholds against the coming of their enemies, round about every city in all the land" (50:1, 6).

ALMA 50:17-23—WHY WAS THIS A "HAPPIER TIME" FOR THE NEPHITES?

Here, Mormon is writing and looking back. He said there "never was a happier time among the people of Nephi, since the days of Nephi" (50:23). What made this such a happy time? The Nephites had endured very difficult circumstances, but never had there been such a mobilized, unified force. Could it be said that the pioneers' crossing of the plains was the happiest time in the Church? It was hard, but they came singing their way across the plains, putting what they had been taught to the test. They were in dangerous circumstances but believed that God would see them safely to their promised land, and He did, on both sides of the veil.

ALMA 51:2-8—WHO WERE THE KING-MEN AND WHAT DID THEY WANT?

The text shows that most of the king-men were of "high birth" (51:8). They may have been unknown descendants of King Mosiah the Elder or King Benjamin or King Mosiah; or they could have been descendants of King Zarahemla, the last king of the Mulekites, as they were called *king*-men (the Hebrew word for *king* is *melek*), so there may be a play on words going on here. It is certainly possible that the Mulekites could have thought the Nephite experience was not going very well from their point of view. With the Zoramites now opposing the Nephites, perhaps some Mulekites were wondering why they were getting caught in the middle of all this. We can understand that from a political point of view. These Nephites, after all, had moved into Mulekite territory with King Mosiah 120 years ago, and had been in charge for a long time. Maybe some of the Mulekites were thinking they ought to reassert their rights.

What did these king-men want? They wanted power, and they again wanted a king. The ending of Alma 51:2 reveals their plan to accomplish this. They did not try to change everything at once, but only claimed that a few "particular points of the law should be altered." Small changes administered subtly and strategically over time can have larger consequences than one would think.

ALMA 51:33-35—AMALICKIAH IS KILLED ON THE FIRST DAY OF THE NEW YEAR

The twenty-sixth year of the reign of the judges in the land of Zarahemla began in a most unusual way. Teancum had crept alone "into the tent of the king and put a javelin to his heart" (53:34). The book of Alma identifies the precise date of that occurrence, noting that when the Lamanites awoke the next morning, which was "on the first morning of the first month," they found their king dead. And looking across the battle terrain, they also "saw that Teancum was ready to give them battle on that day" (52:1), which was New Year's Day. It is not certain, but it appears that the normal new-year kingship rituals may have had something to do with Teancum's choosing to slay Amalickiah on that very day, which was unconventional but crucial. On the day when the king would normally have been re-enthroned and celebrated as a demigod, Teancum chose to leave a javelin in his heart. He knew that nothing could have demoralized Amalickiah's soldiers more dramatically.

TAKEAWAYS

- What can we do to be sure that we "preach the word and the truth according to the spirit of prophecy and revelation" (43:2)?
- Moroni was smart and faithful enough to both gather information and to consult with the prophet before going into battle (43:23). Have you ever done the same when facing an important decision in your own life?
- Did Moroni show mercy to Zerahemnah and his soldiers? Is this a model of how God shows mercy?
- What questions did Alma ask Helaman when he interviewed him before blessing him, prophesying to him, blessing and cursing the land, and blessing the church? (45:2-8)? How important are interview questions like these for us today?
- The chief captains of Amalickiah decided to attack Ammonihah and Noah because they thought they were weak places. What weaknesses do you think Satan is attacking right now in your life and family? How can we anticipate Satan's attacks?
- After great successes, Moroni did not stop preparing for further attacks. How can we prevent our temporary successes from lulling us into a false sense of security?
- Mormon says "there never was a happier time among the people of Nephi, since the days of Nephi, than in the days of Moroni." What circumstances have brought about the happiest times in your life?

34: ALMA 53-63

The authors of these war chapters knew the realities of ancient warfare down to minute details, including traditional skills that included the elevation of heroes who excel, the perpetuation of the military arts by a military caste, counting the troops and knowing how to deploy them effectively, the compulsion of subjugated people to support the war effort, and even wars of extermination and the annihilation of opposing populations. Portrayed also are the powers of captains and chief captains, tense interactions between the officers in the field and the political leaders at home, warnings and exchanging of taunts and offers of peace, and the irreconcilable enmity between certain leaders leading to prolonged eras of intense militarization to gain power and control. Natural influences were depicted: restrictions on the freedom of travel during seasons of war, geographical constraints and significant targets, and the seasonality of war during specific months due to weather. Ethical problems were evaluated in the use of stratagems, and there was a prominent use of religious rituals in regularly seeking divine intervention and protection. The importance of burying the dead and the economic costs and public-health consequences of war and grudges were all considered.

ALMA 53:10-22—THE STRIPLING WARRIORS VOLUNTEER TO SERVE

One of the most remarkable and memorable parts of the Book of Mormon is about the young men who entered into their own covenant, pledging to fight for the liberty of the Nephites, "yea, to protect the land unto the laying down of their lives; yea, even they covenanted that they never would give up their liberty, but they would fight in all cases to protect the Nephites and themselves from bondage" (53:17). They were only one generation removed from those in their fathers' generation who laid down their lives rather than break their conversion covenants. While the fathers were bound by their covenant not to fight, their sons were not. The many afflictions and tribulations of the most recent war had moved these young men with compassion, and it was their desire to volunteer in the war effort. It is interesting to note that these Ammonite youth now called themselves *Nephites* (53:16)—probably adopting this name at the time of their covenant-making.

ALMA 54:1-11—NEGOTIATION FOR PRISONER EXCHANGE

Moroni's terms for the exchange of prisoners required Ammoron to withdraw and go back to the land of Nephi in the south and stop the war (54:10). He also required that the prisoner exchange consist of one man and his wife and children being released by the Lamanites for every man released by the Nephites (54:11). In making that demand, Moroni was following ancient precedent. Capturing women and children was allowed under Israelite law, but they had to be treated humanely and taken as family members (Deuteronomy 21:10–14).

ALMA 54:11-13—"BEHOLD, I AM IN MY ANGER"

Whether it was anger in the sense we use it today, or whether it was great passion for what Moroni believed and knew was right is debatable, but he did call Ammoron "a child of hell," and his tone suggests that this was genuine anger. The letter he sent to Pahoran was even more excoriating than the one he sent to Ammoron. Although such insults may appear to project a strong negotiating posture, hurling insults is usually not an effective way to work out a peaceful settlement.

ALMA 54:20-23—AMMORON AND AMALICKIAH WERE ZORAMITES

On New Year's Eve, Ammoron ends his letter with a standard statement of personal identification, but then added that he was "a descendant of Zoram, whom your fathers pressed and brought out of Jerusalem." (See also the note above on Alma 46:1–4 about Amalickiah's identity.) Interestingly, some of Zoram's descendants were apparently claiming that Nephi and his brothers had forced Zoram to come with them, even though Nephi's record says that Zoram was offered an equal place in the family of Lehi, and apparently Zoram came willingly and never made such a claim, as far as is known, although it is possible.

ALMA 55:4-26—THE NEPHITES RESCUED THE PRISONERS

Moroni was unwilling to accept the "new terms" that Ammoron was suggesting, which was to surrender to the Lamanites and allow them to exercise what they regarded as their right of government. (See 54:1.) As you think about what you know about Helaman and as you read Alma 55–57, what do you find most impressive about his character and how he rose to meet truly amazing challenges? What prepared Helaman to meet those challenging opportunities and responsibilities righteously and successfully? In what ways does the life of Helaman inspire you? What lessons for life do you learn from him? How do his great moments encourage you personally and spiritually? Remember, this is the same Helaman, the son of Alma, whom Alma blessed way back in Alma 36–37.

ALMA 56:16—HELAMAN MARCHED WITH HIS "SONS"

Antipus (who had been appointed the leader of Judea) and the citizens were fighting by day and reinforcing the city by night, and "they were depressed in body as well as in spirit" (56:16). They knew that Judea was next to be attacked. This is a rare occurrence of the term "depressed." The people had suffered many afflictions, and they sensed the inevitability of this next city being taken. Moroni had left the west coast to get up to Bountiful, so there was not much of an army left there to meet the Lamanites.

ALMA 56:18–57—HELAMAN'S SONS FIGHT AND ARE NOT KILLED

"And thus were we favored of the Lord; . . . thus were we preserved" (56:19). Although Antipus was killed in the fierce and deadly battle that ensued, not one of Helaman's sons had fallen. The city of Judea was spared on the third day of the seventh month, about 66 B.C. (56:42), the seventh month of the year being Passover month. Passover was celebrated on the fourteenth [in the evening] and fifteenth days of the lunar month. It was as if the destroying angel passed over these young soldiers—who "did not doubt [that] God would deliver them" (56:47).

ALMA 57:1–4—AMMORON DESIRED A PRISONER EXCHANGE FROM HELAMAN

Note that the date Helaman gives for his negotiations with Ammoron was the end of the "twenty-eighth year of the reign of the judges" (57:5). Helaman refuses to exchange prisoners for the right to possess the city of Antiparah. Surprisingly, this request for a prisoner exchange occurred somewhat before the famous prisoner exchange negotiations between Moroni and Ammoron (54:1–11), which was at the beginning of the twenty-ninth year of the reign of the judges. About a year later, Ammoron wanted to exchange prisoners, this time with Moroni, who refused, and promptly rescued the prisoners.

ALMA 57:6—HELAMAN'S ARMY RECEIVES REINFORCEMENTS

Helaman states that his army was "strong, yea, and we had also plenty of provisions." An army marches on its stomach. This saying, which attests to the importance of forces being well-provisioned, has been attributed to both Frederick the Great and to Napoleon, who said, "C'est la soupe qui fait le soldat" (the soup makes the soldier).

ALMA 57:13–17, 28–36—A PROBLEM WITH UNRULY LAMANITE PRISONERS

Helaman said, "our prisoners were so numerous that, notwithstanding the enormity of our numbers, we were obliged to employ all our force to keep them, or to put them to death" (57:13). Hebrew law forbade the execution of prisoners. Helaman considered the circumstances critical. There were barely enough provisions for the army, let alone the prisoners; but even so, executing prisoners was not Helaman's choice. "It became a very serious matter to determine concerning these prisoners of war" (57:16). Part of the army was given charge over the prisoners to march them from Cumeni to Zarahemla. Gid, the leader of the party, returned the next day, fought to help liberate Cumeni, then explained that the prisoners had been stirred up into rebellion at the news that the Lamanites had an army marching toward Cumeni, and Gid's forces were forced to draw their swords against them. Most of the prisoners died, and the remaining few escaped.

ALMA 58:7-11, 37—DIVINE ASSURANCE

Supplies were apparently not coming; the wait was "many months," and the situation was dire (58:7). Before the provisions and additional troops arrived, Helaman and his officers were strengthened by the Lord, who "did visit us with assurances that he would deliver us; yea, insomuch that he did speak peace to our souls" (58:11). They trusted that "God [would] deliver [them]" despite their desperate situation (58:37). Here is an example of faith at its finest.

ALMA 58:13-38—MANTI IS RETAKEN

The Nephites had been unable to use their previously successful decoy tactics, and attacking the Lamanites in their fort was impractical. The troops of Gid and Teomner hid to cover the right and left flanks in the wilderness. Helaman and his young warriors retreated rapidly into the wilderness area, passing through the hidden troops of Gid and Teomner, drawing the Lamanites after them. Gid and Teomner then slipped in to retake Manti. By marching at night, Helaman's army returned to Manti before the Lamanites returned, and the Lamanites fled into the wilderness and "out of all this quarter of the land." Once again, Helaman's stripling warriors did "obey and observe to perform every word of command with exactness" (57:21).

ALMA 59:3-13—MORONI BECOMES ANGRY AT THE GOVERNMENT

Moroni asked Pahoran for help to strengthen Helaman and the troops that were sustaining that part of the land. However, Moroni then discovered that Helaman had done so well in defending the city of Manti, that all those Lamanite soldiers had fled from Manti to Nephihah, which they easily conquered, causing the Nephite inhabitants to flee to the army of Moroni. This loss caused Moroni to worry about the wickedness of his people, and he feared that they might lose their lands to the Lamanites. "And it came to pass that Moroni was angry with the government, because of their indifference concerning the freedom of their country" (59:13).

ALMA 60:1-36—MORONI WRITES TO PAHORAN

Moroni was discouraged with the people he had tried so hard to teach. This war had been going on now for about a dozen years, so he was likely worn down and weary. He spoke harshly, but due to the circumstances, he felt he was justified. It turns out that for reasons beyond his control, he had little idea what had really been going on in the capital. But he was desperate. They had no supplies, no reinforcements, and many of his people had fallen by the sword. It is obvious that he really cared about his men and his people. Thus, he may have worried that a less pointed or bold correspondence would result in inaction by whoever was responsible for the deprivation of the Nephite armies. After all, he had already written to Pahoran once and received no answer. Pahoran revealed in his reply that he was up to his neck in his own problems. Perhaps the letter was delivered to Zarahemla after Pahoran had left. In any event, it may not have been delivered on time.

ALMA 60:1—WHO WAS DIRECTING THE WAR BACK HOME IN ZARAHEMLA?

It is hard to say. It appears that Pahoran had been rather reluctant to take office and was drafted into his position. When Nephihah stepped down, Pahoran did not even want to take the records. He was not eager to get involved in this situation, but who would have been? They were in a war-torn state of affairs. Unlike Captain Moroni, Pahoran was not eager to dive right into things. But without good people in charge, a democracy is never going to work. This type of government breeds a very real struggle for the voice of the people. Maybe that is one of the overriding themes of the war chapters in the book of Alma—trying to make their limited democratic experiment work. No one had ever tried to do something like what the Nephites were trying to do—having three leaders chosen by the voice of the people. At best, it is not easy to make a democracy work.

ALMA 60:27-29—MORONI'S USE OF WARNINGS IN HIS EPISTLE

Also characteristic of Captain Moroni's firm use of power was his use of warnings of divine retribution: "Except ye do bestir yourselves in the defense of your country and your little ones, the sword of justice doth hang over you; yea, and it shall fall upon you and visit you even to your utter destruction" (60:29). Too often in talking about this letter, people only think of how angry Moroni was and how impetuous he appeared to be, jumping to a conclusion when he did not really know all the facts. Perhaps we need to try putting ourselves in that situation. Moroni had a great reputation, and he had certainly paid a very heavy personal price for everything he had done. He deserved, in a way, to be able to speak his mind openly. He was certainly an honest man. He was not mincing words or hiding behind any kind of protocol, and maybe we can give him the benefit of the doubt, considering his circumstances.

In the end, Pahoran wrote back to Moroni (61:1–21). Pahoran himself had fled to the city of Gideon when Pachus and his deserters had taken over Zarahemla. Holding neither grudges nor animosity toward Moroni (a tribute to the greatness of this man's spirit), he produced and supplied provisions to the army.

ALMA 62-63—THE END OF A TERRIBLE SEVEN YEARS OF WAR

As we reflect on this long campaign, we might wonder what we have gleaned from this that has helped build our character in dealing with the trials and difficulties in our lives. Have our hearts been softened, as we "humble [ourselves} before God, even in the depth of humility . . . [remembering instead] the great things the Lord has done for [us]" (62:41, 50)? This is something that Mormon wants his readers to consider. (See Book of Mormon Central, *KnoWhy* #170.)

Moroni retired and died only two years later (62:43; 63:3). Was his death premature? Was it the result of war injuries, disease, or other stresses of a decade of high-tension conflicts and challenges?

In addition, Helaman regulated the Church but then he also died, only one year later (62:45–52).

Helaman's brother Shiblon took charge of the plates, but he also died three years later (63:1, 10).

Helaman's son Helaman, though still quite young, was able to take charge of the plates (63:11).

Pahoran returned to the judgment seat, but he too died after four years (Helaman 1:2).

Clearly, these seven years of war had taken quite a toll. The weakened condition of the Nephites no doubt contributed to the rise of the opportunistic Gadianton robbers.

In addition, at that time, Hagoth and others, including Helaman's youngest brother, Corianton, began moving to the land northward or sailing away (63:5, 9–10). One might wonder why Mormon thought it important to mention these departures. (See Book of Mormon Central, *Knowhy* #171.)

In looking back over the 63 chapters of Alma, one theme that prevails throughout the book is how crucial it is to avoid the pitfall of pride. Alma's succinct yet forthright words to his son Shiblon serve as a powerful caution for all. "See that ye are not lifted up unto pride; see that ye do not boast in your own wisdom, nor in your own strength" (38:11). Stripping ourselves of pride prepares us to meet God, which is our goal (see Alma 5:28). (See Book of Mormon Central, *KnoWhy* #468.)

TAKEAWAYS

- In these chapters, the many episodes present some interesting morals. Can you list the episodes and their associated morals?
- In these accounts there are also many succinct phrases, such as "having an unconquerable spirit"; "being much confused"; and "they rejoiced in each other's safety." How many can you identify? Ask yourself, "In what context do they appear? What do they say to you personally today? Can you relate to these situations in light of some past experience in your own life?" Select two or three of these expressions and ponder the lessons you can extract from them.
- Moroni wrote a lengthy letter to Pahoran (60:1-36). What adjectives would you use to describe Moroni's letter?
- Pahoran wrote back to Moroni (61:1-21). What adjectives would you use to describe Pahoran's letter?
- Moroni drove the Lamanite army from the land of Lehi to the land of Moroni, where they camped (62:30-32). At night, Teancum killed Ammoron. Teancum himself was also killed (62:35-37), but the war ended (62:38-39). What have you done so that you have been softened and not hardened by trials and difficulties in your life (62:41)?

- As you think back over the entire book of Alma, which of its religious themes and spiritual lessons do you find the most interesting, memorable, and compelling?
- As you think ahead to the end of the Book of Mormon, how has Mormon laid the groundwork for what will come by what he has included in the book of Alma?

35: HELAMAN 1-6

HELAMAN 1—AT WHAT POINT IS A CONSPIRACY TO COMMIT TREASON PUNISHABLE?

The book of Helaman begins with these introductory words: "There began to be a serious difficulty among the people of the Nephites" (1:1). Mormon clearly understated a very dire situation. Within five years, the Nephites had lost several of their most admirable leaders—men who had been pivotal during the long defensive military years. As might be expected, the death of Chief Judge Pahoran had created a disturbance among the people as to who should be his successor (1:2). Three of his sons claimed the right to the judgeship, and one son, Paanchi, took steps to incite rebellion and assure his election.

The legal question became whether Nephite law could punish a person for expressing intent to rebel against the government. This case is only briefly reported, but from it came the Nephite precedent that legally defined the point at which conspiratorial planning became legally punishable as treason. Interestingly, the text says that Paanchi was "about to" set his plan into action: "He was *about* to flatter away those people to rise up in rebellion" (1:7–8; emphasis added). Apparently, he was apprehended. According to other legal documents from antiquity, preparing a rebellion was itself a capital offense. Whether or not the plot ever got off the ground was legally irrelevant. We can surmise that, going forward, this legal concept became a key point in Nephite law.

The execution of Paanchi then evoked a powerful objection among his followers. They sought to overthrow the properly installed chief judge through means of violence, and then blend back into society. As the Nephite government struggled in its campaign against these terrorists at home, external pressures worsened. Within a single year, sensing a moment of weakness in the shaky leadership of the Nephite government, a Lamanite army invaded the capital city of Zarahemla.

HELAMAN 2:4-9—KISHKUMEN THE ASSASSIN

Kishkumen, who had previously assassinated Pahoran$_2$, "went forth toward the judgment-seat" to kill the recently installed chief priest, Helaman$_2$, (2: 6). Near the judgment seat, a co-conspirator turned out to be a double agent and stabbed Kishkumen "even to the heart" (2:9). When dealing with a secret society, one rarely knows who is loyal to whom.

HELAMAN 3:3-7—SOME PEOPLE MIGRATE TO THE LAND NORTHWARD

Many groups of people migrated into the land northward where, the record says, there was not much timber. They solved the problem by becoming experts in building with cement. There are certain locations in Mesoamerica which have cement slabs that were poured 2,000 years ago and that are still in remarkably good condition. Archaeologists date the origin of such building techniques to about the middle of the first century B.C., the exact time of Helaman 3. I like to call this "concrete" evidence for the Book of Mormon.

HELAMAN 3:33-35—FIRMER AND FIRMER IN FAITH?

The righteous Nephites were managing to stay faithful—despite tribulations caused by people at church who "were lifted up in pride, even to the persecution of many of their brethren" (3:34). The text distinguishes that pride did not enter into the church itself, "but into the hearts of the people who professed to belong to the church of God" (3:33). It must have taken great effort to remain strong. The faithful undoubtedly had to be spiritually self-sustaining. Their example is worth noting: "Nevertheless they did fast and pray oft, and did wax stronger and stronger in their humility, and firmer and firmer in the faith of Christ, unto the filling their souls with joy and consolation, yea, even to the purifying and the sanctification of their hearts, which sanctification cometh because of their yielding their hearts unto God" (3:35).

HELAMAN 4:12-13—CAUSES OF FAILURE TO PROSPER

Whatever the economic or political causes, Nephite spiritual failures exposed the Church and the people to impending disasters. Because they boasted in their own strength and did not rely upon the Lord, these people did not prosper. In fact, they lost possession of almost all their lands.

According to these two verses, the Nephite people failed because of:

- The pride of their hearts;
- Their exceeding riches;
- Their oppression of the poor; withholding food from the hungry or clothing from the naked;
- Smiting their humble brethren;
- Making a mock of that which was sacred;
- Denying the spirit of prophecy and revelation;
- Murdering, plundering, lying, stealing, committing adultery;
- Rising up in great contentions; and deserting off to the Lamanites.

We might ask ourselves how we fare when judged against this list.

HELAMAN 5:5-13—HELAMAN'S ADVICE TO HIS SONS

Helaman$_2$ took this opportunity to give direction to his boys, Nephi and Lehi, so that they could carry on the family legacy of righteousness. Helaman$_2$ deeply desired them to remember what he was saying. We cannot overlook the double imperative to "remember, remember." He counseled his sons to remember the significance of their names and then explained the end result he desired for them. We hear urgency in his counsel to do good, not "that ye may boast" but "that ye may . . . lay up for yourselves a treasure in heaven, yea, which is eternal, and which fadeth not away; yea, that ye may have that precious gift of eternal life" (5:7).

HELAMAN 5:11-12—WE MUST BUILD ON THE FOUNDATION OF CHRIST

Helaman gave his sons—and all of us indirectly—crucial advice at the beginning of Helaman 5:12: "Remember, remember that it is upon the rock of our Redeemer, who is Christ, the Son of God, that ye must build your foundation." Throughout history, laying the foundation of a building with a precisely fitted and positioned stone was the key to creating a structure that would stand the test of time. In Helaman's analogy, it is the Messiah, the Son of God, who is our sure foundation. Helaman concluded his remarks to his sons by giving a beautiful description of Christ and his mission. This description gives us hope that if we build our foundation on the rock, which is Christ, we will not be pulled down into the gulf of misery—we "cannot fall."

HELAMAN 5:29-33, 43-49—THE VOICE OF THE LORD

I love the description of the voice these people heard: "It was not a voice of thunder, neither was it a voice of a great tumultuous noise, but behold, it was a still voice of perfect mildness, as if it had been a whisper, and it did pierce even to the very soul" (5:30). A quiet voice is the most dramatic and effective way to get anyone's attention and to prepare them for a message of great importance. In all scriptural instances, the message of the mild voice is the same—it is the message of repentance and faith in the Lord Jesus Christ. From this scripture, we learn that to those who are humble and willing to listen, the voice of the Messenger is also a pleasing voice, gratifying and satisfying in its message. Hearts are softened, and misguided lives are changed. There were 300 people present, the text says, and the voice pierced each one of them to their very souls. Jacob referred to this type of message as "the pleasing word of God, yea, the word which healeth the wounded soul" (Jacob 2:8), souls that are wounded by sin and sorrow and disappointment and loss. It carries with it a message of peace that can be matched by no other source.

This remarkable spiritual event ended with just such a message—the voice from heaven reinforcing a foundational doctrine, "Peace, peace be unto you, because of your faith in my Well Beloved, who was from the foundation of the world" (5:47). We too must put our faith in Christ, the Rock provided from the foundation of the world, who will save us. In times of confusion, pressure, trial, or doubt, you may have received a reassuring feeling of peace. These moments are gifts of the Spirit.

HELAMAN 5:35–39—AMINADAB SEES NEPHI AND LEHI IN THE FIRE

The observers knew that something significant was happening, but it took Aminadab who "had once belonged to the church of God but had dissented from them" (5:35) to explain to the people what was happening. Aminadab was a key player in this prison narrative. He *remembered* enough that he could recognize and explain what was really happening when the others were bewildered. And what did he remember? The words of the prophets Alma, Amulek, and Zeezrom who had unceasingly taught repentance and faith in Christ (see 5:41). We ought not to be surprised when someone like Aminadab steps up to assist in God's work. Well might we remember the words of a beloved hymn: "God moves in . . . mysterious way[s] His wonders to perform" (*Hymns*, no. 285).

HELAMAN 6:1–3—A MAJOR TURNING POINT

There is a short phrase in verse 1 that is easily overlooked. It reports the situation at the end of the sixty-second year of the judges. This phrase signifies a huge swing of the pendulum in Book of Mormon history. Speaking of the large number of converted Lamanites, we read that "their righteousness did exceed that of the Nephites, because of their firmness and their steadiness in the faith." Can you imagine being a Nephite at that time? A few short years ago, the Nephites were fighting the Lamanites. Now the Lamanites wanted to share their testimonies and spiritual experiences, to "fellowship one with another," and to "rejoice one with another" (6:3).

HELAMAN 6:7–13—FREEDOM OF TRAVEL PROCLAIMED

Over two thousand years ago, a very diligent recordkeeper wrote an amazing annual report. Mormon usually summarized such details, but this report is so important and beautifully written that we most likely have it in its entirety and, I think, in its original chiastic form. It is a gem, one of the best examples of chiasmus in the Book of Mormon. The natural balance inherent in a chiastic structure perfectly represents, in a literary way, the newly instituted balance between Nephite and Lamanite lands. Verse 10 marks the absolute middle of the chapter-long chiasm. That turning point states, "Now (a) the *land south* was called (b) *Lehi*, and (c) the *land north* (d) *Mulek*, which was after the son of (e) *Zedekiah*, for the (e) *Lord* did bring (d) *Mulek* into (c) the *land north* and (b) *Lehi* into (a) the *land south*."

Remember, up to this point, if a Nephite or Lamanite stepped on foreign soil, he could be killed or imprisoned on the spot. A theological justification was now offered for this revolutionary policy establishing freedom of travel. Since the Lord brought people into both lands, the Lord intended both lands to be filled with people. Therefore, the people should legitimately be allowed to travel between lands, which is exactly what happened. "And it came to pass that the Lamanites did go whithersoever they would, whether it were among the Lamanites or among the Nephites; and thus they did have free intercourse one with another, to buy and to sell, and to get gain, according to their desire" (6:8).

HELAMAN 6:15-41—THE GADIANTON ROBBERS

Robbers—the perennial plague of ancient civilizations. In the Nephite record, robbers were organized bands who separated themselves from society, opposed the government, and largely subsisted by plundering their enemies. Thieves, on the other hand, were generally members in the community who were guilty of stealing from fellow citizens. Socially and politically, Nephites were squarely enmeshed in a phenomenon identified as "social banditry." Preconditions included disruptions caused by war, famine, economic inequality, sharp social divisions, political marginalization of minorities, and a sense of indignity or injustice. These movements were often rural, led by marginalized military or political figures enjoying the support and protection of their village. They drew strength from people who had been dislocated, displaced, or otherwise alienated from mainstream society. Social brigands were frequently heroes among the poor, acting as defenders and champions of the common people. The record states that a large part of the righteous Nephites was seduced (see 6:38), reminding us of Satan's relentless tactics of leading people "carefully down to hell" (see 2 Nephi 28:21). This concept is reinforced as the Gadianton bandits, working behind the scenes, increased their influence and numbers by quietly infiltrating and finding Nephites who were willing to protect and join them. This is typical *modus operandi* for robbers bringing about the downfall of a great nation. "And thus they did obtain the sole management of the government, insomuch that they did trample under their feet and smite and rend and turn their backs upon the poor and the meek, and the humble followers of God. And thus we see that they were . . . ripening for an everlasting destruction" (6:39–40).

TAKEAWAYS

- **How can we become firmer and firmer in our faith amid trials? Find in Helaman 3:35 a list of steps that begins with humility and ends with yielding one's heart to God. Fill in the steps between these two points and discuss how those qualities build one upon the next.**
- **As we read Helaman 5:12, it is important to note that it says "when the devil shall send forth his mighty winds" not "if the devil shall send forth" Helaman seeks to prepare his sons to face adversity of all kinds. How might this be important advice to everyone?**
- **When have you found that speaking in a whisper (or a quiet voice) is powerful? When in the scriptures does the word "whisper" appear?)**

36: HELAMAN 7-12

In these chapters, we will see that Nephi, the son of Helaman, was a great prophet who tried in various ways to get people to listen to his prophetic voice. What were the main keys to his success?

HELAMAN 7:1-6—NEPHI ARRIVED HOME FROM HIS MISSION TO FIND GREAT INIQUITY

Nephi's teachings had been thoroughly rejected by the people in "the land northward" such that he could no longer stay among them (7:3), so he returned to the land of Zarahemla somewhat discouraged. Seeing the wickedness among the people of Zarahemla, who had been entirely taken over by the Gadianton robbers, "his heart was swollen with sorrow within his breast" (7:6).

HELAMAN 7:6-9—NEPHI LAMENTED OVER THE NEPHITES' WICKEDNESS

Nephi had several great moments in his life. This moment, in which he went up to his tower to pray and mourn the evils of the people and call them to repentance, was certainly one of them. This was a very public expression of sorrow, much like their custom of mourning when someone died.

HELAMAN 7:10—WHAT WAS SIGNIFICANT ABOUT NEPHI'S TOWER?

Ancient American cities had minor market areas in the outlying neighborhoods. There likely would have been main roads that converged to the main market in the center of town. Nephi's tower may have looked like a pyramid of some kind and was probably made of stone. It is possible that this tower also served as a lookout to watch for an approaching enemy. As Nephi bowed himself on the top of this pyramid, "pouring out his soul unto God" (7:11), he was apparently visible enough to be seen by passersby who then spread the word, and multitudes of people gathered to watch.

HELAMAN 7:17-19—NEPHI ASKED, "WHY WILL YE DIE?"

When Nephi was on the top of the tower, he was probably wearing sackcloth and ashes rather than his priestly robes. Many of the people may have thought this was a funeral, and that someone had died. No doubt perceiving the thoughts of their hearts, Nephi asked this intuitive question, "Why will ye die?" He is in fact asking, "Why are you willfully acting in such a way that you are in effect *willingly* dying spiritually?" The question was a time-honored prophetic lament and warning.

HELAMAN 7:25-28—ON HIS TOWER NEPHI PROPHETICALLY CURSES HIS PEOPLE

Nephi, as the prophet, decided to plead with the people and to speak in unequivocal terms to let them know how grim things were going to be for them. He pronounced woes upon them in some rather harsh language: "Except ye repent ye shall perish; yea, even your lands shall be taken from you, and ye shall be destroyed from off the face of the earth" (7:28). It doesn't get much worse than that. When the prophet pleads with us, that is a really good time to listen. Nephi is in that emphatic prophetic pleading mode here on his tower, which was in plain sight.

HELAMAN 8:1-4—CORRUPT JUDGES ATTEMPT TO GET THE PEOPLE TO ARREST AND CONVICT NEPHI

The Gadianton judges were angry with Nephi for stirring up the people to repentance. They began making false accusations and inciting the people to anger against Nephi. In effect, the judges were trying to get the president of the Church—the prophet—arrested. The judges claimed that Nephi had broken the law. They maintained he had illegally reviled against the government. If so, one wonders why the judges did not arrest Nephi. These leaders, as corrupt as they may have been, probably knew that if they dragged Nephi into court, the tide of public opinion and support might very well turn against them. Let us consider an important question. Why did democracy fail in the Nephite world at this time? King Mosiah instituted a form of democracy in Mosiah 29, where judges operated according to the voice of the people. However, as events progressed in the book of Helaman, the government became more and more corrupt. Here are some of the characteristics that are best to have in place in order for a democracy to work properly: The rule of law. A balance between rights and duties. Accountability of rulers to the people. Insulation from bribes. Public events in which everyone can participate. Well-informed and readily available education. It is easy to become a bit cynical about democracy. It is not necessarily a neat, tidy way to run a government. However, in many ways, it offers more hope than just about any other secular alternative.

HELAMAN 8:13-22—NEPHI INVOKED THE TESTIMONIES OF FORMER PROPHETS

After the corrupt judges tried and failed to get Nephi arrested, they pushed a little harder. Nephi took the occasion to speak about prophets and prophecy. Beginning in Helaman 8:16, he began invoking the names of many prophets (eight in all, including Moses, Abraham, Zenos, Zenock, Ezias, Isaiah, Jeremiah, and Lehi) who had spoken the truth as if with a single voice. Just as Jeremiah had prophesied the destruction of Jerusalem, Nephi was now predicting the Nephites' destruction. Here, Nephi uses as evidence for the truthfulness of prophecy the fact that after Lehi departed into the wilderness, he received a vision validating the destruction of Jerusalem.

HELAMAN 8:27-28—NEPHI PROPHESIED THAT THE CHIEF JUDGE HAD BEEN MURDERED

Nephi concluded this speech by prophesying that the chief judge, Cezoram, had just been murdered by his brother Seantum. Unfortunately, some of the people assumed that Nephi must have been complicit in the crime. He firmly challenged them to go and see for themselves the murder of their chief judge.

HELAMAN 9:1-4—FIVE NEPHITES INVESTIGATE NEPHI'S CLAIMS

The people of Zarahemla sent five people to investigate, and of course, they were shocked at the scene that welcomed them. Upon beholding the murder of the chief judge, they all collapsed.

HELAMAN 9:12—A DRAMATIC TWIST OF IRONY

Helaman 9:12 has a touch of dramatic irony. A group of the judges were at the burial of the chief judge and were curious as to why the five investigators had never returned. They were given this as an answer, "Concerning this five whom ye say ye have sent, we know not; but there are five who are the murderers, whom we have cast into prison."

HELAMAN 9:25-38—SEANTUM WAS QUESTIONED AND CONVICTED

In this predicament, where Nephi was brought in as a potential conspirator, he gave the final prophecy of exactly what would happen if the people were to go talk with Seantum. Indeed, they found the blood on Seantum's cloak, Seantum turned pale and answered in exactly the way Nephi prophesied. And then he confessed, exactly as Nephi had predicted. To those who found the five investigators lying on the floor, it looked like the five were the murderers who had been struck by divine judgment. There was a lot of circumstantial evidence that pointed in their direction. Nevertheless, the five suspects could not be convicted on circumstantial evidence under a legal system in which the often-invoked two-witness rule was inviolate. In contrast, Seantum had blood on his garment. He went pale. While this is circumstantial evidence, he eventually did confess, outside of court, having been identified by God. Under biblical law, all those factors counted as witnesses. Meanwhile, there being no witnesses against the five investigators, they had been spared.

HELAMAN 9:39-41—SOME BELIEVED THAT NEPHI WAS A PROPHET

Joseph Smith was a prophet just as Nephi was a prophet, and we can listen to a prophet's voice with confidence. Some of the inhabitants of Zarahemla thought Nephi was a prophet. Interestingly, the five who had been charged with the murder were converted while in prison, so their testimonies also helped to convert other people.

HELAMAN 10:1-3—NEPHI PONDERS OVER THE EVENTS OF THE DAY

The people were amazed at what happened. Some believed, and some did not, but they wandered off and left Nephi standing alone. Left alone, Nephi reacted to this amazing experience by pondering. Notice that he never gloated about how the judges were wrong; he was a humble man who was not seeking his own glory. As he was heading home, he heard the voice of God. "Blessed art thou, Nephi, for those things which thou hast done; . . . And thou . . . hast sought my will and to keep my commandments" (10:4). Is any compliment more precious than this?

HELAMAN 10:4-11—NEPHI RECEIVED SEALING POWER

The next great moment in Nephi's life was when the Lord blessed him forever for his service by granting him the sealing power. "Whatsoever ye shall seal on earth shall be sealed in heaven; and whatsoever ye shall loose on earth shall be loosed in heaven" (10:7). This blessing of the sealing power is the most sublime, personal blessing in all scripture. This power granted Nephi the ability to command virtually anything. "So complete [was] the trust that God [had] in Nephi, so complete [was] the assurance that he would not do or say anything contrary to the divine will, that Nephi [was] granted the promise that all he asks, all that he says, and all that he does in the name of the Lord will be honored. What Nephi prays for he will get, because his hands are clean and his heart pure" (McConkie and Millet, *Doctrinal Commentary on the Book of Mormon*, vol. 4, 385). That is an incredible state of spiritual achievement.

HELAMAN 11:1-4—GOD SENDS A FAMINE INSTEAD OF WARS

Nephi was blessed to be able to "smite the earth with famine" (10:6). In the very next verse, he was given the power to "seal" and "loose" on earth and in heaven. Because "seal" and "loose" can also mean "close" and "open," it is possible that Nephi assumed that his power to cause famine, when necessary, was related to the ability to "close" things up in heaven. It is interesting to note Nephi's motivation for doing so. "O Lord, . . . let there be famine in the land to stir them up in remembrance of the Lord their God, and perhaps they will repent, and turn unto thee" (11:4). Nephi was not the first prophet to use the priesthood to cause drought. Elijah, just like Nephi, used the priesthood to "seal" the heavens to keep it from raining (see 1 Kings 17:1). As the people "saw that they were about to perish by famine, they began to remember the Lord their God; . . . And it came to pass that when Nephi saw that the people had repented and did humble themselves in sackcloth" (11:7, 9), he pleaded with the Lord on their behalf, and the heavens were opened, and the rains came.

HELAMAN 11:18—NEPHI'S BROTHER, LEHI

Throughout this section, there has been no mention of what Lehi, Nephi's brother, was doing. One may wonder where he was during all the amazing experiences Nephi had. Quite unexpectedly, with no more explanation or clarification, we are told, "And behold, Lehi, his brother, was not a whit behind him as to things pertaining to righteousness" (11:19).

HELAMAN 11:23–33—WARFARE TACTICS OF THE GADIANTON DISSENTERS

Despite the great blessings, prosperity, and peace that were then enjoyed in Zarahemla, the lingering political factions opposed to Nephi and Lehi arose again, this time with an even greater vengeance. Those dissenters again commenced war. In these verses, Mormon gives us a clear description of their tactics: raiding, retreating into secret places in the wilderness and the mountains, forming a very "great band of robbers," causing havoc, and following the ancient plans and practices. These tactics have been used throughout time by subversive groups, outlaws, pirates, bandits, and revolutionaries, as the Book of Mormon accurately reflects. Responding to these challenges is never easy. Their mere existence, however, can help people be more watchful, attentive, prepared, and committed to working cooperatively within the frameworks of good laws and collaborative governance.

HELAMAN 11:34–37—THEY DID NOT MEND THEIR WAYS

Mormon did not go into detail about the next few years. After the famine was over, the prosperity of the people and its associated pride caused them to forget God and allowed them to sink once again into the grasp of the Gadianton robbers.

In chapter 12, Mormon can no longer hold back his personal point of view. As an abridger up to this point, Mormon has been very restrained. But in abridging the book of Helaman, he had repeatedly and emphatically encountered sobering evidence of the dark side of human nature.

HELAMAN 12:1—MORMON'S COMMENTARY AND TESTIMONY

Mormon's commentary on the preceding events and behaviors in the book of Helaman comprises the whole of chapter 12. The rest of the chapter expands on these main points, describing the depths of man's folly and the height of the Lord's kindness, patience, and desire to bless the children of men. "And thus we can behold how false, and also the unsteadiness of the hearts of the children of men; yea, we can see that the Lord in his great infinite goodness doth bless and prosper those who put their trust in him" (12:1).

HELAMAN 12:7—LESS THAN THE DUST OF THE EARTH

To illustrate the magnitude of the problems he saw with his people, Mormon demonstrated with imagery from the world around him. He was showing that the story we have just read demonstrated that God keeps his word; if we are righteous, we will "prosper in the land;" and if we let pride get in the way, and harden our hearts, we will suffer, even eternally.

To expand and emphasize his point, Mormon contrasted the obedience of nature with the sinful disobedience of men. Beginning in verse 7 and continuing through verse 17, Mormon vividly describes how the elements of nature are quick to obey the Lord's commands. But not so with man. Joseph Fielding Smith stated: "Everything in the universe obeys the law given unto it, so far as I know, except man" (*Book of Mormon Student Manual* [2018], ch. 37).

HELAMAN 12:13-15—MORMON'S COSMIC VIEW AND IMAGERY

Helaman 12:15 has been viewed as indicating that Mormon had a heliocentric view of the cosmos. However, our modern, sun-centered model of the solar system would have been inconsistent with the beliefs of ancient cultures. The idea that nature was inert was exactly what Mormon did not assume. For him, rocks, hills, mountains, the whole solar system, and even the smallest particles of dust, obeyed the commands of God. Mormon's statements in these verses are evidence that the Nephites understood the earth's motion very differently from the way we understand it today, and that Mormon's commentary was motivated by an awareness of God's active involvement in nature and not from a need to make a scientific correction. We tend to superimpose our view of the cosmos on Mormon's words. There is no mention of the astronomical bodies moving around each other. Mormon is simply expressing a view from his day that resonates with people who believe in the divine Creator, that when God instructs the earth to move in whichever direction He needs it to, the earth moves. Mormon is bewailing that we as people are not as compliant as natural matter. He was not speaking from a scientific point of view, but from a doctrinal and symbolic perspective, a perspective the Lord reinforced when speaking to Abraham. "For I am the Lord thy God; I dwell in heaven; the earth is my footstool; I stretch my hand over the sea, and it obeys my voice; I cause the wind and the fire to be my chariot; I say to the mountains—Depart hence—and behold, they are taken away by a whirlwind, in an instant, suddenly" (Abraham 2:7).

TAKEAWAYS

- **Responding to Nephi's pleas to his people for increased righteousness, we might want to pray asking, "What lack I yet?" as we strive to learn from these chapters.**
- **Why did democracy fail in the Nephite world at this time? How might we strengthen democracy in our own communities, as individuals, as a couple, as a family, or as a neighborhood?**
- **What physical evidence finally justified the legal conviction and execution of Seantum?**
- **In what ways might we understand that the elements of the natural world are obedient to the commands of God?**

37: HELAMAN 13-16

MORMON'S INTEREST IN SAMUEL'S SPEECH RAN DEEP

Helaman 13–16 contains an extensive record of the words of Samuel the Lamanite. It even includes the words that had been added when Jesus gently chided Nephi and the disciples for the omission (see 3 Nephi 23:9–13 and Helaman 14:25). With that level of attention given to Samuel's prophetic speech, readers can be confident that Mormon did not condense this record, or edit it, even if he might have been tempted to do so. In Mormon chapter 1, Mormon explains that he himself "was forbidden to preach unto [his own people], because of the hardness of their hearts" (Mormon 1:17), and that the Gadianton robbers again "did infest the land" (Mormon 1:18), as they had in Samuel's day (see Helaman 11:24–37). Thus, it is even more understandable for him to refer to the fulfillment in his own day "of all the words of Abinadi, and also the words of Samuel the Lamanite" (Mormon 1:19).

HELAMAN 13:1-39–SAMUEL'S MAIN THEMES IN CHAPTER 13

Samuel's speech in chapter 13 includes five themes, which he repeats several times in no specific order several times. The people will (1) harden their hearts against the Lord (13:12); (2) cast out the righteous (13:14); (3) hide up their treasures because they have set their hearts upon riches (13:20); (4) fail to remember the Lord your God in the things "with which he hath blessed you" (13:22); and (5) cast out the prophets, and . . . mock them, and cast stones at them, and . . . slay them . . . even as they did of old time (13:24). Nevertheless, Samuel ended this first section of his speech on a note of hope, "O ye people of the land, that ye would hear my words! And I pray that the anger of the Lord be turned away from you, and that ye would repent and be saved" (13:39).

HELAMAN 13:1-2–SAMUEL PROPHESIES AMONG THE NEPHITES

Samuel arrived in Zarahemla only sixteen years following the famine prescribed by Nephi, the son of Helaman, which had caused the Nephite people to repent. However, the Nephites had again become very wicked. They did not welcome the prophet, and in fact, cast him out.

HELAMAN 13:5-6–SAMUEL ISSUES A TRADITIONAL WAR ORACLE

In verses 5 and 6, Samuel used a common prophetic device known as a "war oracle." "War oracles" are prophetic warnings to the people that God's "army" will be coming after them, or that "the sword of justice hangeth over [them]."

HELAMAN 13:11-13—SAMUEL THEN PRONOUNCES A TRADITIONAL WO ORACLE

Another form of prophetic speech is known as a "wo oracle." The word "wo" is repeated as part of a prophetic warning. Samuel prophesied that Zarahemla would be burned with fire. "Wo unto this great city, . . . I would cause that fire should come down out of heaven and destroy it" (13:12–13).

HELAMAN 13:10,14, 37; 14:10—SAMUEL KNEW HIS SCRIPTURES

In addition to being very adept and inspired in using prophetic speech forms, Samuel also knew and used specific language from previous Nephite prophets, particularly Nephi the son of Lehi, Jacob, Benjamin, Alma, Amulek, and Nephi the son of Helaman. For example, Samuel used a fair amount of "Alma" material, especially from Alma 9 and 42. Alma the Younger had prophesied that the Nephite nation would be destroyed four hundred years after the appearance of the Savior (Alma 45:10–11), and Samuel reflected Alma's words. Of course, that is what happened. Samuel also made use of words of Nephi, the son of Helaman, who stated in Helaman 8:26, "Even at this time ye are ripening . . . for everlasting destruction." Nephi used that phrase twice. Samuel's statement, "then shall ye be ripe for destruction" (Helaman 13:14), likely reflects his familiarity with Nephi's words. While it is understandable that Samuel would have known and used words spoken by his missionary and friend Nephi, it is quite astonishing that these links between Samuel and Nephi were so purposefully used by Samuel, preserved by Mormon, and were included and translated by Joseph Smith with such exactness.

HELAMAN 13:21—SAMUEL WARNS OF DIVINE TALIONIC JUDGMENT

Samuel pronounced a massive rebuke of the pride, greed, and ingratitude of the wicked Nephites who were willing to embrace false prophets while persecuting and rejecting the righteous prophets. He declared God's divine judgment upon the people. His words reflect God's law of reciprocal or "talionic" justice: "an eye for an eye," which was considered as righteous, just, and fair. This basic legal principle is often found in the Book of Mormon (e.g., Mosiah 17:18, 19:20; Alma 12:14, 41:13–15, 49:23).

HELAMAN 13:22—SAMUEL USES ALMA THE YOUNGER'S LAW LIST TO WARN AGAINST SIN

Samuel's warning to the people of Zarahemla reflects Alma 4:9 and 16:18, where Alma, as chief judge and then high priest, twice gave lists of infractions of the law by the Nephites. By alluding to the traditional law of the land, Samuel was perpetuating the rules of public conduct that Nephi's great-grandfather had laid down right there in Zarahemla.

HELAMAN 14:2-7—PROPHECIES OF SIGNS AT THE TIME OF CHRIST'S BIRTH

Samuel gave five signs of the coming of Christ. It would be in five years' time; there would be "one day and a night and a day, as if it were one day" (14:4); a new star would appear; there would be many signs and wonders in the heavens; people would fall to the earth in amazement. As the time approached for Samuel's prophecies to be fulfilled, the prophet Nephi witnessed the growing skepticism of the people concerning the predicted earthly advent of Jesus Christ.

HELAMAN 14:9—AN ANGEL COMMANDS SAMUEL TO PREACH

Angels often quote scriptures. For example, when Moroni first visited Joseph Smith—and many times thereafter—he quoted scriptures and sometimes explained what they meant. As we examine the many forms of Hebrew prophetic speech and scriptural passages in Samuel's material, we can tell that he was using certain conventions and words to make his presentation as formal and official as possible. Samuel had clearly received an education. Israelite prophets were expected to deliver the precise message they had been given, and not deviate one word from what the Lord had told them to say. Here, Samuel had been told, "Cry unto this people, repent and prepare the way of the Lord," and that is exactly what he did.

HELAMAN 14:9-11—SAMUEL'S "PROPHETIC LAWSUIT"

Prophets often delivered God's message by presenting the facts to resemble a legal case against the people. Sometimes they even called witnesses. Samuel issued such a prophetic lawsuit. His entire speech takes the form of a prophetic judgment speech. Typically, as here, the judgment was not revoked, but rather the punishment was suspended in the hope that the people would repent.

HELAMAN 14:12—SAMUEL QUOTES KING BENJAMIN'S TEN-PART NAME FOR CHRIST

Regarding the coming of Christ, Samuel most impressively quotes specific words found in the Nephite scriptures. For example, it is interesting to note that "the name" of Christ in the center of King Benjamin's speech in Mosiah 3:8 is found in Samuel's text in Helaman 14:12. These words are the ten-part (twenty-one-English-word) title for the Lord—"*Jesus Christ*, the *Son* of *God*, the *Father* of *Heaven* and of *earth*, the *creator* of *all things* from the *beginning*." The Nephites had taken the name upon themselves by way of covenant, as they were instructed by King Benjamin.

HELAMAN 14:20-25—SAMUEL PROPHESIES, AS ZENOS DID, OF THE DEATH OF CHRIST

Samuel knew the words of Zenos, who had prophesied about the death of Jesus. This prophecy would have been available only on the brass plates. Samuel was very familiar with Zenos and his prophecies. In contrast to the Savior's birth, His death would be heralded by dense darkness and thunderings and lightnings and all manner of natural catastrophes. In addition, many graves would yield up their dead. The dating of the fulfillment of Samuel's prophecies helps us calculate how long Jesus lived, which is something not known from the New Testament. Using both records—the New Testament and the Book of Mormon—we can state with reasonable certainty that Jesus died on Thursday, April 6, AD 30. His age was 33 years and 4 days at the time of his death. This dating gives profound significance to the timing of the restoration of Christ's church through the Prophet Joseph Smith, which occurred exactly 1800 years later.

HELAMAN 15:5—THE LAMANITES WALK CIRCUMSPECTLY BEFORE GOD

Samuel's description of the religious dedication of the Lamanites is an indication of how completely they were living the law of Moses. There are other formulae for living righteously, but the words here are a precise quotation of Nephi's original instruction to his nation.

HELAMAN 16:1-2—THE SPIRIT OF THE LORD PROTECTS SAMUEL

The book of Helaman concludes with several ominous notes. Many were angry at Samuel, not only because he prophesied that their choices would destroy both them and their great city, but perhaps because he used the sacred name of the Savior revealed at their temple by King Benjamin. They shot arrows and threw stones at him but were unable to hit him because he was protected by the Spirit of the Lord.

HELAMAN 16:3-4—MORE CONVERTS

When the people realized that they could not hit Samuel, God's miraculous protection of His prophet caused more Nephites to accept his teachings. Nephi was busy preaching repentance and baptizing the converts, as well as "showing signs and wonders, working miracles among the people, that they might know that the Christ must shortly come." Samuel fled to his own country and was "never heard of more among the Nephites" (16:8).

HELAMAN 16:14—ANGELS APPEARED UNTO WISE MEN

Mormon reported that three years after Samuel had borne witness of the birth of Christ, "the scriptures began to be fulfilled" as angels began to appear "unto men, wise men, and did declare unto them glad tidings of great joy" (16:14). Despite these prophecies, people still doubted. Their rationalizing portended even greater problems that surfaced five years later. While signs of His birth and death would be seen in the New World, nothing had been said about Jesus coming to visit the Nephites or Lamanites. They argued that if Jesus is in fact "the Son of God, the Father of heaven and of [all the] earth" (as His revealed name said He was, 14:12), then He must "show himself in this land" too and not just "in the land of Jerusalem" (16:19). Mormon knew that our Father in Heaven desires that His children will recognize the signs of the coming of Christ. God has sent and always will send angels to visit worthy individuals who have the faith, strength, and wisdom to declare the "glad tidings" and fortify the faith of those who have not had the same eyewitness manifestation.

TAKEAWAYS

- **What strikes you as impressive about the courage and powerful words of Samuel the Lamanite?**
- **Make a chart identifying all the places where Samuel is quoting or closely paraphrasing the words of previous prophets.**
- **What warnings can we take from Samuel's words about unbecoming behaviors or attitudes about wealth (13:18–23), about rejecting or discrediting the prophets (13:24–29), or about having poor attitudes toward other cultural groups (15:3–14)?**

38: 3 NEPHI 1-7

Third Nephi records one of the crowning moments in all the world's history: the appearance of Jesus Christ, the resurrected Savior and Redeemer, in the New World. The book of 3 Nephi has been called the Holy of Holies of the Book of Mormon because it reports the solemnity of the presence of the Lord at the Nephite temple, which was associated in ancient Israel with Jehovah's appearance in the inner sanctum of the temple. About 3 Nephi, President N. Eldon Tanner said: "Nowhere in scriptures do we have a more beautiful or detailed record of God's dealings with man . . . . [It] will do more than anything else to bring peace and happiness to the world and to the individual."[1]

3 NEPHI 1:2-3—WHO WROTE 3 NEPHI?

It appears that most of 3 Nephi was written by $Nephi_3$, who was an eyewitness to all that is reported here and was also the first of the twelve Nephite disciples. Sometimes Mormon interjects a few words, usually indicating when he does so.

3 NEPHI 1:9—BELIEVERS THREATENED WITH DEATH

Samuel the Lamanite prophesied that the signs of Christ's birth would appear in five years (Helaman 14:2). As the deadline approached, unbelievers decided that if the prophecies of Samuel were not fulfilled by a particular day, Samuel would be considered a false prophet and those who would not repudiate Samuel would be slaughtered. According to the law of Moses in Deuteronomy 18, if a person followed a false prophet, he would get a false prophet's reward—death.

3 NEPHI 1:11-15, 21—SAMUEL'S PROPHECY IS FULFILLED AND A NEW STAR APPEARS

After Nephi cried unto the Lord for an entire day on behalf of his people, the Lord responded, "Be of good cheer; for . . . on the morrow come I into the world." The sign was given: "There was no darkness when the night came." Samuel the Lamanite also prophesied that a new star would appear at the time of Christ's birth (Helaman 14:5). $Nephi_3$ recorded this event: "And it came to pass also that a new star did appear, according to the word" (1:21).

3 NEPHI 2:1-3—THE ROLE OF THE HEART IN APOSTASY

The word *heart* is used five times in these three verses to discuss the influence of Satan over the

---

1 N. Eldon Tanner, "Christ in America," *Ensign*, May 1975.

Nephites who had wandered into apostasy. They became "hard in their *hearts*, and blind in their minds." They now discounted and disbelieved the wonders and miracles they had seen. They imagined it had been "some vain thing in their *hearts*"—something that had been conjured up by men with the aid of the devil to "deceive the *hearts* of the people." Thus, Satan had led away their *hearts* into disbelief. As the people began to resist the gospel of Jesus Christ and ceased to keep some of the commandments, Satan further led away their *hearts*, "tempting them and causing them that they should do great wickedness." Thus, apostasy is largely a condition of the heart. Once the people forgot, took for granted, and rationalized their blessings, they stopped believing and were easily led into sinful behaviors.

3 NEPHI 2:1-3—THE PROPER ROLE OF SIGNS

Jesus taught that signs are not a cure for disbelief (Matthew 12:38–39). The unbelievers in 3 Nephi were not changed by the signs they had seen, including the night with no darkness—they rationalized them away or ascribed them to the devil. Mormon stated, despondently, "And thus did Satan get possession of the hearts of the people again" (2:2). Signs that follow faith tend to strengthen faith, but signs alone do not function well in generating faith and may even lead to rationalization. Well might we say instead of "seeing is believing," that "believing is seeing."

Over the next ten years, unbelief grew among the people. In less than fifteen years from the sign of Christ's birth, the land went from a state of peace, where "the more part of the people did believe" (3 Nephi 1:22–23), to a state of wickedness, casting out and stoning the prophets, making secret oaths, entering into conspiracies, and committing murders. "And the sword of destruction did hang over them" (3 Nephi 2:19)

3 NEPHI 2:4-8—A NEW DATING SYSTEM INTRODUCED

In the one hundredth year of the reign of the judges, it had been nine years since the sign of the Savior's birth and 609 years since Lehi left Jerusalem. From this point on, years in the record were counted from the birth of Christ.

3 NEPHI 3:1-7—GIDDIANHI'S LETTER

The Gadianton robbers now had enormous power and became the chief adversaries of the righteous Nephites. Giddianhi, the robbers' leader, sent a letter to Chief Judge Lachoneus demanding his surrender, claiming that their land and power had been taken unjustly. Giddianhi offered the Nephites the "opportunity" to become part of the secret combination: "Yield . . . and become acquainted with our secret works, and become our brethren that ye may be like unto us" (3:7).

3 NEPHI 3:19-25—RIGHTEOUS PRAYERS

Gidgiddoni (the Nephite general) and Lachoneus (the chief judge) were revered as prophets. The people asked Gidgiddoni to pray to the Lord that they might attack and kill the robbers. Gidgiddoni refused and explained why they should only fight defensively. They should wait to be attacked and be protected by the Lord. After making both physical (weapons of war) and spiritual ("they did put up their prayers to the Lord their God") preparations for the eventuality of an attack, they waited sorrowfully for what might follow (3:25–26).

3 NEPHI 4:1-4—THE NEPHITES STOCKPILE RESOURCES

Lachoneus gathered the Nephites into a defensible space with supplies sufficient for seven years. His plan reflected that of Joseph in Egypt, storing during seven years of plenty for seven years of famine (Genesis 41:46–57). Lachoneus also stressed spiritual preparations: "Except ye repent of all your iniquities, and cry unto the Lord, ye will in no wise be delivered out of the hands of those Gadianton robbers" (3:15). This has inspired people today to prepare for coming challenges. President Ezra Taft Benson has said: "In the Book of Mormon we find a pattern for preparing for the Second Coming. . . . From the Book of Mormon, we learn how disciples of Christ live in times of war" (quoted in Joseph Fielding McConkie and Robert L. Millet, *Doctrinal Commentary on the Book of Mormon*, Vol. 3 [Salt Lake City: Deseret Book, 2007], 321, 327).

Likewise, Elder David A. Bednar has noted that "repeated admonitions to prepare have been proclaimed by leaders of the Church for decades. The consistency of prophetic counsel over time creates a powerful concert of clarity and a warning volume far louder than solo performances can ever produce."[2]

3 NEPHI 4:28—ZEMNARIHAH IS HANGED AND THE TREE IS CHOPPED DOWN

Ancient Israelite law allowed for the execution of people by hanging them on a tree (Deuteronomy 21:22). In later Jewish law, once someone had been crucified, the tree had to be chopped down to remove the wicked person from memory. Likewise, Zemnarihah was hanged from the top of a tree which was then chopped down, obliterating any memory of him.

3 NEPHI 4:29-33—THE NEPHITES SING "HOSANNA"

The Nephites sang "hosanna," praising the God of Abraham, Isaac, and Jacob as they approached their temple (3 Nephi 4:33; compare Psalms 118). The righteous Nephites were still very much involved in God's covenant with Israel, even this far into their history in the New World. But we can also imagine how desperate the Nephites were becoming. They had won

---

2   David A. Bednar, "We Will Prove Them Herewith," *Ensign*, November 2020.

a battle when Giddianhi was killed, but they were soon under siege again. Because the Lord delivered them a second time, the Nephites responded with powerful expressions of piety and worship.

3 NEPHI 5:8-26—"BEHOLD, I AM CALLED MORMON"

Here, Mormon, the compiler and abridger of the Nephite records, identifies himself as "a disciple of Jesus Christ, the Son of God" (5:13). Mormon also noted that he kept the record according to the "will of God, that the prayers of those who have gone hence, who were the holy ones, should be fulfilled according to their faith" (5:14). One of the stated purposes of the Book of Mormon is to show to the remnant of the House of Israel "the covenants of the Lord" (Title Page), and thus it stands as another testament (or covenant) of Jesus Christ. In 3 Nephi 5:25, Mormon used the words *covenant* and *covenanted* five times, presenting this book emphatically in covenant terms.

3 NEPHI 6:10-30—WICKED MEN ENTER SECRET COMBINATIONS

In 3 Nephi 6, peace, righteousness, and prosperity reign for a time. By verse 10, twenty-nine years after the sign of the birth of Christ, contention and pride led again to persecutions. Here we find another complete, rapid example of the pride cycle, which led to lawlessness, corruption, anger, and murder; however, some of the faithful remained "firm, steadfast, and immovable" (6:14). By vv. 28–29, the government had collapsed to the point where the people reverted to their family tribes, and the wicked leaders entered into a false covenant that mimicked the covenants of God.

3 NEPHI 7:15-23—NEPHI RECEIVES ANGELS AND SEES VISIONS

These verses report that in the years before the Savior appeared in Bountiful, many miracles were performed: devils were cast out, people were healed, and Nephi raised his brother from the dead after he had been stoned (mentioned later in 19:4). In addition, because of his great faith, Nephi was ministered to by angels daily. Nephi had been given power "that he might know concerning the ministry of Christ" in Galilee and Judea as Jesus Christ performed miracles, taught, and called Apostles.

3 NEPHI 7:17-18—THE RIGHTEOUS ARE PREPARED

When the great catastrophes came, the righteous were preserved. Nephi "did minister with power and with great authority"; he taught so powerfully that "it were not possible that they could disbelieve his words, . . . so great was his faith on the Lord Jesus Christ." When the calamities struck and when Jesus appeared, Nephi and his righteous followers were prepared to receive His teachings, to begin exercising the authority that He bestowed upon them, and serve Him, having prepared the way before Him.

TAKEAWAYS

- From the events and challenges that arose in the years between the birth of Jesus and his Resurrection, identify three factors that served well to strengthen the conversion and testimonies of those who stayed faithful, even though there was intense trouble and persecution. Discuss how one of those factors could be of help to you as you strive to prepare for the Second Coming of Jesus.
- From 3 Nephi 5, what do you learn from Mormon's first-person introduction, from his personal actions, and from his guiding principles as a disciple of Jesus Christ? What might you prepare as a personal statement of your own guiding principles that you could consider keeping, sharing, or posting?

39: 3 NEPHI 8-11

3 NEPHI 8:3-23—DESTRUCTION AT CHRIST'S DEATH

The destruction at Christ's death had been prophesied by Zenos (1 Nephi 19:10–12) and Samuel the Lamanite (3 Nephi 8:3; Helaman 14:20–29). The three days of impenetrable darkness (8:20–23), and the three hours of tempests, thunder, lightning, and earthquakes (8:6–7) were unprecedented. These were appropriate markers that the "God of nature" suffers (1 Nephi 19:12), and that the "light and the life of the world" (9:18) had died.

3 NEPHI 9:3-12—JESUS NAMES THE DESTROYED CITIES

In a voice heard by all, Christ named the cities that had been destroyed in the region around Bountiful (9:3–12). He repeated five times that this was done "to hide their iniquities and their abominations from before my face, that the blood of the prophets and the saints shall not come any more unto me against them" (9:5, 7, 8, 9, 11). Still, He knows them all, and remembers them by name. Is there anyone who is removed from His loving-kindness?

3 NEPHI 9:19-20—SACRIFICE OF A BROKEN HEART AND A CONTRITE SPIRIT

Jesus proclaimed that He would no longer accept animal sacrifices and burnt offerings. Instead, He defined the new law of sacrifice as the giving of "a broken heart and a contrite spirit" (3 Nephi 9:19, 20). It was stated again in the Book of Mormon not only by Jesus in His Sermon at the Temple (3 Nephi 12:19) but later as well (Mormon 2:14; Ether 4:15; Moroni 6:2). This phrase does not appear in the New Testament, but it was in the Old Testament: "The sacrifices of God are a broken spirit: a broken and a contrite heart" (Psalms 51:17), and "the Lord is nigh unto them that are of a broken heart; and saveth such as be of a contrite spirit" (Psalms 34:18). This ancient formulation of the law of sacrifice therefore may have been included on the plates of brass that Lehi's family brought from Jerusalem, for it was used by Lehi and Nephi (2 Nephi 2:7; 4:32). Other Old Testament references to this principle include the statement by Isaiah, speaking messianically, that the Lord's mission was to "bind up the brokenhearted" (Isaiah 61:1). This expression remains the essence of the law of sacrifice as obeyed by Latter-day Saints today.

3 NEPHI 10:4-6—AS A HEN GATHERS HER CHICKENS

Reinforcing the principle of gathering that had served the Nephites so well under Lachoneus, Jesus used the image of a hen gathering her chicks as a symbol of His continuing loving-kindness. After His Resurrection, Jesus expanded His lament to say how He had (in the past) sought to gather His children, and how He would now do so (in the present) if they would let Him, and how He will yet (in the future) gather His children on condition of repentance and returning to Him with full purpose of heart (3 Nephi 10:4, 5, 6). At and around the temple in Bountiful, Jesus appeared several times to gather and instruct His faithful followers.

3 NEPHI 11:3-7—GOD THE FATHER SPEAKS THREE TIMES

The people who had gathered at the temple early in the morning heard a voice—a soft voice that pierced them to the center and left them speechless, and their hearts began to burn within them (11:3). It was the voice of the Father, which they understood on the third time, "Behold my Beloved Son, in whom I have glorified my name–hear ye him" (11:7).

3 NEPHI 11:8—THE SAVIOR DESCENDS

Following His introduction from God the Father, Jesus descended, apparently slowly, as the people were awestruck. The 2,500-person multitude (see 17:25) turned to Christ in silence. The ancient temple has been called a sanctuary of silence. People sang hymns and there were noises associated with the preparation and burning of sacrifices, but for the most part, the worshippers were silent so they could hear the words of the Lord and the priests. We are encouraged to be silent in our latter-day temples, as well. A verse from Habakkuk states, "The Lord is in his holy temple: let all the earth keep silence before him" (2:20).

3 NEPHI 11:10—JESUS INTRODUCES HIMSELF

The risen Lord said: "Behold, I am Jesus Christ, whom the prophets testified shall come into the world." Much of the book of 3 Nephi from this point forward is Jesus speaking in the first person. The multitude responded in this instance by falling to the earth. In our latter-day temples, we sometimes kneel or, more often, bow our heads in symbolic recognition of our obedience and submission to God's will.

3 NEPHI 11:12—THE PEOPLE REMEMBER THE PROPHECY THAT CHRIST WOULD COME TO THEM

Alma had prophesied that the Messiah would appear in the New World (Alma 16:20). Even so, the arrival of Jesus was a surprise to the people in Bountiful. Their current prophet, Nephi, had not referred to such a prophecy. When the incident occurred, they "remembered" what Alma had said (11:12); but they had not come to the temple expecting this to happen.

3 NEPHI 11:14-15—THE PEOPLE MEET THE RESURRECTED SAVIOR ONE BY ONE

There can be nothing more profound or intimate than having one-on-one, direct physical contact with the Savior—to have Him embrace you and allow you to touch Him. They all came forth, one by one, or family by family, to know with surety that He was the One who was crucified and now stood before them in His resurrected glory.

3 NEPHI 11:16-17—THE PEOPLE SHOUT "HOSANNA!"

Following that amazing experience, "they did cry out with one accord" (11:16). They knew the hosanna shout from Psalms 118:25—it was part of their ancient temple liturgy.

No better expression could welcome Jehovah into their midst—"Hosanna! Blessed be the name of the Most High God!" The ancient interpretation of the word "hosanna" means "save us now." They had heard the Savior explain that He had completed the mission He was foreordained to accomplish. They understood that His suffering had been done for them personally. The hosanna shout was the best expression of their deep love and gratitude to the Lord.

3 NEPHI 11:18-21—NEPHI IS CALLED AS THE FIRST DISCIPLE

Nephi (the former high priest) was then called out of the multitude by Jesus Christ (the eternal high priest; see Psalms 110:4). About thirty-four years earlier, Nephi had prayed to the Lord on behalf of the believers, who had been threatened with death if the signs of Christ's birth did not appear. At that time, Nephi heard the reassuring voice of the Lord, saying that the time of His birth had come (3 Nephi 1:10–14). The two of them were now permanently reunited.

3 NEPHI 11:22-24—JESUS CALLS THE TWELVE DISCIPLES

The twelve men that Jesus called as His disciples had been tested. They had remained faithful through blood and terror and the collapse of the government, followed by the disasters accompanying Jesus's death. Society, as it had been, was obliterated. Now, the disciples could enjoy the peace of Christ's presence. Jesus knew that these Twelve were trustworthy, and that He could reveal to them greater things pertaining to God's kingdom.

3 NEPHI 11:24-28—CHRIST ESTABLISHES THE ORDINANCE OF BAPTISM

The Savior described the process of baptism (11:23–28) and counseled: "According as I have commanded you thus shall ye baptize. And there shall be no disputations among you, as there have hitherto been" (11:28).

3 NEPHI 11:27-37—JESUS EXPLAINS THE UNITY AND ROLES OF THE MEMBERS OF THE GODHEAD

Jesus then teaches the doctrine of the Godhead (11:27–36). The Book of Mormon affirms the unity and oneness of the three members of the Godhead. Jesus emphasized that, while unified in purpose, each member of the Godhead is a separate being, each bearing record of the other two (11:32, 36).

TAKEAWAYS

- Record some notes, either individually or with your family, about what you learn in 3 Nephi 9 about the law of sacrifice.
- What is significant about Jesus coming to the temple in Bountiful? What does it mean to you?
- Review and discuss two or three ways in which Jesus interacted with these people and what you feel as you imagine being there with them on this momentous occasion.
- In what ways are the baptismal instructions given to the disciples in 3 Nephi 11:23–28 the same as or different from the baptisms performed by Alma at the Waters of Mormon (see Mosiah 18)? What things are new here?

40: 3 NEPHI 12-16

3 NEPHI 12-14—READING THE SERMON AT THE TEMPLE ON SEVERAL LEVELS

These chapters can be understood on several levels:

- The first level is private and spiritual—we read to determine where we can be better individuals by trying to develop these kinds of spiritual attributes.

- A second level encourages us to be good members of our families and of society. These wisdom rules will make life more pleasant socially and culturally.

- A third level can be called a covenantal approach, where step-by-step requirements and expectations are given for entering a covenant community.

- A fourth level sees it as a temple text, where we learn to become like God and enter His presence.

Importantly, the Sermon at the Temple lasted all that first day. It begins in 3 Nephi 11 and continues to the end of chapter 18, when Jesus gives everyone the sacrament and places them under covenant to keep the commandments He has just given them. Seeing this experience in that day-long context helps unfold the text's sacred temple covenant-making nature.

3 NEPHI 12:1-11—BLESSED ARE ALL THEY . . .

The Beatitudes in the Sermon on the Mount do not include the word "all" as they do in the Sermon at the Temple. There, Jesus emphatically and repeatedly declares, "Blessed are *all* they . . ." in five places—all those who mourn, all those who hunger, all the pure in heart, all the peacemakers, and all they who are persecuted for His name's sake. Significantly Jesus includes all—everyone—who is willing to come to Him through the strait gate and narrow way He has prescribed.

3 NEPHI 12:18-20—KEEP THE COMMANDMENTS

Jesus taught the covenant to obey and to teach the fullness of "the law and commandments of the Father" (12:19), including repentance. He pointed out that we must keep every "jot and tittle" of the law, since it was not destroyed, but fulfilled (12:18). He asked us to offer a "broken heart and contrite spirit" as a sacrifice (see 3 Nephi 9:20), and to come to Him and be saved. He presented both a law of obedience and a law of sacrifice. Jesus would teach higher aspects of the law once these foundational laws were understood and accepted.

Jesus gives us many important commandments, ranging from keeping the Sabbath day holy to loving your neighbor as yourself. The laws and doctrines of the kingdom of God constitute an interwoven fabric. As Neal A. Maxwell wrote, "The doctrines of the Church need each other as much as the people of the Church need each other. We dare not break the doctrines apart or specialize within them, because we need them all."[1] They are essential to each other, and can all be gathered in one great whole.

3 NEPHI 12:25-26—WHO IS YOUR ADVERSARY?

While we should always seek to agree quickly with our neighbors, another way to understand who the "adversary" is may come from the Hebrew term for an adversary, prosecutor, or plaintiff. In Jewish law the term is *satan*. Lucifer is called Satan because at the final judgment, he will be our accuser. Against him, we will have Jesus as our Advocate, if we have retained Him through our repentance and acceptance. Jesus may be encouraging us to put Satan aside quickly and find refuge in the temple, beyond his reach.

3 NEPHI 12:27-32—A HIGHER ORDER OF CHASTITY, MARRIAGE, AND DIVORCE

Next, Jesus taught the law of chastity as it pertains to covenant marriages. Spouses bound to each other and by covenant with God are to keep their thoughts pure and to divorce only under limited conditions. Ultimately, what God has put together, only God can put apart (Matthew 19:11). Such covenant marriages are not to be taken lightly, but "He that is able to receive it, let him receive it" (Matthew 19:12).

3 NEPHI 12:48—JESUS INVITES US TO STRIVE FOR PERFECTION EVEN AS HE OR OUR FATHER IS PERFECT

The word "perfect" is often misunderstood in our modern, materialistic world. In 3 Nephi 12:48, we are not commanded to be perfect in some absolute sense, but we are invited ("I would that ye should be . . .") "finished" or "at peace with" God, "even as" Jesus is. And what manner of people ought we to be? Even as He is. With His help, we can do that. He has marked the path and led the way, and can love us perfectly, forgive us graciously, and guide us willingly on our journey toward perfection. Elder Jeffrey R. Holland lovingly reassures us: "Every one of us aspires to a more Christlike life than we often succeed in living. . . . If we persevere, then somewhere in eternity our refinement will be finished and complete—which is the New Testament meaning of perfection" ("Be Ye Therefore Perfect—Eventually," *Ensign* or *Liahona*, November 2017).

---

1 Neal A. Maxwell, *Whom the Lord Loveth: The Journey of Discipleship* (Salt Lake City: Deseret Book, 2003), 160.

3 NEPHI 13:9-13—JESUS TAUGHT THE LORD'S PRAYER

Jesus then gave what is known as the Lord's Prayer. It demonstrates how we should pray as a group. Jesus begins: "When *ye* [plural] pray." Several early Christian texts document the use of sacred group prayers, with the participants standing in a circle with Jesus at the center. The Lord's Prayer was undoubtedly intended as a pattern or model for group prayers. Jesus probably used something like this prayer on several occasions, as reflected in the fact that no two texts of the prayer are quite the same (see Matthew 6:9–13; Luke 11:2–4; and 3 Nephi 13:9–13; other early Christian texts offer additional versions). Thus, as the early church father Origen understood the Lord's Prayer to be a model or outline, we too should regard it as a sacred pattern and not a fixed prayer.

3 NEPHI 13:28-30—GOD WILL CLOTHE US

After speaking about washing, anointing (13:16–18), laying up treasures in heaven (13:19–21), and serving only one master (13:22–24), Jesus concluded this section of the Sermon at the Temple by telling the twelve disciples that God would clothe them in glorious garments. The word for "raiment" and "[what ye shall] put on" in Greek is *endumata* and *enduo*, from which we get the word "endow." When you are endowed, you are literally robed or dressed. Here Jesus says, "I will robe you in garments more glorious than Solomon's."

3 NEPHI 14:24-27—WE MUST BUILD ON THE ONLY SURE FOUNDATION

Finally, at the end of this instruction, Jesus invites His followers to build their houses upon a rock. The King James Version says that the wise man built his house on *a* rock, but the Greek version says, upon *the* rock. Helaman 5:12 says, "Remember that it is upon *the* rock of our Redeemer, who is Christ, the Son of God, that ye must build your foundation."

3 NEPHI 15-16—A COVENANTAL PROMISE

Much more can be said about Jesus's instructions on this occasion at the temple in Bountiful. In these two chapters, He testifies that in Him the law is fulfilled (15:4), and He emphasizes that He does not destroy the prophets (15:6–7). He charges the people to be a "light" that cannot be hid (15:12) and to be "the salt of the earth" that is not defiled (16:15). All these elements are presented and deliberately embedded in a holy, covenant-making context. He charges these people, "Therefore, whoso *remembereth* these sayings of mine and *doeth* them, him will I raise up at the last day" (15:1). This is a covenantal promise. It is not enough just to *hear* these words; the teachings must be *remembered* and *followed*. You will then be able to come into the presence of God.

3 NEPHI 16:1-3—ONE FOLD, ONE SHEPHERD

Finally, Jesus explains that He will go to yet "other sheep" in addition to these people at Bountiful, so that all may be "one fold and one shepherd" (16:1, 3). He commands the Nephites to write His teachings so they can come forth and bring others "to a knowledge of [Christ], their Redeemer" (16:4). Jesus concluded these teachings by saying that, in all of this, the words of Isaiah (in Isaiah 52:8–10) "shall be fulfilled." As he was about to leave, He saw that the people were in tears. Moved with compassion, He benevolently decided to stay longer, as we will learn in 3 Nephi 17–19.

TAKEAWAYS

- Identify three or four insights you gleaned from reading 3 Nephi 11–16 in a temple context.
- Mark or highlight several specific words in your scriptures that now have new importance to you as they are seen in the light of the temple.
- Select one commandment Jesus gave in these chapters (11–16) and decide what you can do to keep that commandment more meaningfully.

41: 3 NEPHI 17-19

These three chapters continue the Nephites' holy experience with the resurrected Lord Jesus Christ. Chapter 17 shows Him attending to "the one" and ministering, blessing, and healing in very personal ways. There is an emphasis on family relationships here, as well as on individuals. In chapters 18 and 19, the Nephites enter into a new covenant relationship with the Father as they partake of the sacrament and are baptized and receive the Holy Ghost.

3 NEPHI 17:6-10–FILLED WITH COMPASSION, JESUS HEALED THEM ONE BY ONE

When Jesus was about to leave, He looked upon the people and saw that they were in tears. Jesus Christ then interacts with these people at a very personal level, as His "I-You" statements help us appreciate: "I perceive that **ye** desire that **I** should show unto **you** what **I** have done unto **your** brethren at Jerusalem, for **I** see that **your** faith is sufficient that **I** should heal **you**" (17:7–8). They needed no further encouragement. The throng moved forward with "one accord," and in individual acts of love, Jesus healed them, "every one" (17:9). Jesus had already announced His plan to depart for the night, and He mentioned other "appointments" on His "schedule." His choice to remain with them to bless and heal them one by one speaks volumes about Christ's priorities.

After they had been healed, those people came forward and bathed His feet with their tears. I can only imagine that this was everyone—men, women, and children—wanting and trying to reciprocate the love that He had shown to them. If we desire to follow the example of Jesus, we too need to minister one by one, looking at others' circumstances, and loving and serving them.

3 NEPHI 17:14-15, 19-25–JESUS BLESSED THE PARENTS AND THE CHILDREN

Jesus then "commanded that their little children should be brought" to Him, and He set them on the ground around Him. Then, Jesus stood in "the midst" of them, with the parents kneeling in a large circle around them (17:11–13). Before turning to the children, Jesus blessed their parents and prayed inconceivable things over them. The record of the incident says, "No one can conceive of the joy that filled our souls when we heard him pray for us unto the Father" (17:17). Jesus appreciated the sacrifices and devotion of parents. As Jesus looked around after blessing them, He said to those parents, "Blessed are ye because of your faith. And now behold, my joy is full" (17:20).

Jesus next turned to the children and blessed them one by one, and after that, He turned back to the parents and He said, "Behold *your* little ones" (17:23; emphasis added). Had they become theirs in some eternal way that they had not been before? These blessings were given in the presence of God, angels, and all these witnesses (17:24–25).

Further Reading: Book of Mormon Central, "Why Did Jesus Minister to the People One by One? (3 Nephi 17:21), *KnoWhy* 209 (October 14, 2016).

3 NEPHI 18:3-7—JESUS'S WORDS IN BLESSING THE SACRAMENT

As Jesus administered the sacrament of the bread and the wine, these people covenanted to remember Him always and to keep the commandments that He had just given them. This clearly created a covenantal relationship between the Savior and the Nephites. Naturally, as Jesus offered the sacrament prayers, He spoke in the first person. He told everyone gathered there that they did this "in remembrance of *my* body which *I* have shown unto you. And it shall be a *testimony* unto *the* Father" (18:7; emphasis added). As you hear the sacrament prayers pronounced in Church, listen for Jesus's voice and words in these beautiful prayers. You will find new appreciation for how close the current prayers are to Jesus's original words.

3 NEPHI 18:15-21—HELPFUL INSTRUCTIONS ON PRAYER

Under the old Nephite and Jewish laws, people prayed three times a day. As long as they prayed morning, mid-day, and night, that was good (see Alma 34:21). Now, in 3 Nephi 18:15, Jesus taught the Twelve to *pray always* to avoid temptation. Then Jesus focused His instructions on the multitude, "Verily, verily . . . ye must watch and *pray always* lest ye be tempted by the devil" (18:15; emphasis added). The words "verily, verily" signal double importance. Asking to avoid temptation probably should be a part of many prayers.

In 3 Nephi 18:19, Jesus next taught that they should always pray *to the Father in His name*. Here Jesus offers to unite us with the Father through His name. In 18:20, we are also taught that in prayer, the petitioner should believe they will receive, and ask for what is right.

In 3 Nephi 18:21, the people were next instructed to pray in their families. Nowhere in the Bible does it talk about praying in the family, and to this, Jesus added, "that your wives and children may be blessed." Our Heavenly Father is waiting to bless us, but He wants us to ask.

3 NEPHI 18:37—AUTHORITY TO GIVE THE GIFT OF THE HOLY GHOST

At the beginning of this day, Jesus ordained twelve Apostles and gave them the power to baptize, to cleanse with water. At the end of this day, before He ascended back into heaven, He gave them a second power—the power to cleanse by fire, or with the Holy Ghost. The words used by Jesus in giving the Twelve the power and authority to bestow the gift of the Holy Ghost can be found in Moroni 2. And likewise, Joseph Smith and Oliver Cowdery received the power to baptize from John the Baptist on one day, and the power to give the Holy Ghost was given on a later day.

3 NEPHI 18:38-39—JESUS ASCENDED INTO HEAVEN

In this holy envelopment, the twelve disciples were able to see and testify that Jesus ascended back into heaven. They had seen Him come down, and they testified that He had returned to that holy place and promised to come again.

3 NEPHI 19:1-3—THE PEOPLE SPREAD THE WORD OF CHRIST'S MINISTRY

At the close of the first day, the disciples were told to go out and bring as many as they could for the next day. We know that the crowd was larger on the second day, meaning that people came when someone ministered to them and invited them to this spiritual feast.

3 NEPHI 19:19-23, 27-29—JESUS OFFERED AN INTERCESSORY PRAYER

As Jesus pours out His heart to His Father on behalf of His disciples in these tender verses, we are reminded of His other great intercessory prayer, which He offered on the occasion of the Last Supper as found in John 17, and where He clarified His oneness with and distinctness from the Father (see v. 17). In this Book of Mormon setting, we learn more about the nature of the Godhead by carefully noting how Jesus prays to the Father and what He prays for. This interaction gives us a rare look into the Godhead, Their distinctness and yet Their oneness.

3 NEPHI 19:25—THE PRIESTLY BLESSING

How do words in 3 Nephi 19:25 relate to the priestly blessing in Numbers 6:24–27? Here is the traditional high priestly blessing: "The Lord bless thee, and keep thee: The Lord make his face shine upon thee, and be gracious unto thee: The Lord lift up his countenance upon thee, and give thee peace" (Numbers 6:23–26).

Similarly, the text of 3 Nephi 19:25 says: "His countenance did smile upon them, and the light of his countenance did shine upon them." In fact, the face of God is what the ancient blessing was all about: that you may see His face, that He will smile upon you with His face of approval, that you will know that He loves you, that He accepts you, and that He will be gracious to you. What greater blessing could there be?

Further Reading: Book of Mormon Central, "Why Did Jesus Allude to the Priestly Blessing in Numbers 6? (3 Nephi 19:25), *KnoWhy* 212 (October 19, 2016).

TAKEAWAYS

- **Why did Jesus teach people things that He says they would not be able to understand?**
- **What does it mean to "ponder upon the things" that one hears in Church settings?**
- **Above all, what would you want the Lord to ask for, if He were to pray for you?**
- **What have you learned in these chapters that strengthens eternal family relations?**
- **How can you get more from the sacrament by noticing details found in 3 Nephi 18?**
- **What can we learn in 3 Nephi 19 about the Godhead?**
- **How do the words "and they were filled with desire" strike you (19:24)?**

42: 3 NEPHI 20-26

These chapters have been called Jesus's "Covenant Sermon." It is deep and dense and delightful. These notes will help you unlock its structure and wonderful messages. Here, Jesus draws on passages in Isaiah, Micah, and Malachi 3–4. He gives the covenant people a crucial role in helping the plan of the Father to bless people throughout the world. And the Father promises that He will fulfill all His promises and will never forget His people.

You will want to study these chapters for deeper understanding. Above all, remember that the Spirit teaches line upon line.

3 NEPHI 20:10-22:17—THE FATHER'S COVENANT WITH ALL ISRAEL

On this solemn occasion, Jesus shifts His attention to the collective well-being of the entire covenant people, of which this people, in Bountiful, are just one remnant (20:10). Jesus wants to tell these people that they are a crucial part of God's covenant people, that God has not forgotten them, that He would never forget them, that they will be gathered and blessed with all the blessings He has promised. Interestingly, Jesus never uses the word *covenant* here in the plural. This covenant sermon focuses on only one covenant, namely the Father's covenant with His people through the seed of Jacob, Isaac, and Abraham (20:25, 27), promising them eternal posterity and a place of everlasting inheritance through "the fulness of [Christ's] gospel," which "shall be preached unto them; And they shall believe" that Jesus Christ is "the Son of God" (20:30–31).

Throughout this extended discourse, Jesus speaks on behalf of the Father more directly than He had before. The resounding use of first-person pronouns personalizes this powerful text: "I will establish," "I will return," "I would give," "I will cut off," "I will go before them," speaking by divine authority on behalf of the Father, with whom (of course) Jesus is one.

3 NEPHI 20-25—THE "PROPHETIC WORLDVIEW" OF THE NEPHITES

To understand what Jesus is communicating, it is helpful to remember the outline of "the Nephite prophetic worldview" which basically would have been familiar to the people gathered to hear Jesus in Bountiful. As developed and used by Nephi and others, this "worldview" anticipated the future in four main stages:

1.) The scattering of Israel,

2.) The coming of the Messiah and His rejection by those in Jerusalem,

3.) The day of the Gentiles, and

4.) The victory of God over evil through the reestablishment of Israel and the judgment of the world.

By the time the resurrected Lord delivered this discourse in 3 Nephi, stage 1 (the scattering of Israel) and stage 2 (the coming and rejection of the Messiah) had already occurred. On Day 1 at Bountiful, as Jesus spoke to His disciples, He had begun by focusing on parts of stage 3 (covered back in 3 Nephi 15–16).

Now on Day 2 at Bountiful, Jesus dwells deeply on stage 4 (about the victory of God and the reestablishment of Israel). He does this by quoting Isaiah 52:7–8, about the "watchmen" who will lift up their voices in a day of fullness (covered in 3 Nephi 20:32, 40–41). He also quotes Micah 4:12–13 and 5:8–9 about the Gentiles repenting and receiving blessings (covered in 3 Nephi 20:15–20). He finally quoted all of Isaiah 54 (in 3 Nephi 22:1–17) about the end of times, allegorically telling of the barren or childless woman (symbolizing the church during the Great Apostasy) who will be comforted, become fruitful, and will enlarge and richly adorn her tent (or tabernacle) with seed (children) who will eternally inherit. Jesus then concludes by quoting Malachi 3–4 about the earth not being wasted at His final coming (covered in 3 Nephi 24–25). Obviously, this can be hard to follow, but just knowing these passages in Micah 4–5, Isaiah 54, and Malachi 3–4 makes all this much easier to follow and to appreciate. Here are some of the details and how Jesus illuminates those prophecies in particular.

3 NEPHI 20:16-25—THE LORD'S PEOPLE MAKE, KEEP, AND RENEW COVENANTS WITH HIM

Jesus first quotes Micah after saying that there will be many "remnants" scattered abroad (20:13–14). One remnant of Israel (or Jacob) in particular "will return" unto the Lord and it will be a great sign when "these things" will come forth "unto them" (21:4). Then, in verses 22–27, Jesus goes on to teach about the covenant made with Jacob regarding the land, and also the covenant made with Abraham regarding the blessing of all the kindreds of the earth through his seed. It is interesting that he lists these two patriarchs in the reverse order from our normal expectations. In Leviticus 26:42, about the Holy of Holies in the book of Leviticus, the Lord likewise promises, in reverse order, "Then will I remember my covenant with Jacob, and also my covenant with Isaac, and also my covenant with Abraham will I remember." I think we have here in the Book of Mormon a credible and appropriate reference back to the holiest spot in the book of Leviticus, which is the holiest of all places in the Old Testament.

3 NEPHI 20:29-30—THE LORD WILL GATHER ISRAEL

This covenant speech next emphasizes the role of the Nephites in the Father's plan of salvation and of the fulfillment of God's covenant. Jesus began by explaining how all of Israel will be scattered and lost, but that the Gentiles would be the nursing fathers to help bring the gospel back to the people who had been scattered. The key point is that the coming forth of the Book of Mormon will be the sign (3 Nephi 21:5, 7) whereby everyone can know that the word of God is coming forth again to the scattered Israelites, and that the Gentiles, if they will believe, can then become members of the house of Israel. Jesus explained how this will happen, how people will rejoice and be gathered in, how a New Jerusalem will be formed, and how the victory of God over the forces of evil will eventually be complete (covered in 3 Nephi 22). This promise would have been especially meaningful to the Nephites, who had survived massive destruction and tragedy. As members of this covenant, we are the children receiving the blessings that God promised to Abraham, Isaac, and Jacob, through the gospel of the Lord Jesus Christ. As members of The Church of Jesus Christ of Latter-day Saints, we are the inheritors of this record. We are to take it to all the world as an ensign (a banner) to the nations, to bring to pass the fulfillment of the great covenants and promises of God. The Lord has promised that people from all the nations of the earth will flow unto the House of the Lord and unto the covenant of the Lord, so that they may be blessed eternally.

3 NEPHI 20:35-36—WHAT IS THE MEANING OF THE WORD "HOLY" IN JESUS'S SERMONS?

It is revealing to look at where the word "holy" appears and what it means. The word "holiness" in both Greek and Hebrew has no synonym, making it difficult to define. To understand holiness, we must look contextually at how this word is used. We encounter here several references to God's holy arm, to a holy city (the New Jerusalem), to holy prophets, and to holy angels, along with the Holy Ghost. Prophets mention a holy calling, a holy ordinance, the holy order of the high priesthood, holy scriptures, holy commandments, the Holy of Holies, and more.

Thus, the Lord's visit to these righteous Nephites at their temple can well be termed the Holy of Holies of the Book of Mormon. In 3 Nephi we encounter the holy presence of God and the words of the Lord as, previously, only the high priest was allowed to experience while in the Holy of Holies. The tablets of the Ten Commandments had been stored inside the ark of the covenant, but now Jesus preaches openly of new commandments. The rod of Aaron, also inside the ark of the covenant, had represented the holy Aaronic priesthood authority, and now Jesus gives the higher priesthood authority to His disciples. The shewbread of the temple, which previously could be eaten only by the high priest, anticipated Jesus's miraculous administration of the sacrament; here it was given to all the covenant people. The Holy of Holies is described in Jewish literature as a place of the fullness of joy. Above all, holiness is a state of joy and rejoicing. In 3 Nephi, this now was certainly a time of immense joy and happiness for those Nephite people. Today, we too are striving to be true and faithful Latter-day *Saints,* or *holy ones.* Holiness should define our relationship with God, our relationships within our families, our conduct within Church circles, and our dealings with all other people.

3 NEPHI 22:13—THE COVENANT IS A FAMILY COVENANT

The covenant of God with Abraham and Sarah is not just a national promise; it is also a family promise. In 3 Nephi 17:23, Jesus said, "Behold your little ones," and the multitude saw their children in a sacred environment.

When Jesus returned for Day 2, the people apparently brought their children with them again. Indeed, Jesus continued to minister to them, for the children spoke "unto their fathers great and marvelous things" (26:14), and the people "both saw and heard these children; yea, even babes did open their mouths and utter marvelous things" (26:16). After years of war and the recent natural disasters, imagine the children in attendance hearing the words, "Great shall be the peace of thy children" (3 Nephi 22:13).

3 NEPHI 23:6–25:6—OTHER SCRIPTURE GIVEN, NEPHITE RECORD CORRECTED

Up to this point, Jesus had quoted and expounded scriptures that were known among the Nephites. After Jesus "had expounded all the scriptures unto them which they had [previously] received," He discussed "other scriptures . . . that ye have not" (23:6). Accordingly, in these chapters, Jesus added one missing point regarding the prophecy of Samuel the Lamanite, and then He recited to them Malachi 3–4, which they evidently did not already have.

As a first matter of business, the Lord asked Nephi to "bring forth the record which ye have kept," and Nephi presented to the Lord the records his people had kept. The Lord "cast his eyes upon them" and accepted them (23:8), with one needed correction regarding Samuel's prophecy. That point was then added and now appears in Helaman 14:25.

Jesus specifically asked if Samuel the Lamanite's prophecies were *fulfilled*. He was concerned that the Nephites noted the *fulfillment* of Samuel's prophecies. Think of all the times in the New Testament gospels when the author says, "because it was written," "as it was written," or "to fulfill that which was written." It is important to the Lord that we take note of when prophecy is fulfilled. This is also meaningful evidence that in scriptural text, every word is important. Sometimes we read the scriptures too quickly; the slower we read them, the more we will look at each word and wonder: Why did the Lord or His prophets want these particular words in this text? The answers will speak to our hearts and souls, with meaning far beyond what ink on the printed page might give.

3 NEPHI 24–25—JESUS QUOTES MALACHI 3–4

What reasons might Jesus have had for giving the Nephites these two chapters in particular? Remember that He met again with these people, on Day 2, near their temple and with their children. As you read these two chapters from the book of Malachi, see how many correspondences you can spot between words in Malachi and the words or themes of the temple. Here are a few examples:

Malachi 3:3–10 making pure consecration of tithes and offerings
Malachi 3:18 being able to discern between good and evil
Malachi 4:5–6 bringing parents and children, ancestors and posterity together

And remember also that when Moroni appeared to Joseph Smith, he quoted Malachi 4:5–6 (see Doctrine and Covenants 2), which we can now understand, because Jesus had emphasized those words in speaking to the Nephites, the very record which Moroni had kept and treasured.

3 NEPHI 26:13-21—THE TONGUES OF CHILDREN ARE LOOSED

I believe those little children who were present on this occasion are the key to understanding 4 Nephi. There were four generations of collective righteous living, peace, and happiness following the appearance of Jesus among these people. Those little children would have lived long enough to testify of their experiences to future generations. Four generations of people could have been taught by those little children who grew up, married, and had children and grandchildren.

TAKEAWAYS

- Amidst the explanations given in this covenant sermon, Jesus uses several key words and memorable expressions. Watch for these interlocking pieces, especially as they are sometimes used more than once. In general, as you read these chapters, ask yourself on each page, "What do I learn here about Jesus Christ? About the Father and the Godhead? About the meaning of prophetic words of Isaiah and Micah?
- What do the words and assurances in this chapter mean to you personally?
- What are your roles in God's covenant plan?
- As prophecies are fulfilled in our day, how do we move ourselves from being spectators to being witnesses or agents of their fulfillment?
- Have you had some experiences in which recordkeeping proved especially crucial?
- What is significant about expounding things "both great and small" (3 Nephi 26:1)?
- How does seeing "all things even from the beginning until the time [Jesus] should come in his glory" help people to live righteously and happily (3 Nephi 26:3)?
- Why does Mormon not write any more about what Jesus taught to the Nephites (3 Nephi 26:9)?

43: 3 NEPHI 27-4 NEPHI

3 NEPHI 27:1-3—THE NAME OF THE CHURCH

When Jesus returned to them again, His ordained leaders especially understood that Christ's fulfillment of the law of Moses now required them to abandon much of the old organization and many of the rules that had applied to them based on their membership in one of the tribes of Israel. For example, under the law of Moses, Israelites had needed to know their lineage to fulfill marriage requirements and make sense of land ownership and inheritance rights. Now, the people were living in a new day of no "-ites." Naturally an early question was, "Then what is our new name as a people?" They wisely went to Jesus for the answer.

3 NEPHI 27:4-9—THE CHURCH SHALL BE CALLED AFTER JESUS CHRIST

Jesus answered the disciples' question with a question of His own: "How be it my church save it be called in my name?" (27:8). The sacredness and importance of the name of the Lord is one of the first lessons of holiness. When you bear the name of Jesus Christ—the name of Jehovah—that makes you a holy person. On the crown or headpiece of the high priest officiating at the Temple of Solomon were the words: "Holiness to Jehovah." The name of Jehovah was on his forehead because he, as the high priest, represented Jehovah, which made him a holy being.

3 NEPHI 27:13-22—THE LORD'S DISCOURSE ON HIS "GOSPEL" IS CONTINUED

In 3 Nephi 11, Jesus had defined what He called His "doctrine": faith in Jesus Christ as the Son of God, repentance, baptism, receiving the witness of the Holy Ghost, enduring to the end, and living together without disputation. Those precepts are what people today speak of as the first principles and ordinances of the gospel, and that is what the Nephite disciples had been teaching. However, the points in 3 Nephi 11 were only the initial requirements. Nowhere in the four gospels of the New Testament did Jesus define what He meant by "the gospel." In 3 Nephi 27:13–22, we have a full statement of what the Lord considers the gospel to be.

Now the Savior used the more expansive word "gospel" rather than "doctrine," and He presented more detail on the central points of the plan of salvation in which "the doctrine of Christ" is embedded. The "gospel" includes not only what Jesus will do to deliver salvation to all mankind (27:13–15), but also what people must do to "be lifted up at the last day" (27:16–20). Altogether, this is "my gospel; and ye know the things that ye must do" (27:21). Jesus's central purpose is to bring us all back, worthily, into the presence of the Father, through obedience, ordinances, and covenants. Throughout 3 Nephi, there is an escalation of teaching, beginning with the simplest first principles and progressing to more complex requirements and more expansive teachings. His later statements especially include principles that clarify how and why one can prepare to successfully pass through the process of God's judgment (27:15–19).

3 NEPHI 28—THE THREE NEPHITES

In its entirety, 3 Nephi 28 demonstrates Jesus's power over death. He granted requests regarding the timing and transition of nine of the disciples into life beyond death. He sensed the desires of the three others to never taste death but to remain as special servants to assist with the establishment of the kingdom of God on earth. As evidence that He indeed had power over mortality, Jesus granted and carried out these righteous and appropriate requests at a time when it was needed to ensure that the work of the kingdom would endure (28:9; compare Doctrine and Covenants 7). All of 3 Nephi can be seen as a book about Jesus's conquest of death. He controlled the timing of His birth. He controlled the destructions and deaths at the time of His Crucifixion. He took up His gloriously resurrected body. He had power over His coming and going. Seeing all of 3 Nephi as a temple text, one remembers that the final sealing ordinance in the temple pertains to promises of coming forth in the resurrection, overcoming death, and going forth into eternal life. And thus, it makes sense that 3 Nephi should end by talking about and giving actual reports of overcoming death. As 3 Nephi is the Holy of Holies of the Book of Mormon, it culminates here on its holiest pinnacle of the mountain of the Lord at heaven's gate.

3 NEPHI 28:4-26—THE SPECIFIC DESIRE AND BLESSING OF THREE NEPHITES

In 3 Nephi 28, the three Nephites (who desired to remain on the earth until the return of the Savior) received their assignments and blessings. They were never to "taste of death," but were to be "changed in the twinkling of an eye" at the Second Coming (28:7–8). Mormon may have had personal as well as prophetic reasons for recording so much about the Three Nephites. The events of 3 Nephi occurred about AD 34–35; Mormon began his work and writings around AD 350—more than 300 years later. As recorded in 28:26, the Three Nephites personally ministered to Mormon—he knew them and knew their mission. They were present when the Savior came to the Bountiful temple. They had personally witnessed Christ's appearance, had heard Him, and had talked with Him in the era about which Mormon was abridging and writing. They might have helped Mormon, supplying input to his account, or perhaps checking his accuracy. Moreover, Mormon lived in a time of great apostasy and hardship; it must have been a great comfort when these three men came to minister to him.

3 NEPHI 28:36-40—MORMON DESCRIBES THE CHANGE WROUGHT ON THE THREE NEPHITES

In the temple, we are endowed with power—particularly power to overcome the adversary. This power to command Satan to depart exists in holy beings. This power is referred to in the Psalms

(Psalms 6:8), in the Sermon at the Temple, and in the Sermon on the Mount (3 Nephi 14:23; Matthew 7:23). The Three Nephites were holy men endowed with power over Satan "that he could not tempt them; and they were sanctified in the flesh, that they were holy, and that the powers of the earth could not hold them." These verses tell us something about being holy, and how holiness is a power that is the opposite of the forces of Satan. With this holiness, we not only neutralize the forces of Satan, but we can also overcome them.

3 NEPHI 29-30—MORMON'S CONCLUDING WORDS OF WARNING

In these concluding chapters, Mormon speaks to all people who are not of the house of Israel. He alerts all readers that when "these sayings shall come unto the Gentiles," all should expect the beginning of a major, long-promised event. They should not think that the Lord delays His coming. They should know that the Father will absolutely keep His covenants, especially with "the Jews [or] any remnant of the house of Israel" (3 Nephi 29:8), and that the coming forth of this book is a sign that the sword of His justice is in His right hand (3 Nephi 29:4; as was similarly set forth at the center of Jesus's Covenant Speech in 3 Nephi 21:2–7).

4 NEPHI 1:2—THEY ALL CONVERTED TO THE LORD AND LIVED HIS GOSPEL

"The people were all converted unto the Lord." To "be converted" means "to change." The root "con" means "with," and "vert" means "turn"—not just "turn around"—but to "turn with" or "turn together." A person must turn toward the Lord and adapt his or her life to the Lord's way. There were also to be "no contentions and disputations" or fighting and quarreling among these Christians, as Jesus had stressed in 3 Nephi 11. Perhaps they avoided a great deal of contention because they were able to repent and recognize their part in their problems. The influence of the Holy Ghost helps reduce contention. This same behavior occurred among the early Christians in Palestine and Asia Minor. In Acts 4:32, the record reads, "And the multitude of them that believed were of one heart and of one soul." Elder Dallin H. Oaks taught, "The fact that something is true is not always a justification for communicating it. . . . The use of truth should also be constrained by the principle of unity. One who focuses on faults, though they be true, fosters dissensions and divisions among fellow Church members in the body of Christ."[1] A Zion community is maintained by relationships, but contention tends to become personal and leads to the breakdown of relationships.

4 NEPHI 1:3—THEY HAD ALL THINGS IN COMMON

Like the early Christians as described in Acts 4:32, 36–37 and Acts 5, these Nephites found that having all things in common was crucial to creating a Zion society. There is no information on how the Nephites managed such a system. Did they bring their crops into a central storehouse

---

1 Dallin H. Oaks, "Criticism," *Ensign,* February 1987. https://www.churchofjesuschrist.org/study/ensign/1987/02/criticism?lang=eng.

and redistribute them? That may have been impractical. Maybe they were willing to share the things over which they had stewardship. Perhaps they viewed themselves as holding things in trust for the benefit of other people. They may have recognized all property as belonging to the Lord—dedicated to Him—and therefore usable by the steward for the benefit of others. No doubt they acted similarly to the members of the Church in the time of Alma the Younger:

> In their prosperous circumstances, they did not send away any who were naked, or that were hungry, or that were athirst, or that were sick, or that had not been nourished; and they did not set their hearts upon riches; therefore they were liberal to all, both old and young, both bond and free, both male and female, whether out of the church or in the church, having no respect to persons as to those who stood in need. (Alma 1:30)

These Christians now had a higher set of priorities than they had before Christ's visit. They no longer placed so much emphasis on material things and personal status—on who had the most money or who was the king or best soldier.

4 NEPHI 1:5—COMPASSIONATE SERVICE AND HEALING IN THE NAME OF JESUS

This Zion community truly cared about taking care of the poor, the sick, and the needy. The disciples of Jesus used the priesthood to bless others in the name of Jesus—healing the lame, blind, and deaf. Compassionate service is a necessary component of Christlike living.

4 NEPHI 1:7—MAKING COMMUNITY IMPROVEMENTS

In 4 Nephi 1:7, it is recorded that the people rebuilt the cities that had been destroyed. City building and city planning were important to improving the community. The people pulled together and built tight-knit communities where people lived close together to serve and benefit one another.

4 NEPHI 1:10—THEY BECAME A FAIR AND DELIGHTSOME PEOPLE

Verse 10 states that "the people of Nephi . . . became an exceedingly fair and delightsome people." The words "fair and delightsome" probably refer to their being clean (pure) and happy.

4 NEPHI 1:16—THEY BECAME A HAPPY PEOPLE

Mormon observed that "there could not be a happier people among all the people who had been created by the hand of God." In the temple, we learn that one of the first commandments given to Adam and Eve was the commandment to "be happy." When we strive to be happy, the Lord will help us to fulfill this commandment to the greatest extent possible. In summary, Mormon provided a detailed description of the Nephites who created a peaceful and righteous society by the way they believed, behaved, and lived. Mormon had seen our day. Undoubtedly, he recorded the ideas he felt would be most valuable to his future audiences.

4 NEPHI 1:18—THEY WERE BLESSED BEYOND MEASURE

How did they create a Zion community? It takes a temple, it takes a church of God, and it takes the priesthood to have a society like this. Of course, it takes all members in such a society to be willing to operate all those things and make these beautiful, happy blessings a reality.

4 NEPHI 1:14-49—BUT THE ZION SOCIETY BEGINS TO CRUMBLE

By verse 22, Mormon reported that "two hundred more years had passed away" and most of the second generation of people since the appearance of Christ had also passed away, along with all those having firsthand testimony of Christ's ministry in the New World. Mormon then described a deterioration of the Zion society as the people become exceedingly rich. In the two hundred and first year, "there began to be among them those who were lifted up in pride, such as the wearing of costly apparel, and all manner of fine pearls, and of the fine things of the world" (1:24). That signaled the end of people having all things in common. "Memory loss" was also a strongly contributing factor in 4 Nephi, and we must strive hard to avoid a similar spiritual amnesia. In the 1890s, a general call went out throughout the Church for anyone who personally remembered the Prophet Joseph Smith to send in their memoirs, diary entries, or any other record that preserved the historical reality of what Joseph thought, said, and did during his ministry as the prophet of the Restoration. The recollections of hundreds of the early Saints regarding Joseph Smith were compiled in a book titled *Remembering Joseph*.[2] The people in 4 Nephi may not have had access to written accounts of the Savior's visit to their parents and grandparents, but a strong oral history tradition could have helped prevent their downfall.

TAKEAWAYS

- **Make a thoughtful comparison of what Jesus said about the definition of His "doctrine" in 3 Nephi 11 and what He said about the more expanded meaning of His "gospel" in 3 Nephi 27. How are both definitions useful in different ways?**
- **Record for further reflection a few points taught by Jesus in 3 Nephi that you want to remember and contemplate the next time you go to the temple.**

---

2   Mark L. McConkie, ed. and comp., *Remembering Joseph: Personal Recollections of Those Who Knew the Prophet Joseph Smith* (Salt Lake City, UT: Deseret Book, 2003).

44: MORMON 1-6

WHAT DO WE KNOW ABOUT MORMON? WHO WAS MORMON?

Consider the following notes as you read these six autobiographical chapters. What other points might you add?

Mormon knew history, and it influenced his choices as he selected which records to transcribe or to abridge onto his plates.

Mormon remained stalwart amid unthinkable hardships and tragic disappointments, one after another. He introduced himself, first and foremost, as "a disciple of Jesus Christ, the Son of God" (3 Nephi 5:13), and, accordingly, throughout his composition of his abridgment, Mormon features Jesus Christ as the focus of Nephite doctrine, worship, religion, and civic and social order. Mormon personally wrote the ten chapters found in Mormon 1–7 and Moroni 7–9.

Mormon was much more than just a nominal Christian.

Ammoron trusted Mormon. There is no information on the age of Ammaron or on his immediate kinship to the young Mormon, though they both descended from Nephi. However, this older man knew that this ten-year-old boy was very precocious, and he trusted him. Being trusted with a major assignment can be very influential in developing confidence in the formation of a young person's character, and indeed Mormon remembered that description. Being told that he was a trustworthy and responsible person likely made Mormon even more so.

In Mormon 1:2, Ammaron told Mormon plainly that he was a "sober" child. Likewise, Alma, when speaking to his sons Helaman and Shiblon, had ended his blessings and instructions by encouraging them to "be sober" (Alma 37:47; 38:15); and Nephi, Jacob, Benjamin, and Alma spoke words with "soberness" (1 Nephi 18:10; Jacob 2:2; 6:5) or with "truth and soberness" (Mosiah 4:15; Alma 42:31; 53:21). So, in Nephite vocabulary, this word carried high praise and honor.

The word "sober" meant being "moderate, frugal, continent, reasonable, and sensible." Mormon was by nature all these things. His disposition was calm and level-headed, even in the worst situations.

Ammaron also referred to Mormon as being "quick to observe" (1:2), implying perhaps that he was good at accurately perceiving his surroundings, and maybe also quick to learn and obey.

The Nephites were not living their religion very well at this time, and they were making poor choices. An observant person sees his surroundings, considers them, and decides to do something better. Mormon continued in this vein, even stepping down as the commander of the Nephite armies when their behavior fell below his standard.

Mormon was also patient and obedient, and remembered his duty, all of which he attributed to his being a descendant of Nephi. At the age of ten years, he was asked to take stewardship of the records when he reached the age of twenty-four, in AD 334.

Describing himself, Mormon commented that at the age of ten, he was "learned somewhat after the manner of the learning of my people," using a phrase that is similar to the words Nephi used to describe himself (1 Nephi 1:1–2).

Mormon's calling as a prophet and religious leader occurred when he was fifteen years old, in AD 325–326. In Mormon 1:15, he related, "And I, being fifteen years of age and being somewhat of a sober mind, therefore I was visited of the Lord, and tasted and knew of the goodness of Jesus." The similarity here to Joseph Smith's life is worth noting. Joseph was visited by the Father and the Son around that same time in his life.

Mormon then went through a period of growth and preparation for the fulfillment of his calling. Having been visited by Jesus Christ, he immediately desired to begin teaching what he had learned but was forbidden for a time because of the unrighteousness of the people. Instead, the next year, at the age of sixteen, Mormon was acclaimed as the military leader of the Nephite forces.

Based on Mormon's evident precociousness, spirituality, lineage, and physical stature, Ammaron was certainly inspired five years earlier as he confidently selected Mormon at such a young age as the next recordkeeper. Ammaron needed someone reliable and competent to make and edit records. It is likely that his positive statements about Mormon's strengths encouraged Mormon to develop those strengths further.

MORMON 2–MORMON'S MILITARY LEADERSHIP

When Mormon was selected to lead the military system at the young age of sixteen, he had been prepared to assume this position. Looking mature and being responsible were basic foundations, but he needed to be groomed and trained for the role. What else must have prepared him to be able to accomplish his phenomenal mission?

As he explained in Mormon 1:5, he was a direct descendant of Nephi, which, according to the book of Jacob, meant that he had the right to be a king or leader. That right belonged to the direct descendants of Nephi. This may explain how he could have been selected at such a young age to fulfill that role.

It is feasible for a precocious and serious-minded young man like Mormon, particularly one who had been both trained by his father and called of God, to become an important leader at a young age.

The series of skirmishes between AD 326–331 provided a great victory for Mormon, who did not win many battles during his lifetime. Several issues preceded these events: robbers, over-population, intense militarism, and intense fear (Mormon 2:3). The Nephites had resorted to sorceries, witchcrafts, and magic (Mormon 1:19); they were no longer relying on the Holy Ghost, and they turned to superstition to find a successful strategy. Divination, augury, and their associated crafts are surrogates for the lack of the influence of the Holy Ghost. These factors came together to cause the Nephite crisis.

As recorded in Mormon 2:9, however, Mormon regrouped the army and prevailed for a moment of victory against Aaron. Mormon reported, "He came against us with an army of forty and four thousand. And behold, I withstood him with forty and two thousand. And it came to pass that I beat him with my army that he fled before me." The Nephites were slightly outnumbered, but Mormon wanted us to know that he won at least that once.

Very little is said about the things Mormon did between AD 331–345 as recorded in Mormon 2:18, but the points that Mormon touched on were the most crucial. For example: The Nephites became worse, and the day of grace was past; they were sorrowful, but not unto repentance. Mormon's diagnosis of the serious spiritual decline of his people thus identifies their strong rejection of the basic teachings of Jesus in 3 Nephi. While using words sparingly, Mormon is excellent at remembering and using significant key phrases that he obviously knew from his study of the records and teachings of his people.

In the year AD 344, the Nephites fled again, and Mormon led them up to the land of Jashon, where there was a deposit of the Nephite records. In Mormon 2:17 he recorded, "Behold I had gone according to the word of Ammaron and taken the plates of Nephi and did make a record according to the words of Ammaron." By the time he returned in AD 344, Mormon, at the age of 24, had already obtained access to the plates.

Between AD 334 and 344, Mormon worked somewhat on the records. He was apparently finishing the record of what he called the large plates when, in Mormon 2:18, he wrote: "and upon the plates of Nephi, I did make a full account." That is, he wrote on what for centuries had been called the large plates, recording "all the wickedness and abominations" of his own people. But upon *these* plates (the plates of Mormon), as he also wrote, he "did forbear to make a full account."

In the year AD 350, the Nephites (led by Mormon) made a ten-year peace treaty with the Lamanites and even with the Gadianton robbers. They bought those ten years of peace at a very high price, promising to give up the entire land south of the narrow neck of land.

In Mormon 3:1 we learn that during that decade, Mormon had made sure that his people were employed in preparing for the inevitable resumption of battle. Nevertheless, that decade was the only time in Mormon's life that he had a peaceful period long enough to work on a major project, such as the Book of Mormon. Mormon was forty years old in AD 350, and he was fifty years old when the ten-year peace expired. It was during this Jubilee decade that he had time and the opportunity to work on the abridgment.

At the same time, if he had married in about AD 331, his son Moroni could have been born a year or two later, and he would have been about 18 or 19 years old in AD 350—old enough to have been taught and trained by Mormon in the languages of his people and in the skills required to abridge records and to make and inscribe plates. When Mormon died in AD 385, Moroni knew exactly how to pick up where Mormon had left off. It makes sense that Moroni would have grown up as his father's research and writing assistant.

Promptly after those ten years, in Mormon 3:4, the king of the Lamanites wrote a letter warning of impending hostilities. And, indeed, it was not more than two years after this ten-year timeout that Mormon would utterly refuse to lead the Nephites any longer because of their vengefulness and hatred.

MORMON 3-THE NEPHITES' DOWNFALL

In Mormon 3:2, Mormon tells us that he was specifically asked by the Lord to "cry unto this people—Repent ye and come unto me, and be ye baptized, and build up again my church, and ye shall be spared." This was the last warning for his people.

Mormon began, as instructed, to teach about repentance. In his earlier sermon, recorded in Moroni 7, while speaking to a band of believers, he had taught the higher law from the Sermon in the Temple, but now he focused on the first principles of the gospel—faith, repentance, and baptism. The ten-year ceasefire would have been a great time for people to have regrouped and returned to Christ, but apparently, they had not done so.

Mormon commented in Mormon 3:3 that he had done what he had been commanded to do. "I did cry unto the people," but his efforts were in vain. His people did not recognize that the Lord had spared them and granted them a time for *repentance*. However, "behold they did harden their hearts against the Lord" (3:3).

It becomes clear in Mormon 3:9 that the Nephites became proud and boastful because of their success. Not only were they interested in revenge, but they even swore before the heavens that they would "avenge themselves of the blood of their brethren."

The war, to the Nephites, became an offensive action. It is quite possible that their choices were based partly on a desire to step into a position of advantage, and win, but their motivation and trust in themselves precluded the help of the Lord.

Mormon retired at the age of 53 because he could no longer stand at the head of the wicked and abominable Nephites, who would neither hear his cry for repentance nor cease being avengers. In Mormon 3:11–16, he announced that he would stand down. Twenty years later and at the very end of his life, Mormon was called back into service and again accepted the role of leader.

Mormon withdrew from the battle and stood on the sidelines. His words were resolute. "I utterly refused to go up against mine enemies; and I did even as the Lord had commanded me; and I did stand as an idle witness to manifest unto the world the things which I saw and heard" (3:16). Mormon was not going to be a partisan. He was not going to try to persuade people. He was simply going to record the effects of their choices without being able to alter their course.

His testimony is the kind that would be expected from a person who had watched the horrors that he had to watch, knowing the hopelessness and his lack of power to change the inevitable consequences.

He had tried to get his people to repent, but now they had uprooted and moved, had been attacked and won, but then were attacked again and lost, and became proud and unruly. In Mormon 3:17–22, after washing his hands of further responsibility and pronouncing himself an idle witness, he stated only the following remaining purposes that he hoped to accomplish as he served as that witness:

- "And for this cause I write unto you, that ye may know that ye must all stand before the judgment-seat of Christ, yea, every soul who belongs to the whole human family of Adam; and ye must stand to be judged of your works, whether they be good or evil" (17:20)

- "And also that ye may believe the gospel of Jesus Christ, which ye shall have among you" (17:21)

- "And also that the Jews, the covenant people of the Lord, shall have other witness besides him whom they saw and heard, that Jesus whom they slew, was the very Christ and the very God." (17:21)

In Mormon 3:22, he forewarned all to repent and prepare for the time of judgment. Repentance is what the Lord had commanded him to preach (3:2). It is apparent that this urgent message of the need to repent was in Mormon's mind the whole time he was editing, abridging, and producing the Book of Mormon.

The fact that all will stand to be judged is really the only thing Mormon had left to say to his own people. The status of being an idle witness left nothing more for him to do than bear testimony and remind people of their accountability to God. He knew they had received their last chance.

Mormon did not get angry; he calmly and coolly stepped to the sidelines and stood as an idle witness. That is a sober person. This is also characteristic of the way Mormon handled the accounts of the destructions in 3 Nephi 8, and other conflicts with the Gadianton robbers. He presented a factual, purposeful, sober history. He was decidedly suited for the task of abridging the history of his people into our Book of Mormon.

MORMON 4—MORMON RELUCTANTLY DESCRIBES A HORRIBLE SCENE

In Mormon 4:11 we read, "It is impossible for the tongue to describe, or for man to write a perfect description of the horrible scene of the blood and carnage which was among the people, both of the Nephites and of the Lamanites."

He was surrounded by wickedness and slaughter all his life, and yet he was visited by the Savior and was an Apostle, a sensitive person, the leader of the Church, and a prophet. Thus, his reluctance to graphically describe the evils was in keeping with his role and character. After Mormon had lived with the experiences of war for some time, and it was somewhat in the past, he wanted people to know how bad it really had become. He wanted them to know that God was no longer justified in standing by these people.

MORMON 5—A RECORD AS A WARNING

Mormon explains why he writes only a few things—because the sorrow would be too great (5:9). But he knows that people who are concerned for the house of Israel will sorrow for the calamity of these distant kinsmen who would not repent and be "clasped in the arm of Jesus" (5:11). Mormon had been commanded to write to the "unbelieving of the Jews; . . . that they may be persuaded that Jesus is the Christ," the anointed Messiah, through whom God will keep His promises "unto the fulfilling of his covenant" (5:14).

Mormon concludes by admonishing the Gentiles to repent, humble themselves, turn from their evil ways, "lest a remnant" will tear them to pieces (5:22–24). Mormon's words here echo the woes and warnings in 3 Nephi 29–30, but in Mormon 5 he relates those more general curses and commandments to the Gentiles' specific mistreatment of the Nephite remnant and seed that will scatter and survive the institutional collapse of the Nephite nation as a people.

MORMON 6—GREAT LAMENTATIONS

The words of sorrow and mourning in Mormon 6:16–22 can be seen literally as a powerful formal lamentation. In Mormon 6:16–20, Mormon first addresses the dead:

> O ye fair ones, how could ye have departed from the ways of the Lord! O ye fair ones, how could ye have rejected that Jesus, who stood with open arms to receive you! Behold, if ye had not done this, ye would not have fallen. But behold, ye are fallen, and I mourn your loss. O ye fair sons and daughters, ye fathers and mothers, ye husbands and wives, ye fair ones, how is it that ye could have fallen! But behold, ye are gone, and my sorrows cannot bring your return.

The central narrative is in Mormon 6:21: "And the day soon cometh that your mortal must put on immortality, and these bodies which are now moldering in corruption must soon become incorruptible bodies; and then ye must stand before the judgment-seat of Christ, to be judged according to your works; and if it so be that ye are righteous, then are ye blessed with your fathers who have gone before you."

Then follows a return to a final direct address in 6:22: "O that ye had repented before this great destruction had come upon you. But behold, ye are gone, and the Father, yea, the Eternal Father of heaven, knoweth your state; and he doeth with you according to his justice and mercy."

When one is in the deepest moments of sorrow and grief, not much can be said. However, Mormon has embraced what can be said as he looks back on not only the thousands who have died right before his eyes, but on the lost potential of this great nation. This is a sublime elegy.

TAKEAWAYS

- **Write an introduction you would use in introducing Mormon to speak at a devotional in your stake or at some important public occasion.**
- **From the standpoint of leadership, what would you list as the top three characteristics that made Mormon a great leader? For each item on your list, give one anecdote.**
- **Think of several important leaders who have been influential in your life and how you have benefitted from their leadership. How have you imitated them when facing questions or challenges?**
- **How did Mormon make use of the ten years of peace between 350 and 360 AD? Choose two goals you would like to accomplish in a specified amount of time (days, months, or years).**

45: MORMON 7-9

MORMON 7–FINAL FAREWELL

Everyone can learn many lessons from Mormon's life and personality. One might wish to emulate Mormon's devotion to duty. One might strive to remain positive and faithful when facing difficulties and disappointments. One might mourn and lament, openly recognizing sorrows and tragedy. One might likewise think what one can do today to help descendants and future generations learn lessons of truthfulness and testimony, looking forward to the ultimate victory in the eternal battle in which we are led by Jesus Christ in obedience and charity.

After his formal lament in Mormon 6, Mormon offered his final words of farewell. He was giving all he had left to the posterity of his people, and he was also most likely trying to strengthen his only son Moroni in these last words of his final book within the Book of Mormon.

Mormon had four specific statements detailing what he wanted his audience to know, and he expressed those four points tersely and clearly, each preceded by the phrase "Know ye that":

- Know ye that ye are of the house of Israel (7:2).

- Know ye that ye must come unto repentance, or ye cannot be saved (7:3).

- Know ye that ye must lay down your weapons of war, and delight no more in the shedding of blood, and take them not again, save it be that God shall command you (7:4).

- Know ye that ye must come to the knowledge of your fathers, and repent of all your sins and iniquities (7:5).

In verse 5 he expanded upon his fourth desire which was in and of itself a lucid summary of the mission of Jesus:

- Believe in Jesus Christ, that He is the Son of God, and

- Believe that He was slain by certain of the Jews, and

- Believe that by the power of the Father He hath risen again, and

- Believe not just that Jesus is risen, but that from the Father He hath gained the victory over the grave; and that in Him is the sting of death swallowed up.

Mormon's summary statement here and its expansion illustrates his sincere love for his people and his powerful testimony of the details of Christ's Atonement. He wanted his people to know:

- that Jesus will bring to pass the resurrection of all the dead,

- that all mankind will be resurrected to stand before the divine judgment seat,

- that Jesus will provide redemption for all who will repent and accept His Atonement, and
- that those who accept it and are thus found guiltless will dwell in the presence of God.

In referring to the gospel of Jesus Christ, Mormon then prophesied of the coming of the Bible through the Jews to the Gentiles, and thence to the descendants of the Nephites and Lamanites. He stated that if his audience believed his records, they "will believe that [namely, the Bible]." He knew that this would be one of the great missions of the Book of Mormon—to help establish the truth of the Bible. Doctrine and Covenants 20:11 similarly states that one of the main missions of the Book of Mormon is "proving to the world that the holy scriptures [including the Bible] are true."

Lastly, Mormon gives yet another statement of "the intent" for which the Book of Mormon was written on durable metal plates. Through these plates, the remnant of his people will eventually "know concerning [their] fathers, and also the marvelous works which were wrought by the power of God" (7:9)

Remembering who we are and what the Lord has done for us is indeed of crucial importance. President Spencer W. Kimball (1895–1985) taught that the most important word in our religious dictionary is *remember*. "Because we have made covenants with God," he said, "our greatest need is to remember" them (Henry B. Eyring, "Always Remember Him," *Ensign*, February 2018).

MORMON 8-9—MORONI CONTINUES THE RECORD

In these two chapters, Moroni finishes the record of his slain father. In finishing the record of his father, Moroni did not stay at or around the location of the final battle, where he would have been killed. The final battle took place in AD 385, and Moroni finally buried these records in AD 421, thirty-six years later. He apparently spent those thirty-six years in exile and likely, for the most part, alone.

Moroni never had an opportunity to speak face-to-face with the people to whom he so yearned to deliver this message, but he used exceptionally effective rhetorical techniques to make his message clear to an audience that was widely spread in distance and over time—even centuries. He felt an urgency to reach them [us], then and now, and he reiterated his phrases, wondering if we are hearing him.

Moroni produced three conclusions to the Book of Mormon. One is here in Mormon 8–9, another is found in Ether 12, and his final farewell can be found in Moroni 10. These three conclusions were written at different times, and they are very different from each other. However, we can learn many lessons from each of them. He was doing his duty and closing the record as his father had charged him to do. He was warning us. He was commanding us. He issued challenges and asked questions.

When Moroni was abridging the book of Ether, he inserted his second farewell as an extended commentary on the fact that the people of Ether would "not believe" the great and marvelous things which he prophesied "because they saw them not" (Ether 12:5). He then discourses, teaches, worries about the Gentiles mocking, prays that the Gentiles will have charity, and bids farewell for the next thirty-six verses (12:6–41), then lets Ether have the last word in the book of Ether (15:34).

But when he wrote Moroni 10, he was not doing it out of a sense of duty or because he had been told to do it, and he was not worried about what his readers might think. Moroni simply pours out his heart to us. That is where we will eventually find his series of seven pleading exhortations to us.

Moroni wisely began in Mormon 8:14 with blessings and accompanying curses. In verses 14 to 22, he warned people not to condemn the record because of potential mistakes or faults of men (8:17). He also warned people that no one shall have these records to get gain (8:14), and he blesses those who will bring this book to light with an eye single to God's glory (8:15; invoking 3 Nephi 13:22). He warns people not to try to destroy the work of the Lord or to claim that God has forgotten His covenant (8:21), for "the eternal purposes of the Lord shall roll on" (8:22), and the words and prayers of the righteous dead shall cry from the dust (8:23–25).

In Mormon 9:31, Moroni likewise ends his first farewell by again pointing out how fortunate the readers are that, through this record, God has made manifest their—Moroni's contemporaries'—imperfections, "That ye may learn to be more wise than we have been." He may have been concerned that people would condemn the book as unrighteous because the people who produced it had been destroyed, thus making it the work of a sinful people. Moroni asked readers not to condemn the record because of who the people were, because of their weakness in writing, or because of their weakness in many other ways.

He also wrote a blessing to the person who would bring forth the book, "Blessed be he that shall bring this thing to light" (8:16). So, Joseph Smith was given a blessing, and that will recur in Moroni 10:24–25: "Wo be unto the children of men because of unbelief" which will exist at the time when the Book of Mormon comes forth, for "there shall be none that doeth good among you, no not one," which words will be fulfilled as the Savior spoke to Joseph Smith in the First Vision. Then Moroni continued and clarified, "For if there be one among you that doeth good, he shall work by the power and gifts of God" (10:25) which is another reference to Joseph Smith and the only way in which the Book of Mormon could possibly come forth.

In chapter 8, verses 26 to 32, Moroni began to talk about the time when the Book of Mormon would come forth. Six times, he wrote, "It shall come in a day when . . ." He forecasts clearly:

- *It shall come in a day when* it shall be said that miracles are done away (8:26)

- *It shall come in a day when* the blood of the saints shall cry unto the Lord (8: 27)

- Yea, *it shall come in a day when* the power of God shall be denied (8: 28)

- Yea, *it shall come in a day when* there shall be heard of fires, and tempests (8: 29)

- Yea, *it shall come in a day when* there shall be great pollutions (8: 31)

- Yea, *it shall come in a day when* there shall be churches built up . . . for your money (8: 32)

A section of questioning begins in verse 33. Seven times he asked, "O why? Why? Why?" Why have you done this? Why are you this way? Why do you continue to do this?

- *Why have ye* built up churches unto yourselves to get gain? (8: 33)

- *Why have ye* transfigured the holy word of God? (8:33)

- *Why have ye* polluted the holy church of God? (8:38)
- *Why are ye* ashamed to take upon you the name of Christ? (8:38)
- *Why do ye* not think that greater is the value of endless happiness? (8:38)
- *Why do ye* adorn yourselves with that which hath no life? (8:39)
- *Why do ye* build up your secret abominations to get gain? (8:40)

In verse 35, Moroni wrote, "Jesus Christ hath shown you unto me." He has seen our day, our problems, our wickedness, and our weakness. That is why he repeats himself in trying to get his point across to us, so that we will truly take note and behold:

- Behold, look ye unto the revelations of God; for behold, the time cometh (8:33)
- Behold, the Lord hath shown unto me great and marvelous things (8:34)
- Behold, I speak unto you as if ye were present, and yet ye are not (8:35)
- But behold, Jesus Christ hath shown you unto me, and I know your doing (8:35)
- For behold, ye do love money . . . more than ye love the poor and the needy (8:37)

Four times, Moroni used a declarative mode preceded by "*I speak.*"

- *I speak* unto you as if you were present. (8:35)
- *I speak* concerning those who do not believe in Christ. (9:1)
- *I speak* unto you who deny the revelations of God. (9:7)
- *I speak* unto you as though I spake from the dead. (9:30)

Obviously, Moroni liked repetition. In what ways does repetition help drive points home?

MORMON 9–MAY IT BE SO

Moroni switches into a challenging mode for nonbelievers. He now provides a long list of various questions aimed at different audience, namely people who do not believe in Christ. He asks sixteen questions of those who do not believe.

- Will ye say? (9:2)
- Will ye longer deny? (9:3)
- Do ye suppose? (9:3)
- Do ye suppose? (9:3)
- Have all these things passed? (9:15–19)
- Has the end come yet? (9:15)

- Are not these things marvelous? (9:16)
- Who can comprehend? (9:16)
- Who shall say? (9:17)
- Who shall say? (9:18)
- Why has God ceased? (9:19)
- Who can stand? (9:26)
- Who can deny? (9:26)
- Who will rise up against the almighty? (9:26)
- Who will despise the works of the Lord? (9:26)
- Who will despise the children of Christ? (9:26)

Why would Moroni, personally, have been so intently interested in our need to be believing? We read in Moroni 10 that without belief, we cannot have faith, hope, or charity. Unbelief is the enemy of all those good things. He wanted us to know that we must believe and "deny not the gifts." He knew that the Book of Mormon would have to come forward by the gift and power of God.

True to his rhetorical form, Moroni ends his first farewell with a three-fold petition. Three times he prays: "*May* the Lord Jesus Christ grant that [our brethren's] prayers may be answered according to their faith." "*May* God the Father remember the covenant that he hath made with the house of Israel." "*May* he bless them forever, through faith on the name of Jesus Christ." His fervent petitions for the Lord's blessings are given not only for our benefit but for any and all readers. May it be so. "Amen."

TAKEAWAYS

- **Regarding chapter 7, How are Mormon's final farewell words here either consistent with, or different from, the attitudes and purposes that he stated in his earlier editorial comments?**
- **In Mormon 7:9, Mormon says that the Book of Mormon is written for the intent that people will believe the Bible, and that if people truly believe the Bible, they will also believe the Book of Mormon. Describe three or four important ways in which you have found the Bible and Book of Mormon to be mutually reinforcing.**
- **From chapter 9:27–31, make a list highlighting Moroni's admonitions to future readers. Then make a post-it note to remind yourself of the importance of heeding any one of Moroni's instructions. If you feel creative, make a meme or illustration, and share it with someone you love, spotlighting one of these admonitions.**

46: ETHER 1-5

SEEING THE UNDERLYING RECORD OF ETHER AS AN EPIC

It appears that the Jaredite story was originally told and written in the manner of an epic. In *A Glossary of Literary Terms*, M. H. Abrams defines characteristics of literary epics as follows (the examples from Jaredite literature are added):

- The hero is a figure of great national or even cosmic importance. In *The Iliad,* he is the Greek warrior Achilles, the son of the sea nymph Thetis. Sometimes there are two brothers who stand in contrast with each other. In the story of the Jaredite origins, there were two brothers, Jared and his brother, rather like Romulus and Remus, or other such pairs.

- The setting is ample and even huge in scale, possibly even cosmic. With help from the gods, Odysseus sails or wanders over the Mediterranean basin, the whole of the known world. The Jaredites, with divine assistance, cross a huge ocean to an unknown land.

- The action involves superhuman deeds either in battle, as in *The Iliad*, or long arduous journeys, as in *The Odyssey.* The Jaredite journey was certainly arduous, dangerous, and long.

- In these great actions, the gods or other supernatural beings take an interest or an active part. The Olympian gods are involved in Homer's epics. Jehovah, the Son of God who will come to earth, provides guidance for the Jaredite journey.

- An epic is a ceremonial performance narrated in a ceremonial style, not given in normal speech. The text of the brother of Jared, who goes up into a high mountain where he sees not only the finger but also the face of God, is extraordinary, and it beckons to its readers to also strive to find an opening through the heavenly veil.

This last point does not mean that epics are, of necessity, only fictional literature. For many years, people believed that all components of *The Iliad,* including the siege of Troy, were mythological. The Homeric epics were validated when in 1868, Heinrich Schliemann discovered the city of Troy, now well excavated at the archaeological site of Hisarlik. The excavation demonstrated the existence of many levels of occupation, city gates, and city walls. Many of the things Homer described are there. Indeed, history and human experience fundamentally precede poetry and theology.

Typically, the purpose of an epic was not simply entertainment. Epics were crucial in the reflection of essential needs and in the formation of a particular culture. For example, there are Maya creation epics such as the *Popol Vuh.* Such stories tell of the origin of that civilization, as seven ships sail across the sea and arrive in Central America. In addition, the great Israelite epic is the exodus from Egypt. The liberation, the plagues, the wandering in the wilderness, crossing the Red Sea, and acquiring their land contribute to their becoming a people.

ETHER 1:1-2—SEEING MORONI AS ABRIDGER, EDITOR, COMMENTATOR, AND AUTHOR

Because the text of the book of Ether is obviously "layered," it is interesting to notice, at the outset, that in any given verse, various "voices" may be speaking to us or influencing the text's wording and meaning. Those possible voices would include (1) Jared or the brother of Jared, (2) other ancient Jaredite recordkeepers or storytellers, (3) the final Jaredite prophet, Ether, (4) King Mosiah as translator, (5) Moroni as abridger or editor, (6) Moroni as commentator or as author adding his own thoughts and impressions, and finally (7) Joseph Smith as translator bringing it forth in English. Facing this complexity, the gift and power of the Holy Ghost can help us as readers to discern and hear the inspired messages of these voices reaching out to us.

Although Moroni says in Ether 1:2 that he is taking his account from the twenty-four gold plates, it is not likely that Moroni retranslated Ether's plates. He would probably have said so if he had. It is not clear that he even had those plates with him, though he would have known of them.

Ether 5:1 then contains an important disclosure by Moroni: "And now I, Moroni, have written the words which were commanded me *according to my memory.*" Apparently, he knew these Jaredite origin stories very well, if not by heart, as was common in ancient cultures. Parts of Moroni's book of Ether may reflect things that he and his father, Mormon, had discussed. As they were engrossed in wars, the final chapters of the Jaredite history would have been particularly relevant to them.

In Ether 2:11, Moroni states one of his main purposes here: "that ye may know the decrees of God—that ye may repent." The call to repentance is a persistent theme throughout Moroni's writings.

Interestingly, Moroni was honest enough to tell readers when he was chiming in, when he was abridging, and even when he was quoting. For example, in Ether 2:13, Moroni did not say, "And now I proceed with Ether's record," but rather, "Now I proceed with *my* record" (emphasis added). Moroni's abridgment produced what one might thus call "Moroni's Book of Ether." In addition to his abridgment of existing material, Moroni took occasion to interject his own commentary, asides, and sometimes prophecies. The main ones are found in Ether 1:1–6; 4:1–6:1; 12:6–41; and 15:33.

Mormon and Moroni usually state clearly when they are interjecting their own commentary. Thus, there is not the same amount of uncertainty or confusion here as there can be in parts of the Old Testament, where dissecting its layers of redaction and editing is often uncertain.

Another intriguing feature is the source text's underlying continuity. If one were to mark everything spoken by Moroni in one color, and mark everything that is Jaredite in a contrasting color, one can take the Moroni material out, and the remaining Jaredite text flows seamlessly together. This careful splicing of the text is very difficult to do without a word processor. The result is, from a text-critical point of view, a powerful testimony of the antiquity and the editorial process by which the book of Ether came to us.

ETHER 1:6-32—ETHER'S GENEALOGY IS LISTED BACK TO JARED

This king list could originally have been either written or oral. Similar king lists appear among the earliest written records in ancient Mesopotamia, and many Mesoamerican monuments have now been shown to contain historical information about royal lines. Some early peoples also orally transmitted memorized king lists and stories about their origins. While it is not clear whether Ether worked in this respect from a written royal record, an oral tradition, or a combination of both, the integrity of the Jaredite king list as a separate source is underscored by its apparent insertion as a unit amid Moroni's introductory materials (Ether 1:3–5, 33). The words in these verses follow very closely the words of Mosiah$_2$ in Mosiah 28:17.

The genealogy in the book of Ether (Ether 1:6–33) is a prime example of these ancient king lists. The list, which served as an identification and reference for the author, is listed from the author down to his most ancient ancestor. Thus, Ether is named first, Aaron is tenth, Shiz is twentieth, and Jared is thirtieth. Whether the number thirty is important is not clear, but it is significant in many Polynesian cultures for leaders to be able to recite their lineage, sometimes as far back as thirty generations.

Culturally, king lists were especially important in ancient Mesopotamia, the place where the story of the Jaredites begins. In Mesopotamia, their number system was based, not on the number 10, but on the number 60. Throughout the ancient Near East, for commercial and legal purposes, there were 60 shekels in a mina, and 60 minas equaled 1 talent. The number 60 was conveniently divisible by 2, 3, 4, 5, 6, 10, 15, 20, and 30. And thus, the number 30, being the number of names in this king list, may well have had some cultural currency.

Other names will appear in the history chapters in the book of Ether that are not listed in this royal lineage (the brother of Jared, for example), and sometimes the names of these kings appear in the narrative history more than once. But none of the names in the king list appear *their first time in the narrative* out of this order. Thus, the thirty names first given in *the list* from Ether back down to Jared are then introduced *into the narrative* from Jared back up to Ether in exactly the opposite order, and not even one of them is left out. Quite amazing.

Also, in this context, think of Joseph Smith dictating the translation of Ether 1–12 to Oliver Cowdery, presumptively over the four days from May 25 to 28, 1829. Imagine anyone telling a story, beginning with a list of 30 names, and then over the next four days elaborating the histories of those 30 leaders in exactly the opposite order, interspersing various side stories, interactions between parties, conflicts, and editorial asides. There is no evidence or reason to believe that Joseph had any notes or even access to Oliver's manuscript page for Ether 1 as he revealed the text of Ether 6–12. And, reported interviews from Emma Smith and David Whitmer indicate that there were no outlines or notes.

ETHER 1:33—WHO WAS THE BROTHER OF JARED?

Temple priests served an important role in Mesopotamian society. Perhaps Jared and his family had a priestly connection of that nature through the brother of Jared. He may have been involved in religious worship and he had faith necessary to be able to get the answers and blessing from the Lord that he needed.

At the time of Jesus's life in Jerusalem, Flavius Josephus, a Jewish historian, wrote the *Antiquities of the Jews*. In it he wrote of the effects of the fall of the tower of Babel:

> After this they were dispersed abroad, on account of their languages, and went out by colonies everywhere; and each colony took possession of that land which they light upon, and unto which God led them; so that the whole continent was filled with them, both the inland and the maritime countries. *There were some also who passed over the sea in ships, and inhabited the islands.* And some of those nations do still retain the denominations which were given them by their first founders: but some have lost them also. (Book 1, Chapter 5)

ETHER 2:1—THE VALLEY NORTHWARD

The "valley which was northward" that the people of Jared went "down" to was named the valley of Nimrod (see Genesis 10:8–10). In another interesting statement, Josephus, in his *Antiquities of the Jews*, said,

> Now it was Nimrod who excited them to such an affront and contempt of God. He was the grandson of Ham, the son of Noah: a bold man, and of great strength of hand. He persuaded them not to ascribe it to God, as if it was through his means that they were happy; but to believe that it was their own courage which procured that happiness. He also gradually changed the government into tyranny; seeing no other way of turning men from the fear of God, but to bring them into a constant dependence on his own power. He also said, "He would be revenged on God, if he should have a mind to drown the world again: for that he would build a Tower too high for the waters to be able to reach; and that he would avenge himself on God for destroying their fore-fathers." (Book 1, Chapter 4)

ETHER 2:4-5, 14—THE LORD SPOKE THROUGH A CLOUD (OR VEIL)

At one point, the brother of Jared had neglected to consult with the Lord for four years. The text explains in Ether 2:14 that the Lord came to him, and "stood in a cloud and talked with him." The Lord spoke to and chastened the brother for three hours. For the Israelites going through the desert, the Lord was in a cloud at the tabernacle, protected from their vision. They could only speak with the Lord though the appropriate authority of the high priest, in this case Moses. Their cloud appeared as a pillar of fire at night, leading them both physically and spiritually. This calls to mind the burning bush from which the Lord addressed Moses.

ETHER 3:6-13, 19-20—THE BROTHER OF JARED IS ADMITTED INTO THE PRESENCE OF THE LORD

In Latter-day Saint doctrine, we speak of a symbolic veil that has two applications. In one case, the veil is a mechanism that shades the memory as we transition to earth from our pre-earth life. In a second, but related, application, the veil provides a protective barrier to protect us from unauthorized interaction with the Lord in the present. In each instance, the veil is penetrable under circumstances such as the brother of Jared's great faith that allowed him to see beyond it.

ETHER 3:15—WAS THE SAVIOR'S APPEARANCE TO THE BROTHER OF JARED UNIQUE?

In Ether 3:15, the statement by the Lord, "Never have I showed myself unto man whom I have created, for never has man believed in me as thou hast," raises a question as to what the Lord meant by this, for He had shown himself to certain of the patriarchs such as Adam and Eve. Enoch and Noah had preceded the brother of Jared and spoken with God. A *BYU Studies* article by Kent Jackson presents several different views for how this may be understood. For example, Bruce R. McConkie interpreted the verse as, "Never have I showed myself in the manner and form now involved. . . . Never before has the veil been lifted completely so that a mortal man has been able to see my spirit body *in the full and complete sense of the word.*" As another interpretation, Sidney Sperry thought that the word "man" might mean "an unbelieving man," but "to the faithful, he had indeed shown Himself" (Kent P. Jackson, "'Never Have I Showed Myself unto Man': A Suggestion for Understanding Ether 3:15," *BYU Studies*, 30 no. 3 [1990], 71). Available at: https://scholarsarchive.byu.edu/byusq/vol30/iss3/13.

ETHER 4:19—WHY DO SO MANY OF MORMON'S TEACHINGS APPEAR IN ETHER 4 AND 5?

Obviously, Moroni read, knew, and treasured the record he had of his father's great sermon found in Moroni 7. Although, at the time that Moroni wrote Ether 4 and 5, he had not yet decided to include that record in his final book of Moroni, and here it is evident that Moroni draws on some of his father's rhetoric and vocabulary in Ether 4 and 5, as he will do again in Moroni 10. Clearly, Moroni had taken seriously the training and instruction he had received from his father, Mormon. And he hopes that all his readers will do so as well.

ETHER 5:1-4—THE PLATES WILL BE SHOWN TO THREE WITNESSES

Likewise, in Doctrine and Covenants 6:28, the Lord affirmed the validity of this law of witnesses, declaring in April 1829, that "in the mouth of two or three witnesses shall every word be established." Witnesses, together with physical and written evidences, still play crucial roles in religious life, as well as in legal systems throughout the modern world, in coming to recognize and know the truth.

ETHER 5:5-6—YE SHALL SEE ME, AND WE SHALL STAND BEFORE GOD AT THE LAST DAY

Many people are looking forward to greeting and thanking Moroni, "when ye shall see me, and we shall stand before God at the last day" (5:6). Here Moroni puts himself on the line as a witness on the day of God's judgment. To quote 2 Nephi 33:15, "For what I seal on earth, shall be brought against you at the judgment bar." Moroni later will likewise say, "Ye shall know that I lie not, for ye shall see me at the bar of God" (Moroni 10:27).

TAKEAWAYS

- If you were writing a history of a fallen civilization, make a brief wish list of the sorts of stories or details you might want to be sure to include or exclude. Does the book of Ether line up with any items on your list?
- Ponder what you think Moroni hoped his readers would learn and remember most from the positive Jaredite experiences. What might his top three desires be?
- What, in your opinion, are the two or three most significant aspects of the brother of Jared's encounter with the Lord?

47: ETHER 6-11

In these chapters, we learn the history of the Jaredites. They contain no doctrinal discourses, but they do teach solemn admonitions about the evils of wickedness, immorality, idolatry, political strife, power struggles, secret oaths, violence, failing to heed prophetic warnings, and refusing to repent, and thus these chapters are relevant today, even though they come from a very different time and place.

ETHER 6:2-3—THE LORD PROVIDES LIGHT FOR THE JAREDITE BARGES

The brother of Jared went to the Lord concerned about the lack of light in the barges. The Lord did not provide a solution to the problem, but asked, "What will ye that I should do that ye may have light in your vessels?" (Ether 2:23). In response, the brother of Jared "did molten out of a rock sixteen small stones; and they were white and clear, even as transparent glass" (Ether 3:1). He then went back and asked the Lord to touch each stone, causing them to "shine in darkness, to give light unto men, women, and children, that they might not cross the great waters in darkness" (Ether 6:3).

Referencing this account, Hugh Nibley commented, "Who gave the brother of Jared the idea about stones in the first place? It was not the Lord, who left him entirely on his own; and yet the man went right to work as if he knew exactly what he was doing."

Both Nibley and John A. Tvedtnes have found a substantial body of ancient literature containing legends or histories of stones that provided light. In the Babylonian Talmud, a Jewish commentator reported that the Lord instructed Noah to "set therein precious stones and jewels, so that they may give thee light, bright as the noon." Another ancient Jewish rabbi explained, "During the whole twelve months that Noah was in the Ark he did not require the light of the sun by day or light of the moon by night, but he had a polished gem which he hung up." Jewish accounts of a shining stone being used in Noah's ark are of particular interest, considering that Ether 6:7 made a direct comparison between the Jaredite vessels and Noah's ark: "There was no water that could hurt them, their vessels being tight like unto a dish, and also they were tight like unto the ark of Noah."

Further Reading:

Hugh Nibley, *The Collected Works of Hugh Nibley*, Vol. 6, *An Approach to the Book of Mormon*, (Salt Lake City and Provo, UT: Deseret Book and FARMS, 1988), 285, 337–358.

John A. Tvedtnes, "Glowing Stones in Ancient and Medieval Lore," *Journal of Book of Mormon Studies* 6, no. 2 (1997): 99–123.

ETHER 6:4-11—PERSONALLY APPLYING LESSONS FROM TWO OCEAN JOURNEYS

The narratives of the Jaredites and Lehi's family crossing the ocean in their vessels share similar conditions and outcomes, yet the tales themselves serve two separate purposes.

The Jaredite record states that *the Lord God* caused furious winds, and that the people were "tossed upon the waves of the sea" as their vessels were pushed forward to the promised land. By contrast, we know that disobedience caused the great storm on the voyage of Lehi's family to the promised land. In other words, it was not an easy voyage—they had their trials, but they ultimately made it to their desired destination. In both narratives, the people were traveling to their promised land for the same general purpose. In one scenario, the Lord provided the tempest that pushed the Jaredites toward the promised land. Those people were allowed to learn and grow through trials and tribulations—not of their making—along the journey. In the other scenario, the disobedient choices of a few caused unnecessary delay and difficulty for everyone aboard the ship.

We can metaphorically apply this situation to ourselves. When we face trials, tribulations, or trauma, it may be for a greater purpose. We may undergo difficult experiences to reach our desired destination. We can also slow our own progress through haughtiness and disobedience.

ETHER 8:4—HOW DOES A KING SPEND HIS LIFE IN CAPTIVITY?

This ancient society structure included class distinctions, as did many ancient near-eastern cultures. With class distinction came privileges and legal benefits—particularly for royalty. Enemies of a king could confine him and other royal members in a restricted area where they were required to stay—in a palace or a specific part of the land. Even though they were restricted in their movement, they lived their lives in comparative ease. They were not put into slavery, nor were they required to work for other people. Therefore, the many kings over several generations living "in captivity" in the Book of Ether were likely in restricted areas but were permitted to live and act with relative freedom.

ETHER 8:20—"AND NOW I, MORONI . . ."

It appears that Moroni left the Jaredite record largely intact. When the texts of Moroni's five "And now I, Moroni" comments are removed from the book of Ether, the remaining text flows flawlessly. For example, even though there is almost an entire chapter of commentary from Moroni separating the text of Ether 12:5 and 13:2, when they are placed back together, they read: "Ether did prophesy great and marvelous things unto the people, which they did not believe, because they saw them not. . . . For behold, they rejected all the words of Ether; for he truly told them of all things, from the beginning of man."

ETHER 9:1-12—THE EVIL PLOT AND DESTRUCTION OF AKISH'S KINGDOM

Many years after arriving in the promised land, Jared and his brother asked the people for their preference of government and the people requested that one of their sons be anointed king. We often see the glamorous side of kingship, but in the Book of Ether we see it was a curse for this civilization. Sons and daughters rise up against fathers, brothers against brothers—all to gain power.

The conspiracy by Akish and his friends came to fruition when Omer was overthrown as king and Jared was installed as ruler. Jared was grateful, no doubt, so he allowed Akish to marry his daughter. Jared's success, however, was short-lived. Akish recruited fellow conspirators to behead Jared while he sat on the throne. As king, Akish, jealous of his own son, starved him to death.

In short order, the kingdom of Akish, which he had used treachery to obtain, was destroyed by that same treachery. The spread of the "wicked and secret society" had "corrupted the hearts of all the people" (9:6). His own sons began a war that went on for "many years," resulting in the obliteration of all but 30 people in that kingdom. For a short period of time, Akish's plans looked successful, but evil soon wrecked an entire nation.

ETHER 9:28-35—POISONOUS SERPENTS UPON THE FACE OF THE LAND

Prophets warned that a "great famine" would come if the people did not repent, but they were persecuted and cast out. As predicted, "there was no rain upon the face of the earth." Amid the great famine, an interesting series of events followed. First, the land was infested by "poisonous serpents," next, "flocks began to flee" southward, and the serpents followed the flocks (Ether 9:31). The serpents then stopped pursuing the flocks and "hedge[d] up the way," preventing people from passing into the land southward (Ether 9:33). Ether's record states that when the people had eventually suffered enough to repent and the famine ceased, the serpents were no longer a threat.

As strange as this series of events may seem, the details are ecologically sound. In times of drought, snakes will often migrate to populated areas in search of water or prey. If the drought does not subside, the snakes, as well as other animals, will continue to migrate in search of water. When rain again showered the land, snakes and other animals would find their natural habitats, and populations would return to their proper balance. Thus, the serpents would no longer pose a barrier to the land southward.

This narrative can also be used as a parable, showing that real repentance can end a spiritual famine and tear down the barriers that keep us from returning to the Lord. The Atonement of Jesus Christ can overcome any barrier.

ETHER 10:5-8—KING RIPLAKISH IN CONTRAST TO KING BENJAMIN

Riplakish was the second king following a famine which had decimated the Jaredite kingdom (Ether 9:28–35). His father had begun to rebuild the kingdom (Ether 10:1–4), and by the time Riplakish took over, he wielded considerable power. The record describes oppressive taxation and extravagant building projects during Riplakish's reign. We read of Riplakish's behavior as king in Ether 10:5: "He did have many wives and concubines, and did lay that upon men's shoulders which was grievous to be borne; yea, he did tax them with heavy taxes; and with the taxes he did build many spacious buildings." Then in verse 7, "even his fine gold he did cause to be refined in prison; and all manner of fine workmanship he did cause to be wrought in prison." In many ways, King Riplakish stands in direct contrast to King Benjamin. When reading the Jaredite record, King Mosiah must have noted the stark contrast between his father, Benjamin, and the behavior of Riplakish.

ETHER 11:1-21—THE FALL BEGINS, WARNINGS OF DESTRUCTION AND THE SOLUTION

The Book of Mormon is a divinely appointed warning for modern days, twice illustrating the downfalls of two societies that succumbed to wickedness and corruption. Various Jaredite royal descendants ruled in great wickedness, persecuting the prophets until those prophets withdrew from the people. And sure enough, severe destruction followed. Eventually, prophets again came among the people warning that "God would execute judgment against them to their utter destruction," and would bring other people to inherit the land of promise.

In the Book of Mormon, we see the fulfillment of that warning. The Jaredite nation was destroyed, and Lehi's descendants possessed the land. But eventually, the Nephite nation was also destroyed because of unrighteousness. As found in 3 Nephi and elsewhere in scripture, one solution can turn the tide of social decay and destruction—when the people hear the word of the Lord, repent, and adhere to the principles taught by Jesus Christ.

TAKEAWAYS

- **How much divine instruction and guidance did the Jaredites have to prepare their vessels? How much divine help is available to us as we journey toward our "promised land"?**
- **It is clear that the Lord cared about the people having light during this long journey. How does this account help us identify what steps we can take to obtain that light?**
- **What does Moroni prophesy about nations that "uphold secret combinations, to get power and gain"? What does Moroni suggest we should do when we see "these things come among you"? What are some solutions for us in our day (8:20–26)?**

- Why are evil plans often successful in attaining their goals? Did the success last? To what did it lead?
- What behavior prevented them from listening to the Lord and his prophets?
- Can wickedness among the leaders cause decline in a nation?

48: ETHER 12-15

ETHER 12:3, 6—THE AGONY OF INADEQUATE FINAL FAREWELLS

Steve Walker, a faculty member in the Brigham Young University English department, has written several articles on literature and belief. He once wrote an essay titled "Last Words," as an introduction to the books of 4 Nephi, Mormon, Ether, and Moroni, in which farewells are given by Mormon (Mormon 6–7) and Moroni (Mormon 8–9; Ether 12; and Moroni 10). Steve is a master of literary analysis. This is what he said about these farewells:

> Looked at from a literary perspective, for its impact in our personal lives, I find the final section of the Book of Mormon to be particularly engaging. Like any good climax, it tends to be the most intense part of the book. It is arguably the most significant section. This culmination of a thousand-year chronicle puts the whole volume into over-view mode—the summary at the end of the book encapsulates what has mattered most. T. S. Eliot ("Little Gidding," *The Four Quartets*) observed that, "What we call the beginning is often the end. And to make an end is to make a beginning. The end is where we start from." Endings re-orient us as when Sam from *Lord of the Rings* returns to the Shire with all those world-altering adventures involving the ring. "Well, I'm back."
>
> The small books that wrap up the Book of Mormon—Fourth Nephi, Mormon, Ether, and especially Moroni—give us the conclusion to the whole matter. Their endings are emphatic because they take up the theme of endings in a series of death-bed statements, famous last words. That's dramatic because of the 'last, the best of all the game' effect, because of our expectation that the final things said distills overall implications, as in Sidney Carton's last words in *A Tale of Two Cities*: "It is a far, far better thing that I do than I have ever done." The final Book of Mormon words put me in mind of the last words of Rabelais, for instance, who said: "I'm going to seek a great perhaps"; and of Lord Nelson's, "Thank God I have done my duty"; and Goethe, "More light". I especially like Pancho Villa's expression that final statements matter, "Don't let it end like this. Tell them I said something."
>
> Unlike the apocalypses we're used to, the kind of arcane theoretical symbolizing we get in Ezekiel or Revelation, this apocalypse invades actual experience. (Walker, Steve, "Last Words" in *The Reader's Book of Mormon: Last Words: 4 Nephi–Moroni*, eds. Robert A. Rees and Eugene England [Salt Lake City: Signature Books, 2008], vii–xxii.)

In Ether 12, Moroni offers for a second time what he thought at that time would be his final farewell. He had already signed off once in Mormon 8–9, but by the grace of God, Moroni was still alive, having now appended the book of Ether to Mormon's record. But even at that, it would not be Moroni's final farewell.

Moroni may have been inspired (or sobered) by the failure of Ether to stem the tide of destruction and mutual annihilation of the warring Jaredite factions. Ether had cried repentance, from morning until night, but without success. He had prophesied many things, which people did not believe (Ether 12:3, 6). This caused Moroni to ponder, why would they not believe? Why had his own people failed to believe? In response to his musings, Moroni was inspired to write about faith. He wants to show the whole world that "faith is things which are hoped for and not seen," and that people "receive no witness until the trial of [their] faith" (12:6). Moroni provides a long list of cases where good things happened only after people had faith, including the appearance of Christ to the Nephites, and miracles brought about by the faith of Moses, Alma and Amulek, Nephi and Lehi, the Three Nephites, and the brother of Jared (12:11–21). Moroni includes himself in the process, as he too has been walking alone exclusively by faith, hoping that his work on the records in the Book of Mormon would someday see the light of day.

But Moroni worries that people will mock what he has awkwardly written (12:23–24). And here is where the Lord says to Moroni, "Fools mock, but they shall mourn; and my grace is sufficient for the meek, that they shall take no advantage of your weakness; And if men come unto me I will show unto them their weakness. I give unto men weakness that they may be humble; . . . and if they humble themselves before me, and have faith in me, then will I make weak things become strong unto them" (12:26–27). Many lessons can be learned from Moroni's examples and his candid musings here.

ETHER 12:23-41—MORONI FEARS THAT GENTILES WILL MOCK HIM

Why was Moroni so concerned about the Gentiles mocking "the placement of our words"? Of course, inscribing records on metal plates would have been tedious work. With no erasers, Moroni must have worried constantly about misplacing a character or leaving something out. He may also have worried about composing texts using the optimal standard arrangements, such as parallelism and chiasmus. Again, the art of "placing" words optimally was a highly sought scribal skill.

After examining the excellent Hebrew poetry of the earlier writers (such as King Benjamin and Alma), it is no wonder that Moroni was concerned about the placement of his words. He recognized and had directly quoted many brilliant poetic writings. C.S. Lewis, referring to Hebrew use of parallelism said, "It is (according to one's point of view) either a wonderful piece of luck or a wise provision of God's, that poetry which was to be turned into all languages should have as its chief formal characteristic one that does not disappear (as mere metre does) in translation" ("Introductory" to C. S. Lewis, *Reflections on the Psalms,* 6th imprint [London: Collins, 1969], 12). I think we have plenty of reasons to believe that Moroni had very high personal standards. Maybe he expected a little too much of himself, and maybe he was worried about every little detail, but indeed he had given attention to so many details. Normally, by the time we get to the Book of Ether, we tend to rush through it. Reading it from the perspective of Moroni, we realize that it contains numerous gems, properly presented and infinitely inspiring.

ETHER 13:25—SURPRISED BY TRUTH

As Hugh Nibley was riding the troop transport ships that were crossing the English Channel on the morning of June 6, 1944, he was one of the first to hit Utah Beach as one of the intelligence officers. He was to get behind German lines so he could let everybody know what was happening. He had smuggled a small copy of the Book of Mormon into his intelligence pockets. They were told that they could not put anything into these pockets except for classified materials. As he was riding across the choppy waters, he could not stop thinking about the war chapters at the end of the book of Ether. On several occasions, as Brother Nibley told this story, he would emphasize that, although he had read those chapters before, what had previously seemed so far out of the realm of reality suddenly became profoundly true, beyond anything he had ever experienced. It was at that darkest moment that his testimony of the truthfulness of the Book of Mormon became indelibly real for him. It was true in ways that no one could have just made up. Of course, Moroni himself, had experienced the painful realities of the crushing defeat of the Nephite armies, and his detailed accounts in these three chapters were grounded on the horrors of war that he had personally experienced. And like Brother Nibley's experience, Moroni's personal encounter with the darkness of war allowed him to rejoice even more in the ultimate contrast to be found in the wonderful testimonies of Christ throughout the Nephite records and on the twenty-four gold plates of Ether.

ETHER 15:31—SHIZ STRUGGLED AFTER CORIANTUMR SLEW HIM

One final event included by Moroni at the end of the book of Ether is the strange account of the decapitation of Shiz. It is often noted and has been wondered about, even mocked. In the final Jaredite battle, the head of Shiz was chopped off, but then he rose up, and collapsed. People suppose that this account must be mythological or has been embellished through the ages and doesn't represent an accurate account of what had happened. But reporting on the plausibility of this reported physiological phenomenon, Gary Hatfield, a professor of neuropathology, explains,

> Shiz's death struggle illustrates the classic reflex posture that occurs in both humans and animals when the upper brain stem (midbrain/mesencephalon) is disconnected from the brain. The extensor muscles of the arms and legs contract, and this reflex action could cause Shiz to raise up on his hands. In many patients, it is the sparing of vital respiratory and blood pressure in the central (pons) and lower (medulla) brain stem that permits survival.
>
> The brain stem is located inside the base of the skull and is relatively small. It connects the brain proper, or cerebrum, with the spinal cord in the neck.

Coriantumr was obviously too exhausted to do a clean job. His stroke evidently strayed a little too high. He must have cut off Shiz's head through the base of the skull, at the level of the midbrain, instead of lower through the cervical spine in the curvature of the neck. . . . Significantly, this nervous system phenomenon (decerebrate rigidity) was first reported in 1898, long after the Book of Mormon was published (Hadfield, M. Gary, and John W. Welch, "The 'Decapitation' of Shiz," in *Pressing Forward with the Book of Mormon: The FARMS Updates of the 1990s*, eds. John W. Welch and Melvin J. Thorne [Provo, UT: FARMS, 1999], 266–268).

Apparently, when the brain stem is cut at a certain point there is still enough of the nervous system left that it could give these impulses before the victim dies. Modern scientific knowledge thus offers corroboration of this gruesome account in the Book of Mormon, making this "weak thing" strong.

TAKEAWAYS

- **Why do you think Moroni interrupts the flow of Jaredite history to insert a discourse on the theme that "ye receive no witness until after the trial of your faith" (12:6), concluding after 13:1?**
- **Read Ether 12:37–40 aloud in a small group and discuss what significance one might see in the fact that Hyrum and Joseph Smith chose to read Ether 12:37–40 in the Carthage Jail, shortly before their martyrdom.**
- **Ether's final testimony is simply powerful and powerfully simple (15:34). How is it significant in helping us decide what is most important to us?**

49: MORONI 1-6

Moroni's first farewell, recorded in Mormon 8–9, was written "four hundred years" after "the coming of our Lord and Savior" (Mormon 8:6). Notably, this was approximately fifteen years after the battle at Cumorah (see Mormon 6:5). Moroni's final farewell, contained in the book bearing his own name, was written "more than four hundred and twenty years" after "the sign was given of the coming of Christ" (Moroni 10:1). By this time, nearly thirty-five years had passed since the battle at Cumorah. So, Moroni was at least middle-aged by this point and had wandered for many years to escape death at the hands of the Lamanites and to fulfill the commandments of the Lord (Moroni 1:1–4).

MORONI 1:1-4—WE SHOULD NOT DENY THE CHRIST

Above all, Moroni states clearly that he will not deny the Lord, no matter the cost (1:3). He certainly knew the words of his father and perhaps he had even helped him record the series of "woes" that included the following: "Wo unto him that spurneth at the doings of the Lord; yea, wo unto him that shall deny the Christ and his works!" (3 Nephi 29:5). So often we express confidently that we would do as Moroni did and refuse to deny Christ even at the pain of death. But we might well think: In what smaller things do we show less faith? In what ways are we leaving a legacy for future generations, as Moroni so admirably and so arduously did? We can learn a great deal from Moroni's example of courage and faith. He knew what the Savior had taught at the temple in Bountiful. He understood the covenants he had made, and he knew what taking the name of Christ upon himself meant. By his declaration, he tells his readers how he would handle being captured. He was not going to deny Christ, even at the expense of his own life. As we partake of the sacrament and renew our baptismal covenants, we take upon ourselves the name of Christ and promise to remember Him always. Remembering implies that we will not deny—in other words, forget or pretend that we cannot remember what we once knew. There is a covenantal dimension to Moroni's statement. He wants us to remember that life will be difficult. There will be real challenges. We need to be prepared to stand with Christ no matter what. This is typical of Moroni's masterful style of understatement, where you must stop and consider each of his words.

MORONI 1:2—WHY WERE THE LAMANITES STILL FIGHTING?

Why were the Lamanites now fighting amongst themselves? They had finally gotten rid of the pesky Nephites. Things should have been wonderful for them, but what was happening? There had been great unity, and there was no manner of *ites*, but then corruption entered. Everyone split off into their own social, economic, or ideological groups.

Many of these groups had a common enemy—the Nephites. They were ready to get rid of them. However, once they did, we see the occurrence of a familiar pattern. If a political group is only brought together by an enemy, once that enemy is gone, there is not much to hold them together any longer. They begin dividing up the spoils until they inevitably turn on each other and start fighting. If a civilization is not peaceful to begin with, it is unlikely that it will become peaceful when they achieve power and success.

MORONI 1:4—"PERHAPS THEY MAY BE OF WORTH"

Moroni decided to write a few things, "perhaps they may be of worth unto my brethren, the Lamanites, in some future day" (1:4). He started by sharing the words of Christ spoken to His disciples, commanding them to "call on the Father in my name" (Moroni 2). Prayer in the name of Christ is always the starting point of righteous living. Then he gave the sacred words used by Jesus in giving the disciples the authority to give the Holy Ghost (Moroni 2). He also gave the words used to ordain priests and teachers (Moroni 3), the words of the sacrament prayers (Moroni 4 and 5), and instructions for holding church meetings (Moroni 6). These are indeed of utmost worth.

MORONI 2:1–3—AUTHORITY TO BESTOW THE HOLY GHOST

In these verses, Moroni records how the Nephite disciples were given the authority to give the gift of the Holy Ghost, and the way that ordinance should be performed. These instructions were given by the resurrected Savior. In 3 Nephi 18:36–37, Jesus touched the Twelve, but the multitude did not hear what He said. The disciples witnessed that He gave them the power to give the Holy Ghost.

Joseph Smith was once asked by U.S. President Martin Van Buren, in what ways Latter-day Saints "differed from other religions of the day." The prophet's answer was that we have the gift of the Holy Ghost and that it is given by the laying on of hands, and "all other considerations were contained in the gift of the Holy Ghost" (Joseph's letter to Hyrum, December 5, 1839).

MORONI 3:1–4—ORDAINING PRIESTS AND TEACHERS

In chapter 3, Moroni provides the instructions and words for ordination to the priesthood. Jesus told the disciples, "after they had prayed unto the Father" (3:2), they should place their hands on the heads of the persons being ordained and ordain them. This manner of conducting ordinations can remind us of the importance of preparing prayerfully before performing any priesthood ordinance or service unto the Lord.

The main charge then given to the priests and teachers was that they should "preach repentance and remission of sins through Jesus Christ, by the endurance of faith on his name to the end" (3:3).

These ordinances required the laying on of hands. This is reminiscent of Moses laying his hands upon Joshua: "And Moses did as the Lord commanded him: and he took Joshua, and set him before Eleazar the priest, and before all the congregation: And he laid his hands upon him, and gave him a charge, as the Lord commanded by the hand of Moses" (Numbers 27:22–23).

In Deuteronomy 34:9, we read of the effect this had on Joshua: "And Joshua the son of Nun was full of the spirit of wisdom; for Moses had laid his hands upon him." This method of ordination was also used by Alma (see Alma 6:1). It was a common practice of early Christians, especially in the New Testament.

MORONI 4-5—"WILLING TO TAKE UPON THEM"

One particularly noteworthy phrase appearing in the prayers in Moroni 4–5 that was not included in the recorded words of Christ in 3 Nephi 18: "that they are *willing to take upon them* the name of thy Son" (Moroni 4:3; emphasis added). That phrase parallels King Benjamin's words as he put his people under covenant to take upon themselves the name of Christ (Mosiah 5:8) about 150 years before the appearance of Christ at the temple in Bountiful. It seems that Nephite texts and traditions had combined and coalesced beautifully into the final sacrament prayers in Moroni 4–5. Elder Dallin H. Oaks emphasized the word *willingness*, pointing to a future consummation. Elder Oaks said: "By partaking of the sacrament we witness our willingness to participate in the sacred ordinances of the temple and to receive the highest blessings available through the name and by the authority of the Savior when he chooses to confer them upon us" (Dallin H. Oaks, "Taking upon Us the Name of Jesus Christ," *Ensign,* May 1985, 81).

MORONI 6:2-3—MORONI SETS FORTH THE REQUIREMENTS OF BAPTISM

The requirement for baptism is given in 4 Nephi 1:1: "As many as did come unto them, and did truly repent of their sins, were baptized in the name of Jesus; and they did also receive the Holy Ghost." Moroni 6:2–3 clarifies the expectations, stating: "Neither did they receive any unto baptism save they came forth with a broken heart and a contrite spirit, and witnessed unto the church that they truly repented of all their sins. And none were received unto baptism save they took upon them the name of Christ, *having a determination to serve him to the end*" (Moroni 6:3; emphasis added). Moroni's people also helped all Church members remain faithful to their baptismal covenant: "As oft as they repented and sought forgiveness, with real intent, they were forgiven" (6:8).

MORONI 6:5-9—THE CHURCH IS TO MEET TOGETHER OFTEN

When followers met together, it says in verse 9 that their meetings were "conducted by the church after the manner of the workings of the Spirit and by the power of the Holy Ghost; For as the power of the Holy Ghost led them whether to preach, or to exhort, or to pray, or to supplicate, or to sing, even so it was done." Singing and music were also part of their worship services. This carried over the traditional uses of the Old Testament Psalms and other hymns of praise and joy that were long-standing parts of ancient Israelite family and temple worship. Throughout the scriptures, hymns play an integral role in worship—a heartfelt outpouring of testimony and gratitude by Saints in all dispensations and in all circumstances. Alma spoke of "the song of redeeming love" (Alma 5:26), a spontaneous acknowledgement of gratitude for the Lord's atoning sacrifice; Hosea spoke of a song of remembrance for the Lord's tender mercies (Hosea 2:15); the Psalmist entreated us to "come before [the] Lord's presence with singing" (Psalms 100:2); a heavenly choir heralded the birth of the Savior with praises of "glory to God in the highest" (Luke 2:14); we read of the Savior and His disciples on the sacred occasion of the Last Supper singing a hymn before going "out into the mount of Olives" (Matthew 26:30); faithful Saints of the Restoration, who had suffered every form of trial, deprivation, and persecution, united their voices in thanksgiving as they sang, "All is well" (*Hymns*, no. 30); and the Prophet Joseph Smith invited the very earth to "break forth into singing" in praise of the Restoration (Doctrine and Covenants 128:22). Singing and praising God (see 3 Nephi 4:31) was endorsed by Jesus as He quoted Isaiah (see 3 Nephi 16:18–19; 20:32–34; and 22:1).

In addition, at the end of verse 5, it says that when they met, it was "to speak one with another concerning the welfare of their souls." One may hope that in the study of scriptures, in priesthood and Relief Society classes, concentration centers on the welfare of souls, and how well everyone is doing, and that the lessons focus on the real purpose of getting together. In that case, the Spirit can guide us more specifically. Using the methods given for ordinances and meetings and applying the guidance in Moroni 1–6 will give us the means to become closer to becoming the Zion society we know is possible.

TAKEAWAYS

- **Write a thank-you letter to Moroni. Write what you would like to say to him when you will meet him at the judgment bar of God, as he says we all will.**
- **Closely compare the first-person words used by Jesus, as He blessed the sacrament in 3 Nephi 18, with the words now used by the priests in blessing the bread and the water (see Doctrine and Covenants 20:77–79). Discuss with others their insights, impressions, and feelings about the history of our sacrament prayers, from Mosiah 5:10–12, to 3 Nephi 18, and finally in Moroni 4–5.**
- **For this week, try beginning each day with a hymn and record the difference it makes.**

50: MORONI 7-9

Moroni must have treasured the words found in these chapters. After being alone for an extended time, he included three writings from his father, Mormon, the great historian, prophet, military leader, and custodian of all sacred records. We can understand Moroni's loneliness and imagine the comfort he felt while reading the counsel from his righteous father. The three writings are: Mormon's sermon testifies boldly of Jesus Christ and urges true followers to live in the light of correct principles despite Satan's pronounced influence on society (found in Moroni 7). The two other epistles, private correspondence from father to son, unfold in candid language Mormon's eventual resignation to the fate of a wicked society; they also instruct plainly how to continue in individual righteousness. This is not embellished rhetoric. Mormon's vocabulary is very straightforward. Probably due to his many years of military leadership, Mormon was a forthright speaker of truth. These two letters deal with the problems of infant baptism (Moroni 8) and the final degeneration of the Nephites (Moroni 9).

MORONI 7—MORMON'S SERMON IN THE CONTEXT OF THE TEN-YEAR PEACE TREATY

In approximately AD 350, the Lamanites, the Gadianton robbers, and the Nephites made a serious, inviolate peace treaty that lasted ten years (Mormon 3:1). If, as scholars believe, it coincided with a great sabbatical celebration of peace and jubilee, what better time for a prophet like Mormon to have given his magnum opus—the most important words that he could give to his people, dealing with the crucial topics of prayer, faith, hope, and charity. The occasion must have been very solemn, as everyone on both sides of the war was willing to take a sabbatical from the killing and violence.

Moroni described this as a speech given in a synagogue "which they had built for the place of worship" (7:1). One may glide over that little statement, not noticing that these people had been on the run. The Nephites had been driven to a land northward (Mormon 2:29), where they lived during the ten-year peace treaty. It would have made sense for them to build a synagogue, and it also makes sense that Mormon would have been the most appropriate candidate to have spoken, perhaps at its dedication, as people tried to reclaim their faith, rebuild their hope, and try to love everyone, even their enemies.

MORONI 7:3-4—MORMON'S AUDIENCE

Any Nephite listening to Mormon would have been weary from being on the run. They were a war-torn generation; all they had known was strife and instability. Mormon's wording was aimed right at the hearts of his audience. He said, "I would speak unto you that are of the church, that are the peaceable followers of Christ, and that have obtained a sufficient hope by which ye can enter into the rest of the Lord from this time henceforth until ye shall rest with him in heaven." Yearning for the peace that comes from entering into the rest of the Lord would have been a very powerful way for him to begin his talk, especially as a ten-year period of peace had been negotiated. They had a start, yet he wanted to stir them unto greater works.

"And now my brethren, I judge these things of you because of your peaceable walk with the children of men." He is speaking to his synagogue, his beloved brethren, his church, and his people. He was blessed with an inner group of faithful believers. He was leading Nephites, Jacobites, Josephites, Zoramites, and many different people; but here, he is likely addressing the leaders, the ones who really held the Nephite tradition together. They were people who had hope in the "Rest of the Lord." They had a start, and he wanted to stir them to greater works. Fourteen times, Mormon interrupts his train of thought by calling out to his "brethren," and nine of those times he refers to them as "my beloved brethren."

MORONI 7—MORMON'S SERMON ECHOES JESUS'S SERMON AT THE TEMPLE

For his text on this occasion, Mormon parallels Christ's sermon given to the Nephite people at the temple. It contains some of the most sacred words that Jesus taught. And although Mormon frequently used or alluded to the Savior's words, he explained further and added new concepts to meet the local needs. For example, "By their fruits ye shall know them" (3 Nephi 14:20).

Mormon changes only one word, "By their works ye shall know them" (Moroni 7:5). In this case, the word "works" is more active, progressive, and ongoing, whereas "fruits" might be thought of as more final, specific, and result oriented.

Following this reference to the Savior's sermon, Mormon explained that if their works were good, then they were good. He said, in verse 10, "Behold, God has said, a man being evil cannot do that which is good," similar to Jesus's metaphor that a good tree (3 Nephi 14:17-19) cannot bring forth evil fruit. Giving a gift, making an offering, or praying without real intent (i.e., doing so casually or grudgingly) is not counted as righteousness. In Mormon 2:14, Mormon had recorded that the people had refused to offer the ultimate and most desirable sacrifice—that of a broken heart and contrite spirit.

Mormon continued, "For if he offered a gift or prayeth unto God, except he shall do it with real intent it profiteth him nothing" (7:6). Notice further that Moroni also used the phrase "with real intent" in his encouragement to pray to know the truth of the Book of Mormon in Moroni 10:4–5. Moroni had learned this from his father.

Mormon reaches again to the words of the temple sermon to prelude his next main point. "Whatsoever thing ye shall ask the Father in my name, *which is good, in faith believing that ye shall receive*, behold it shall be done unto you" (7:26; emphasis added). This statement repeats, with two qualifications, the Savior's words in the temple sermon: "Ask, and it shall be given unto you" (3 Nephi 14:7). Mormon went on to develop the thought even further. His adaptations of the text came predominantly through developing the concepts and principles to benefit his audience. He often added a new level of understanding to the words and phrases.

MORONI 7:16-18—THE LIGHT OF CHRIST

There must have been some confusion among the people when distinguishing good from evil. In verse 16, Mormon taught a very significant new concept. He explained that the spirit of Christ—or what today is more often called the "Light of Christ"—is given to everyone, and this source of divine light can help us make righteous judgments: "The Spirit of Christ is given to every man, that he may know good from evil; wherefore, I show unto you the way to judge," the criteria being, "Every thing which inviteth to do good, and to persuade to believe in Christ, is sent forth by the power and gift of Christ" (7:16).

In direct contrast, Mormon reminds them, "Whatsoever thing persuadeth men to do evil, and believe not in Christ, and deny him, and serve not God" is promoted by the devil, then he adds, "for he persuaded no man to do good, no, not one" (7:17). Note Mormon's no-nonsense nature when including such pointed emphasis. He likely witnessed many excuses for poor judgments during his life.

There indeed had been significant emphasis on "light" in Christ's Sermon at the Temple. Jesus also taught, "The light of the body is the eye; if, therefore, thine eye be single, thy whole body shall be full of light" (3 Nephi 13:22). Here in Mormon's discourse, he also discusses light and discernment. His ultimate purpose is to help his listeners discern how to "lay hold upon every good thing" (Moroni 7:19).

MORONI 7:21-39—MORMON ON FAITH

Mormon mentioned the recent dearth of miracles three times, in verses 27, 29, and 35, in which he asks three rhetorical questions. In verse 27, he asked, "Wherefore, my beloved brethren, have miracles ceased because Christ hath ascended into heaven?" The people were apparently arguing that the Savior was living up in heaven and had distanced himself from them. Mormon countered in verse 29 with his second question: "And because he hath done this [ascended into heaven], my beloved brethren, have miracles ceased? Behold I say unto you, Nay; neither have angels ceased to minister unto the children of men." As part of his evidence that miracles had not actually ceased, he taught the importance of angels and their mission, their ministry of calling people to repentance and seeing that the covenants of God are fulfilled (see 7:30–31).

After that brief clarification, in verse 35, Mormon again asks: "Has the day of miracles ceased?" In verse 37, he concludes, "It is by faith that miracles are wrought; and it is by faith that angels appear and minister unto men; wherefore, if these things have ceased wo be unto the children of men, for it is because of unbelief, and all is vain."

Mormon made it clear that it was not God, or his angels, or the Holy Ghost who had ceased to appear or to work with humans here on earth. Again, he asks three more rapid-fire questions to show that God will not withhold His power so long as "there shall be one man upon the face [of the earth] to be saved" (7:36). (That reference to "one man upon the face of the earth" may well have haunted Moroni as he wandered as a lone survivor for many years upon the land.) Mormon also encouraged his audience by explaining that he knew that they could be faithful (7:37) and meek, and that they (and also we) could thus be "fit to be numbered among the people of his church" (7:39).

MORONI 7:40-43—MORMON ON HOPE

Following his treatment of faith, Mormon delicately intertwined that theme with his teachings on hope. Here he asks his two final questions: How can a person obtain faith except together with hope? And what should one hope for (7:40–41)? Again, we learn predominantly and specifically from Mormon, as we saw briefly with Alma, that if the power of the Holy Ghost is active, one hopes to be resurrected and to stand again in the presence of God (7:41). That is the last place the wicked want to be. Cleaving to the good and developing faith leads to hope in Christ, and those elements lead to charity. Faith is a necessary and sufficient condition for hope: If you have faith, you must have hope, for without faith there is no hope (7:42). Moreover, a person cannot have faith and hope unless they are "meek, and lowly of heart" (7:43), and that meekness necessarily leads to charity (7:44).

MORONI 7:44-47—MORMON ON CHARITY

Three results of true faith and hope are (1) being "acceptable before God," (2) meekly confessing "by the power of the Holy Ghost that Jesus is the Christ," and (3) having charity (7:44). Mormon's logic here is that if you don't have charity, you are "*nothing*"; on the contrary, when a person *is* "acceptable before God," that person must be *something*, and thus must possess the attribute of charity. This is another way of saying that charity is an essential—even a necessary condition for existence in the presence of God. Mormon emphatically concludes that "charity is the pure love of Christ, and it endureth forever" (7:47).

Then, after concluding, "wherefore, my beloved brethren, if ye have not charity, *ye are* nothing" (Moroni 7:46; compare "and have not charity, *I am* nothing" [1 Cor. 13: 3; emphasis added]), Mormon says, "for charity never faileth" (Moroni 7:46; 1 Corinthians 13:8). Mormon then tells his audience absolutely to "cleave unto charity, which is the greatest *of all*" (7:46; emphasis added). Mormon speaks as a personal witness of the pure love of Jesus and of obtaining "every *good* thing" through Him.

MORONI 8:4-9—INFANT BAPTISMS BEGIN AMONG THE NEPHITES

There is no information about why infant baptism began among the Nephites, but a totally new pattern had arisen. Mormon was astonished, even offended by it. This may well have been intended. People were starving; the gruesome consequences of warfare did not spare children. Parents may have been afraid that their children would never get a chance to be baptized. In the absence of guidance from the Holy Ghost, people do what appears logical at the time.

Whatever motivated this practice, Mormon did not like it; he saw this as an awful wickedness and did not identify any righteous reason for the change. He described it as a "gross error," and "a solemn mockery" (8:9). Mormon was most concerned because infant baptism abrogates the whole purpose of Christ's Atonement, and very clearly denies repentance that allows Christ's mercy to operate. Thus, it creates a bigger problem within the entire Church. If people are not willing to teach their children to repent so that they can be baptized, then they cease repenting, allowing wicked conditions to ensue.

MORONI 9:6—MORMON AND MORONI REMAIN FAITHFUL (SEE MORMON 5:1)

To his son, Moroni, who had also been called to preach to the people, Mormon wrote, "Notwithstanding their hardness, let us labor diligently; for if we should cease to labor, we should be brought under condemnation; for we have a labor to perform whilst in this tabernacle of clay" (9:6). He was essentially saying, "Well, we are still here. God has spared our lives. As long as we are alive, He expects us to be working. We must carry on with the responsibilities He has given us." It is a reminder to cherish the "gift of his calling unto me" (7:2). It is important to remember that our responsibilities before the Lord are also gifts.

MORONI 9:18-22—RECOMMEND THEE TO GOD

One may ask whether order is related to principle. There are signs of ripening destruction. Here, near the end of their civilization, the Nephites were without order, without mercy, without principle, and were past feeling. In fact, their civilization had fallen apart. When these people became unprincipled and past feeling, they became obsessed with killing and lost all sense of obedience or order. Eventually, the military system and society devolved into disorder, disarray, and then chaos. Mormon states bluntly that he "cannot recommend them unto God" (9:21), but even in this extreme condition he does not excuse Moroni from individual righteousness. In fact, he recognizes Moroni's collective actions and choices, saying, "But behold, my son, I recommend thee unto God" (9:22). From Moroni's example, we can be assured that individual righteousness is always a choice.

TAKEAWAYS

- How have your callings been both a gift and a responsibility in your life?
- What more can you do to offer gifts or prayers with real intent?
- What good works allow the Light of Christ to shine through you?
- What other similarities do you notice in Mormon's sermon and Jesus's Temple Sermon? How do these compare to the Sermon on the Mount?

51: MORONI 10

In his final chapter, Moroni begins by stating that he is concluding and sealing up his record: "I seal up these records, after I have spoken a few words by way of exhortation unto you." While his closing words are directed specifically to "[his] brethren, the Lamanites," this powerful chapter has been and will continue to be a life-changing message for all who have or ever will read it. He exhorted the Lamanites—and all readers—to take defined spiritual steps to come unto Christ. Moroni made this clear in 10:24, when he extends his words to "all the ends of the earth," clarifying the principles he had taught, and then inviting *all* to "come unto Christ" (10:30). Each exhortation and every invitation is worth examining and applying to our own spiritual growth.

MORONI 10:1—MORONI'S WORDS TO THE LAMANITES

In urging the Lamanites toward righteousness, Moroni used the word "exhort" eight times as he taught. The word "exhort" can refer to many levels of encouragement, but Moroni avoided using the more pointed questioning and challenging methods he had used in Mormon 8–9.

MORONI 10:3—REMEMBER THE LORD'S MERCY (FIRST EXHORTATION)

Moroni's first exhortation was, "*Remember how merciful the Lord hath been unto the children of men.*" This theme of remembering the mercy of the Lord is found throughout the entire Book of Mormon. For example, Alma, Benjamin, Jacob, and Helaman all addressed this topic. Knowing that God has been merciful in the past provides confidence that He will be generous again. If we remember the love of God, gratitude will soften the heart, making us more receptive to personal revelation.

MORONI 10:4-5—ASK GOD IN THE NAME OF CHRIST (SECOND EXHORTATION)

Moroni's second exhortation was "*ask God the Eternal Father in the name of Christ, if these things are not true.*" Biblical law (see Deuteronomy 17 and 19) required two or three witnesses in order for anything legal, including all important documents, to be enforced. When sealing up an important record, a scribe would call upon other people to testify to its legitimacy. But Moroni was all alone. His exhortation and promise in Moroni 10:4 provide more than an opportunity for testimony-building. Moroni had planned to perform a formal sealing as explained in Moroni 10:2, so he named three witnesses who would testify to the truthfulness of what he had written, though not in the traditional manner. So, he called upon the three members of the Godhead! Moroni 10:4 states, "And when ye shall receive these things, I would exhort you that ye would ask *God, the Eternal Father*, in the name of *Christ*, if these things are not true; and if ye shall ask with a sincere heart, with real intent, having faith in Christ, he will manifest the truth of it unto you, by the *power of the Holy Ghost.*"

These ultimately reliable witnesses will always testify to the correctness of scriptural records in all eras, not only during our earth lives, but also at the judgment bar. Moroni states, "And God shall show unto you, that that which I have written is true" (10:29). The authentication of this record is far greater than that of any other. It is incumbent upon the reader to observe Moroni's seventh exhortation in verses 24 through 27—to believe and trust the record that he has provided.

MORONI 10:6-7—DENY NOT THE POWER OF GOD (THIRD EXHORTATION)

Moroni preceded his discussion about the gifts of God with an exhortation to "*deny not the power of God*," and later explained that when people are unbelieving, "the power and gifts of God shall be done away" (Moroni 10:24). We must have faith before God's power can reveal truth. He declared that God only "worketh by power, according to the faith of the children of men" (10:7).

MORONI 10:8-16—DENY NOT THE GIFTS OF GOD (FOURTH EXHORTATION)

Moroni used the word *deny* seven times in this chapter. He used it three times in three consecutive verses (10:6; 10:7; 10:8) that addressed his Lamanite readers. He used it again four times at the very end of the chapter. If we must not deny Christ, or the power of God, then we must not deny the many gifts of God. Moroni's four other uses of "deny" occur near the end of chapter 10, in verses 32 and 33 (see below).

MORONI 10:17—GIFTS OF THE SPIRIT COME UNTO EVERY MAN SEVERALLY

Moroni teaches that the gifts come by the Spirit of Christ. They come unto every man "*severally, according as he will*" (10:17; emphasis added). "Severally" is an antiquated way of saying "individually." In the Parable of the Talents, for example, the master gave out talents "to every man according to his *several* ability" (Matthew 25:15), that is according to his *individual* or *personal* ability.

MORONI 10:18—REMEMBER THAT EVERY GOOD GIFT COMETH FROM CHRIST (FIFTH EXHORTATION)

Following his list of gifts of the Spirit, Moroni exhorted the reader to remember that "*every good gift cometh of Christ*" (10:18). This statement presumes the existence of bad gifts, and later, in 10:30, Moroni reminded his readers to "touch not the evil gift." Evil gifts may initially look enticing (as worldly pleasures paraded before us), but they lead us down the wrong path and encourage pride. By the fruits that are borne of "good gifts," we can recognize and harvest the benefits or abilities they generate.

MORONI 10:19—REMEMBER GOD REMAINS THE SAME (SIXTH EXHORTATION)

Moroni's sixth exhortation is to remember that God is the same, yesterday, today, and forever. He is constant in sustaining His covenants; God's promises are sure. One of the main reasons the Book of Mormon was written was so that people will know God's covenants and will know that God is the same today as He was when He first made each covenant.

MORONI 10:24-27—REMEMBER ALL THESE THINGS (SEVENTH EXHORTATION)

In verse 24, Moroni addressed "all the ends of the earth." Expounding further on the gifts of God, he warned that if the gifts of God were to be "done away," it would be because of unbelief and unrighteousness. This is followed by his seventh exhortation in verse 27. Speaking still to the entire world, he explained why we must remember these things: "For the time speedily cometh that ye shall know that I lie not, for ye shall see me at the bar of God; and the Lord God will say unto you: Did I not declare my words unto you, which were written by this man, like as one crying from the dead, yea, even as one speaking out of the dust?"

The term "remember" is used throughout the record. King Benjamin also said, "And now, O man, remember, and perish not" (Mosiah 4:30). There is more to remembering, though, than just being able to memorize something. The Hebrew word behind "remember" is the term "obey." When we *really* remember something, we obey it. The word "member" refers to "a part of something." To "re-member," therefore, means "to put the parts back together." Moroni asked us to recall and recollect and feel again what we experienced when good gifts came to us. He was giving us a recipe for building, strengthening, and maintaining our testimony of Jesus Christ

MORONI 10:30-32—COME UNTO CHRIST AND BE PERFECTED BY HIS GRACE (EIGHTH EXHORTATION)

In these verses, Moroni outlined steps to attain the goal of coming unto Christ and being perfected in Him. To become perfected in Christ, Moroni explained, we must deny ourselves of all ungodliness, and love God with all our might, mind, and strength, which Jesus identified as the greatest commandment.

"Perfected" does not mean 100% or flawless. The Hebrew term means "to be at peace, finally settled, everything is calm." In Greek, "to be perfected" means "to come across a finish line." Note also that the scripture says to be perfected "in Christ." This can only be accomplished as we are yoked together with Him through our covenants and harnessing His enabling power. "Our only hope for true perfection is in receiving [our Savior's grace] as a gift from heaven—we can't 'earn' it" (Jeffrey R. Holland, "Be Ye Therefore Perfect—Eventually," *Ensign*, November 2017). He does not expect us to achieve "perfection" alone or in this lifetime.

MORONI 10:30-31—TOUCH NOT THE UNCLEAN THING

Moroni used Isaiah 52:11 here: "Depart ye, depart ye, go ye out from thence, touch no unclean thing; go ye out of the midst of her; be ye clean, that bear the vessels of the Lord." This phrase was also used in Alma 5:57. Jesus quoted it almost verbatim at the temple in Bountiful in 3 Nephi 20:41. Moroni was teaching principles that had been demonstrated and taught throughout the record.

In 10:31, Moroni also used Isaiah 52:1–2: "Awake and arise from the dust, O Jerusalem." He continued with "and put on thy beautiful garments, O daughter of Zion; and strengthen thy stakes and enlarge thy borders forever." He blended three passages from Isaiah 52 and Isaiah 54, all of which Jesus had quoted in 3 Nephi 20 and 22. Moroni echoed the words of Jesus and prophets as he invited us to come unto Jesus.

MORONI 10:32-33—DENY NOT, DENY NOT, DENY NOT, DENY NOT

Four culminating exhortations to "deny not" are included in these last two verses. After having expanded the audience to include people in "all the ends of the earth" (10:24), Moroni goes on to invite everyone to "come unto Christ and lay hold upon every good gift." He then places the next two "denys" at the center of a chiasm in 10:32:

"Come unto [a] Christ,
    and [b] be perfected in him,
        and [c] *deny* yourselves of all ungodliness;
            and if ye shall [c'] *deny* yourselves of all ungodliness, and love God with all your might, minds, and strength, then is his grace sufficient for you, that by his grace
    ye may [b'] be perfect
in [a'] Christ."

And then in 10:32–33, he intensifies his final point using a direct parallelism:

"And if [d] by the grace of God
    ye are [e] perfect
        in [f] Christ, ye can in nowise
            [g] *deny* the power of God" (10:32).
"And again, if [d'] ye by the grace of God
    are [e'] perfect
        in [f'] Christ,
            and [g'] *deny not* his power, then are ye sanctified in Christ" (10:33).

With this final emphasis, Moroni signaled that all readers should make serious efforts to avoid wrongly denying the manifestations of God's spirit to us. As the word "deny" was used prominently in interrogations reported in the cases of Sherem, Korihor, and others in the Book of Mormon, Moroni wants all his readers to never deny what they know to be true. If we deny the truth, our lot will be sad before the judgment bar of God.

MORONI 10:34—MORONI ULTIMATELY INVOKES THE NAME JEHOVAH

The name "Jehovah" appears only once in the Book of Mormon (except when it is in a quotation from Isaiah or another prophet). Moroni takes this final opportunity to call upon the holy name of Jehovah, his last word "until . . . I am brought forth triumphant through the air, to meet you before the pleasing bar of the *great Jehovah, the Eternal Judge of both quick and dead.*"

The name "Jehovah" was extremely sacred to the ancient Israelites. One needed to be careful to never take this name "in vain." Misuse of it was blasphemy. In Jewish observances, the name "Jehovah" was so sacred that it could only be pronounced aloud on the Day of Atonement.

MORONI 10:34—THE PLEASING BAR

Moroni ended by bidding farewell until he will meet us "before the pleasing bar of the great Jehovah, the Eternal Judge of both quick and dead." This phrase is also found in Jacob's farewell in Jacob 6:13. Alma 42 makes it very clear that God is both just and merciful, and that God cannot exist without both attributes. Understanding God as both a just and a merciful judge provides us with great reassurance. Moroni's life was dedicated to bringing all people to stand before God, through Christ, to receive all promised blessings. It is a wonderful privilege for us to have and to be able to discuss this beautiful text. The Holy Ghost bears witness that this sacred book is true.

TAKEAWAYS

- **Why is it important for us to remember and ponder how merciful God has been from the time of Adam until now (10:3)? How does that change our perspective? What kinds of emotions or thoughts does this evoke?**
- **How do Moroni's eight exhortations resonate with you personally?**
    - **to remember how merciful God has been to the children of men (10:3)**
    - **to ask God (10:4)**
    - **to deny not God's power (10:7)**
    - **to deny not God's gifts (10:8)**
    - **to remember that every good gift comes from Christ (10:18)**
    - **to remember that God remains the same (10:19)**
    - **to not be unbelieving, and not to die in your sins (10:24–27)**
    - **to come unto Christ and lay hold on every good gift (10:30)**
- **Moroni's concluding words (10:30–34) give us a wonderful example of how to invite people to come unto Christ. What impresses you the most about what he says in these very memorable verses? Find a way to share a personal testimony of your own experience with any of the verses written by Moroni with someone close to you or with someone who is searching for answers.**

52: CHRISTMAS IN THE BOOK OF MORMON: ANOTHER TESTAMENT OF JESUS CHRIST

MOSIAH 3:3-13, 2 NEPHI 25:6

Let us begin with the famous words spoken by an angel to certain shepherds and repeated each year in Nativity presentations large or small: "Behold, I bring you good tidings of great joy, which shall be to all people" (Luke 2:10–11). This headline was a joyous one, having many facets, being meant to be shared generously. King Benjamin had a similar experience, as reported in the Book of Mormon, when an angel of the Lord visited him declaring "glad tidings of great joy" (Mosiah 3:3). King Benjamin was told to teach these truths to his people, "that they may also be filled with joy" (Mosiah 3:4). And what were those glad tidings? "The Lord Omnipotent who reigneth, who was, and is from all eternity to all eternity, shall come down from heaven among the children of men, and shall dwell in a tabernacle of clay" (Mosiah 3:5). He will come with majesty, power, goodness, and authority.

The "glad tidings" will also include the miracles that Jesus will perform and His culminating Atonement and Resurrection (Mosiah 3:5–10). All this will be done out of love, "that salvation might come unto the children of men even through faith on his name" (Mosiah 3:9). What marvelous tidings! They are unto all people, unto every nation, and unto all the children of God, making it possible for everyone to "receive remission of their sins, and rejoice with exceedingly great joy" (Mosiah 3:13). The angelic message from our Lord is clearly one of happiness and relief, spreading peace, hope, and charity among God's children on earth. As Nephi wrote, "We rejoice in Christ" (2 Nephi 25:26).

1 NEPHI 11:13-18, 2 NEPHI 17:14—A VIRGIN WILL CONCEIVE

Nephi also recorded Isaiah's prophecy, "a virgin shall conceive, and shall bear a son" (2 Nephi 17:14). Here Isaiah prophesied something unusual about this birth; he is saying more than that this mother will be young, as most girls in that time were when they married. Nephi also sees this virgin, "beautiful and fair," and is told by an angel, "Behold, the virgin whom thou seest is the mother of the Son of God, after the manner of the flesh" (1 Nephi 11:18). King Benjamin adds that she would be named Mary (Mosiah 3:4). Alma the Younger teaches, "She being a virgin, a precious and chosen vessel, who shall be overshadowed and conceive by the power of the Holy Ghost, and bring forth a son, yea, even the Son of God" (Alma 7:10). All these descriptions, given to men living in another hemisphere, support and strengthen the recorded events in the New Testament Gospels.

2 NEPHI 19:6—UNTO US A SON IS GIVEN

From the time they were a small group in the wilderness, the Nephite people had an understanding that the Savior of the world would come to earth as a gift from a loving Heavenly Father. Nephi quoted the prophecies of Isaiah from the brass plates, "For unto us a child is born, unto us a son is given" (2 Nephi 19:6). Sent as a deity clothed in mortality, Jesus Christ is Heavenly Father's gift to all His children. Only through this perfect gift can the virtues of faith, repentance, and obedience be efficacious for the rest of God's children. Yet, because He came and fulfilled His mission, it is possible for all of God's children to attain the glory, honor, and dominions of eternal life.

We often think of the word "unto" simply as a replacement for "to," meaning that something is given to someone. Jesus was given to believers as an exemplar, a teacher, a sacrifice for sin, a healer, and so forth. Another meaning of "unto" indicates that the gift of this Savior will continue until a particular time, as in "remain faithful *unto* the end." Certainly, the gift of the Son of God as Mediator and Redeemer remains in force through and unto all generations of time. A third use of "unto" suggests "to bring about or empower." For example, Moroni urges us to have "faith on His name *unto* repentance." This reading becomes very personal. The power and might of the Savior's grace realizes its full potential in us when we receive this gift and use His infinite Atonement for our good. Jesus Christ is indeed a perfect gift given to all God's children through all time for the purpose of empowering imperfect siblings.

CHRISTMAS AND EASTER ARE CONNECTED

At Christmas time it is fully appropriate to also focus also on the miraculous circumstances surrounding the birth of our Savior and to celebrate the arrival of the Only Begotten Son to live among men on earth. Though the birth of Jesus was foretold and anticipated with great excitement, it was never the apex moment of prophetic visions or prophecies. Rather, it was consistently viewed as an essential event building toward the truly climactic Atonement, Crucifixion, and Resurrection of the Son of God.

Notice how each of the prophecies of the birth of Christ also included information regarding His ministry and atoning sacrifice, with a focus on its potential for all mankind. Nephi, for example, sees not only the baby Jesus carried in His mother's arms, but also witnesses His ministry and Crucifixion. Nephi is shown that ultimately, Jesus will visit the Nephite posterity in the promised land. Alma taught not only that Jesus would be born of Mary at Jerusalem, but also explained that He would take upon Himself pains, sicknesses, and sins to know "according to the flesh how to succor his people" and "blot out their transgressions" (Alma 7:10–13). President Gordon B. Hinckley reminded us of this connection when he taught, "There would be no Christmas if there were no Easter," because the Atonement of Jesus Christ "is the keystone in the arch of our existence" (April 2007).

HELAMAN 14:2-7, 3 NEPHI 1:4-22—SIGNS OF CHRIST'S BIRTH ARE GIVEN AND FULFILLED

In the Book of Mormon, the birth of Jesus was also heralded. Samuel the Lamanite gave five signs of the coming of Christ: (1) the five-year prophecy, (2) no darkness for two days and one night, (3) a new star, (4) signs and wonders, and (5) people will fall to the earth. All ancient societies had important calendar units or time periods that were carefully marked. Possibly because the very lives of the believers depended on the fulfillment of those prophecies, Nephi paid careful attention to documenting the precise wording of Samuel's prophecies as well as their exact fulfillments (see 3 Nephi 1:13, 15, 16–17, 21; 2:1). Samuel said they would be able to clearly discern the setting and rising of the sun, yet there would still be no darkness. At the end of those five years, exactly as Samuel had prophesied, "at the going down of the sun there was no darkness" (3 Nephi 1:15). Like any other miracles performed by or connected with the birth, ministry, and Resurrection of Jesus, the way these manifestations happened is unknown.

Samuel the Lamanite also prophesied not only of the great overnight light, but added that a new star, "such an one as ye never have beheld," would also appear (Helaman 14:5). The Book of Mormon records: "And it came to pass also that a new star did appear, according to the word" (3 Nephi 1:21). Elder Neal A. Maxwell taught, "The so-called 'little star of Bethlehem' was actually very large in its declaration of divine design! It had to have been placed in its precise orbit long, long before it shone so precisely!" ("In Him All Things Hold Together," *BYU Speeches*, March 31, 1991). Other natural phenomena, the signs and wonders not detailed, would also have required a great deal of advance planning on the part of the Lord.

3 NEPHI 1:9—THE BELIEVERS ARE THREATENED WITH DEATH

As the time approached for Samuel the Lamanite's prophecies to be fulfilled, Nephi witnessed the growing skepticism of the people concerning the predicted earthly advent of Jesus Christ. This skepticism led to the persecution of those who believed in Christ's coming by those who felt that the time of His birth had already passed. These skeptics threatened to kill the believers unless the sign of Christ's birth appeared before a certain date.

The unbelievers had drawn a line in the sand: if the prophecies of Samuel the Lamanite were not fulfilled within five years, they would take it as evidence that Samuel was a false prophet. If a person followed a false prophet, he would then be considered in violation of a capital law and receive the death penalty. If the faithful had continued to follow what the people regarded as a false prophet, the threat of death makes clear sense when viewed strictly according to their law (see Deuteronomy 18:20–22).

On the night that these signs were given, many who had laid a snare for the believers fell to the earth, fulfilling the last of Samuel's prophecies. The power structure turned on its head in a matter of minutes. Suddenly, the unbelievers were no longer in positions of confidence. Instead, they fell to the earth, astonished and likely afraid. They now feared the consequences of their own unbelief.

2 NEPHI 4:19-20—BE OF GOOD CHEER

Frequently in the Book of Mormon, faith is tested up until the very last moment. Over the centuries, believers endured physical deprivation, social injustice, and imprisonment at the hands of persecutors. Some were martyred. For nearly five years between Samuel's prophecy of the Savior's birth and its fulfillment, believers had to endure a society counting down the days to their execution. It came down to the last day. Things looked pretty grim. The situation begs an honest evaluation of our own level of determination to remain constant in our faithfulness in the face of such an impending peril. Yet, in this last recorded antemortal interaction between Jehovah and His prophet Nephi in Zarahelma, the Lord responded to Nephi's ardent prayer, saying, "Be of good cheer" (3 Nephi 1:13). The solution was known, had been preplanned, was not frustrated. This is a consistent message from God. Regardless of how things look from our perspective, He is in charge; so, we can have hope, take courage, and hold out till the final moment. As Alma the Younger put it, "Whosoever shall put their trust in God shall be supported in their trials, and their troubles, and their afflictions, and shall be lifted up at the last day" (Alma 36:3).

President Russell M. Nelson has warned that for believers, difficult days lie ahead that will test their faith; yet he couples that warning with a promise of peace: "As you truly repent and seek His help, you can rise above this present precarious world. . . . He, and He alone, does have the power to lift you above the pull of this world" ("Overcome the World and Find Rest," *Liahona*, November, 2022).

The Book of Mormon is absolutely clear on the overriding reality that the Lord Jesus did in fact condescend to come and dwell as a mortal among mankind, to suffer and die, bringing to pass the resurrection and immortality of all the sons and daughters of God. Just as the sign announcing His birth brought light and deliverance to the Nephites, His promises remain sure: He will bring light, deliverance, and exaltation to all who come unto Him.

TAKEAWAYS

- **How many Christmas words or messages can be found in the Book of Mormon?**
- **For starters, where in the Book of Mormon can you find:**
    - **the words "glad tidings,"**
    - **the knowledge that a virgin will conceive,**
    - **the words "for unto us a child is born,"**
    - **the mention of a new star appearing,**
    - **though in dire circumstances, being encouraged to be "of good cheer," and**
    - **that His mother will be called Mary?**
- **In how many ways does it change things to view the Savior's entire life and mission as you celebrate His birth? Why did President Hinckley ask us to think of Easter at Christmas?**

- How does knowing that the prophecies about Jesus were fulfilled exactly as promised, and not just approximately, give us confidence in our Savior's saving powers and covenantal promised blessings?
- This Christmas season, how can we intentionally strive to "be of good cheer" in spite of any challenges we might be facing? Note in your journal the difference this conscious effort makes.

ABOUT THE AUTHOR

John W. Welch is the Robert K. Thomas Professor of Law Emeritus at the BYU Law School and former editor-in-chief of BYU Studies. He practiced law in Los Angeles with O'Melveny & Myers, at which time he cofounded the Foundation for Ancient Research and Mormon Studies in 1979. In 2016, he cofounded Book of Mormon Central and now serves on the board of Scripture Central. He was the general editor of the Collected Works of Hugh Nibley. From 1988–1991, he served as one of the editors for Macmillan's Encyclopedia of Mormonism. In 2005, he was one of the organizers of the bicentennial conference for Joseph Smith at the Library of Congress. He has made several important discoveries and advances regarding biblical law, Book of Mormon studies, and LDS history. His publications cover many topics, including chiasmus, the trial of Jesus, biblical laws in colonial America, the preamble to the United States Constitution, the Good Samaritan, the Sermon on the Mount, King Benjamin's Speech, temple studies, and the New Testament books of Matthew, Acts, and 2 Peter. With Covenant Communications, he and his wife Jeannie have recently copublished *The Parables of Jesus: Revealing the Plan of Salvation*.